SHOOT ME FIRST

SHOOT ME FIRST

A cattleman in Taliban country.
Twenty-four years in the hotspots
of Pakistan and Afghanistan.

Grant Lock

Melbourne

First published in 2011

Broad Continent Publishing
PO Box 198
Forest Hill Victoria 3131
Australia
management@broadcontinent.com.au
www.broadcontinent.com.au

National Library of Australia Cataloguing-in-Publication entry
Author: Lock, Grant.
Title: Shoot me first : a cattleman in Taliban country. Twenty-four years in the hotspots of Pakistan and Afghanistan / Grant Lock.
ISBN: 978-0-9805264-9-3 (pbk.)
Subjects: Lock, Grant.
Lock, Janna.
Community development personnel—Australia—Biography.
Pakistan—Social life and customs.
Afghanistan—Social life and customs.
Dewey Number: 361.7092

Cover photograph by Sam Roberts
sam@samrobertsphotography.com.au
www.samrobertsphotography.com.au
Telephone +61 415 179 717

Edited by Owen Salter
Designed by Michael Collie
Map by David Wong
Set in 11 pt Minion

To my wife, Janna Maxine:
You said, “I have done nothing.”
But you did everything.

ACKNOWLEDGMENTS

The story goes that the fabled Mullah Nasruddin was hailed by a friend from across the river. "Hey Mullah, how do I get across to the other side?"

"Don't be a fool, man!" the Mullah shouts back, "you *are* on the other side!"

I thank all of you who have helped this volume get "to the other side".

Janna, my amazing co-traveller, thank you for all your love and support.

My children: thank you, Angela Seewald, Maria Barham and Matthew Lock—particularly you, Maria, for all your early editing and input. Thank you, John Barham, my son-in-law, for being my webmaster at: shootmefirst.com

For you blokes at the Blokes' Breakfast: you read, listened and continually encouraged me. In particular, my huge thanks to you, Len Woodley—you've been a constant, informed mentor and stimulator.

Owen Salter, thanks for your masterful final editing. Thank you, Wendy Noble, for your midstream editing, and Emma Dowden for your encouragement from early days.

Thanks, Sam Roberts—your front cover photography has been admired by many.

Michael Collie, thanks for being my publisher. Your vision, professionalism, creative skills, short emails and long phone conversations have brought it all together.

Thanks to all my colleagues who have participated in and verified my writing.

I wish to acknowledge the friendship and dedication of our long-suffering Afghan and Pakistani friends, as well as our many expatriate colleagues. Thanks also to all who supported and encouraged us from home.

Some names have been changed for security reasons.

Where the heart goes,
there follows the foot.

AFGHAN PROVERB

CONTENTS

Taliban Country
Afghanistan 2004–2008

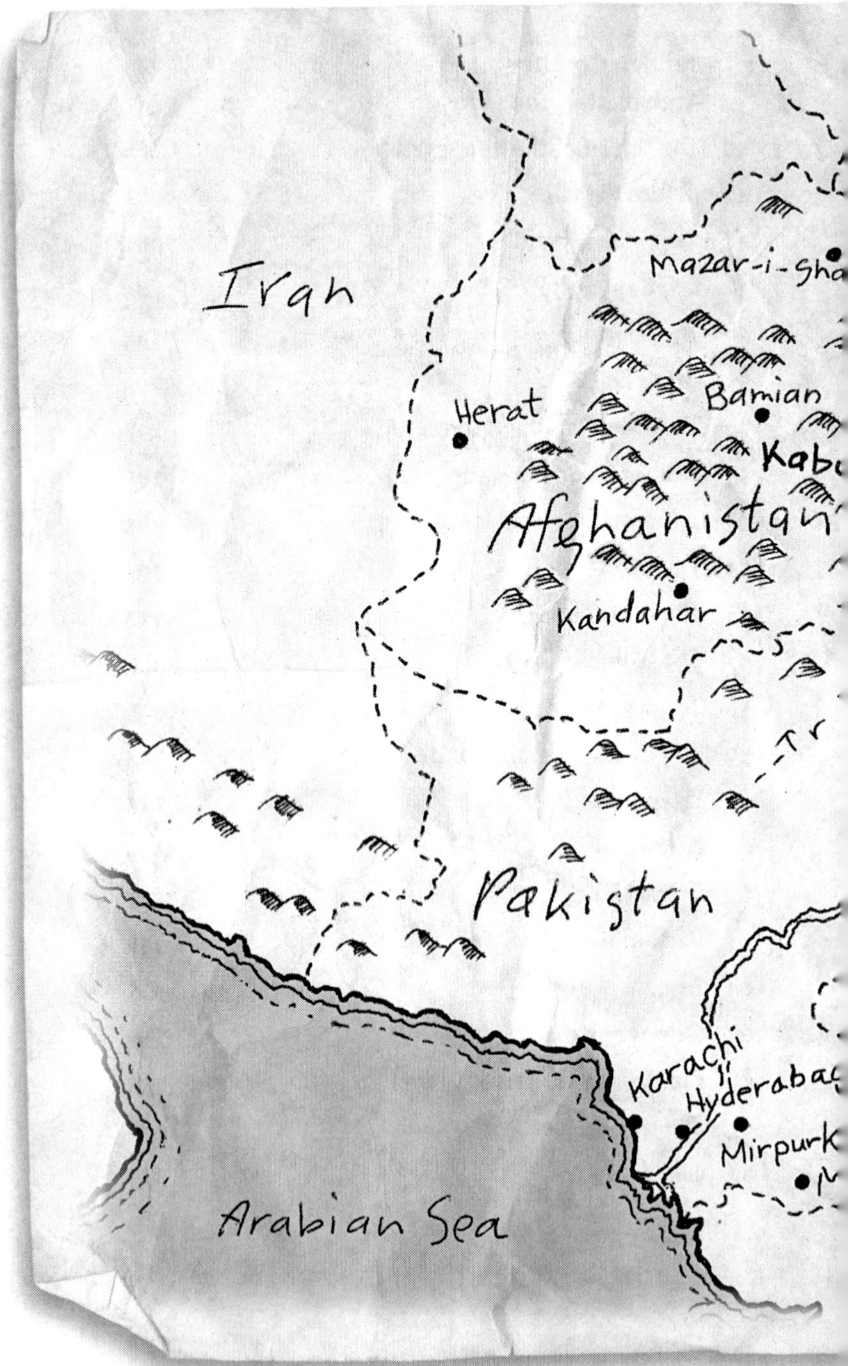

Iran

Mazar-i-Sha

Herat

Bamian

Kab

Afghanistan

Kandahar

Pakistan

Karachi

Hyderaba

Mirpurk

Arabian Sea

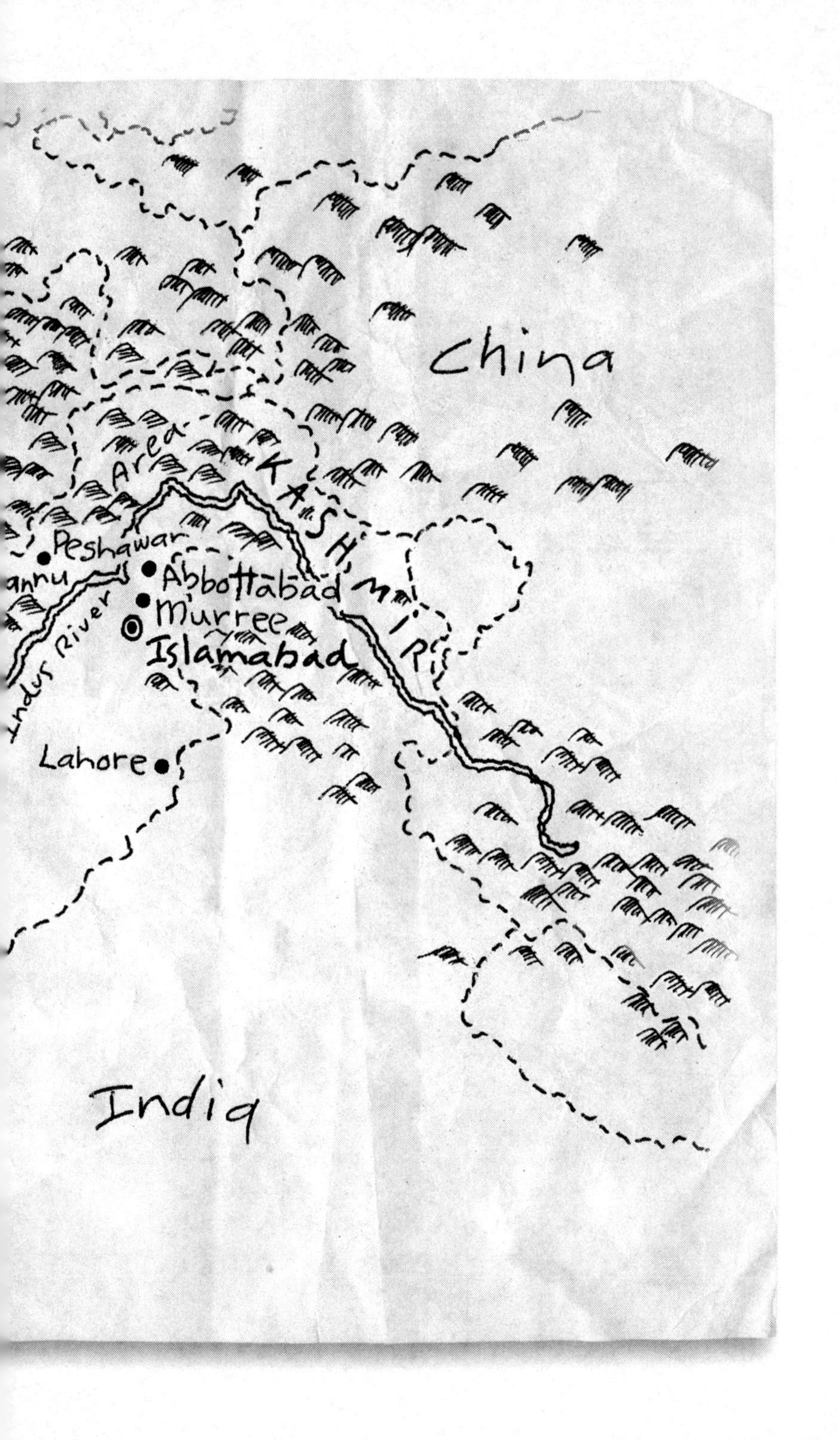

China
KASHMIR
Area
Peshawar
Abbottabad
Murree
Islamabad
Indus River
Lahore
India

PROLOGUE

NORTH-WEST PAKISTAN, 1992

The stench of stale urine rises with the dust as my Pakistani workmen begin to demolish the building. Shovels and picks bear down on the mud bricks, clay rendering and poles. Sweat rolls down their faces, glistening in the sun.

Time is up. The *dukandar* (shopkeeper) has had his chance to demolish it himself. Now I'm doing it for him, as quickly as I can, before there is trouble. I'm dimly aware of the noise of a crowd gathering in the street outside the mud walls of the derelict Pennell High School.

This is Bannu, in Pakistan's Pashtun country, near the border with Afghanistan. Back in the days of the British Raj, Dr Theodore Pennell built a school for boys and later added this segregated compound for girls. Neglected, and closed in recent times, we plan to open it again.

*

It is a challenging region for an *engrez* (foreigner) to work in. Before too many years have passed, the eyes of the whole world will focus on the nearby rugged Tribal Area. The Taliban- and al-Qaeda-riddled mountains span this porous border of the Islamic Republics of Pakistan and Afghanistan. Pilotless drones will circle overhead while Islamic extremism oozes from its mountain fastness. As the Coalition tries to extricate its troops from the Taliban war, Afghanistan will be worried. The United States will be worried. Indeed, the entire world will be worried because the sting of an over-patronised Taliban scorpion will be curling back to strike its mentor, nuclear-loaded Pakistan.

Now in 1992, however, as I watch the walls of the *dukandar*'s illegal storeroom come down, all I'm worried about is getting the job done despite any uncooperative locals.

*

"Sir! Now! You must come *now*! They are very upset!" It's Samson, my dedicated Pakistani assistant. Unlike the long-haired muscle man of Old Testament times, my Samson is frail and sickly. He stands barely as high as my shoulders. But his shrewd understanding of Pashtun ways has got me out of jams before.

"Sir! Sir! You must come outside! They have *guns*!"

So what's new? As with the *naan* bread and chai tea they survive on, Pashtuns and guns are synonymous. Pashtun boys are born with a gun in their hands. Pashtun courage and marksmanship when repelling invaders and settling feuds amongst each other are legendary.

"Look, Samson, this building is coming down. Right now! We need all the space we can get to rebuild the school."

"*Voh bahoot bahoot naraaz!*—They are very, *very* angry, Sir!"

Pashtuns and guns, plus anger. I'd be a fool to ignore that nasty cocktail. I order the workmen to keep up the demolition. Dust from the collapsing clay roof fills the air as I march to the gate. It was hard enough to evict the squatters. We're not stopping now.

Stepping out of the compound, I can see that the influential shopkeepers have indeed stirred up an angry crowd. Mostly bearded, they are gesticulating and shouting in Pashtu. What's all this about? They know their fellow shopkeeper illegally extended his storeroom into the school ground. They know that yesterday he signed a document admitting his fault. He agreed for us to remove the building if he failed to do it himself within twenty-four hours. Surely they know that we are re-opening Pennell's school for their Muslim daughters as well as the minority Christian girls. Don't they realise that this is for them?

But the mob is defending the damaged honour of their colleague, who yesterday had to publicly admit his guilt to an unbelieving foreigner, a lowly *kafir* who stands with the small community of Pakistani Christians, the local *kafirs*.

Hospitality, honour and revenge. That's the age-old mantra of Pashtunwali, the unbreakable code of the Pashtuns. Looking into the black eyes of the shouting beards, I can see that in this dusty Bannu bazaar, honour and revenge have conveniently coalesced.

The mob surrounds us. Samson's glasses seem bigger, and his body smaller, than ever. The mob's burly leader shouts in Urdu, a language that has taken me three years to master. "If you don't stop your workmen from demolishing the building"—and he pauses to add venom to his ultimatum—"we are going to shoot them!"

The crowd falls silent, savouring the imminent back down of the *engrez.* The preservation of all-important male honour trumps female welfare every time. Anger and indignation surge up within me. *Hey, you bellowing misogynists, this is for you. This is for your daughters, for the mothers of your grandchildren.*

I stare back. Who is going to blink first? My brain fleetingly recalls a girl I met the day before. "I want to study," she confided. "One day I want to become a doctor."

The emboldened beard repeats his threat. "If you don't stop your workmen from demolishing the building, we will shoot them!"

I hear my voice answering the challenge. It's surprisingly strong and resolute. "If you are going to shoot my workmen, Sir"—and I jab my forefinger, first at his chest then mine—"you'll have to shoot *me* first!"

They all hear it. The silence thunders in my ears.

THE DESERT

SOUTH-EAST PAKISTAN

1984–1989

3 | 1984 | 1985 | 1986 | 1987 | 1988 | 1989 | 1990 | 1991 | 1992 | 1993 | 1994 | 1995

GHANISTAN OCCUPIED BY RUSSIA | AFGHAN CIVIL WAR

ONE

HALFWAY ACROSS AUSTRALIA

KIMBA, SOUTH AUSTRALIA, 1950

The bazaars of Bannu are a long way from the South Australian country town with the roadside sign that reads "Kimba: Halfway Across Australia". That is where I encountered my first Afghan, the white-bearded cameleer, Afghan Charlie.

I'm standing a safe distance from Afghan Charlie's imperious companion. My twin brother and I are awed by this massive, unusual beast. It's very different to anything Dad has on the farm. We know chooks, turkeys and ducks. And we have pigs, thousands of sheep and a herd of cattle. Daily, before and after school, we have to feed some of them, or help round them up with Mac the sheepdog. This is before reliable electricity, freezer trucks and well-stocked supermarkets become a regular part of country life. If you want it fresh, you have to produce it yourself.

Barry and I sit next to each other on the school bus, and in the classroom, and at lunchtime. As a display of maternal impartiality, my mother always dresses her identical sons exactly alike. "Which is which?" is the commonest of questions. With the air of one who possesses superior knowledge, someone knowingly says, "Barry has a slightly fatter face." I slowly blow air into my cheeks to confuse the onlookers. "Barry is fractionally taller too." That little nugget of hidden truth then evokes, "Come on, boys, back to back," and the embarrassing comparisons continue. It is as if we are rare circus animals. I can identify with Afghan Charlie's camel.

The huge beast of burden growls in protest as once again it kneels to take on board a load of school kids. It then perambulates around the perimeter of the outback schoolyard. Barry and I are in Grade 2. We've already spent our sparse pocket money, but our sister Gaynor, three years our senior, manages to produce the threepence needed for her undulating ride.

Years later she would come to despise Afghan camels. Gay and her husband, Tom, manage a cattle station near the top end of the Simpson Desert. There are now more than one million free-living dromedaries in central Australia. They haughtily plough through fences, damage water troughs and, with aloof alacrity, chomp up 20-kilo mineral blocks intended for cattle.

As evening approaches, bus monitors hustle Barry and me away from the ranks of the gawking schoolkids. "Come on, you Locks, you'll miss your bus."

White-whiskered Afghan Charlie, in his baggy *shalwar kamiz* suit and meticulous turban, camps among the Mallees and Black Oaks on the edge of town while his hobbled income-generator browses through the bush.

❋

Charlie prostrates toward Mecca and again declares, "*Allah O Akbar,* God is great." He is one of the last of the Afghan cameleers who opened up central Australia. Roaring Fords and Chevs have squeezed them out of their silent business of plodding supplies in and hauling wool and minerals out. Rather than shoot their humped friends, the Afghans released them into the desert.

Afghan Charlie boils his chai and bakes his *naan* on the smoky campfire and dreams of his family in his distant village. This same village was visited long ago by the agents of Sir Thomas Elder, the farsighted businessman who introduced camels and cameleers to the new colony of South Australia. They were needed to explore the arid inland, erect the trans-Australian telegraph line and challenge donkeys, horses and oxen as the true ships of the desert.

Little did I know then that one day *camelus dromedarius* would supply my wife, Janna, and me with our daily drinking water in the sandy Thar Desert of southern Pakistan. Nor did I know that later still we would share our lives with the needy in Afghanistan, the land of Afghan Charlie's Pashtun forebears.

TWO

A NAME TO REMEMBER

KARACHI, PAKISTAN, 1984

"What is your good name?"

"Lock," I reply. The baffled official looks at me and Janna with our three children. Twelve-year-old Angela and ten-year-old Maria have been overwhelmed by the sea of gawping male faces in Karachi's sweltering airport.

Angela avoids their gaze. "Haven't they seen Australian kids before?" She doesn't realise that at her age many Pakistani girls are in a family-arranged engagement and will soon be married. Snowy-haired Matthew pokes his eight-year-old nose over the official's desk and cranes to see beyond towering stacks of old visa applications.

*

In the middle of the 1982 wheat planting season, my auburn-haired wife presented me with a serious challenge. We'd been watching the evening news. Janna has always been interested in current affairs. She is a stimulating person to be in love with.

She looked up from her large tapestry. "Grant, do you think there could be more to life than sitting in a tractor and going round and round a paddock until you meet yourself in the middle?"

I wondered what had suddenly caused her to ponder our future aspirations. But then, anyone starting a tapestry that size would have to have a long-term perspective.

It took a while to absorb her question. "Let's just keep our options open," I suggested. "Surely God is big enough to make it clear if we are meant to do something else."

A year later, in 1983, it happened. It was as though a tap was turned from one pipeline named "Kimba" to another named "Overseas" and the word "Pakistan" came gushing out. Breaking the news to Mum and Dad was not easy.

Mum had tears in her eyes. "Grant, you and Janna must follow your own dreams, just as Bill and I have." But Dad was not so understanding. All my life I'd yearned to hear my mother's words, "I'm proud of you", from my father's lips. Whether I was topping my class at school, playing the best tennis in the district or swinging a deal to sell thirty bulls to a cattle station, there was always that wall of generational silence. I *thought* he was proud of me, but it was never verbalised. And it hurt.

"We need you here, son, to keep the beef cattle stud and the cropping going." He snorted off in a huff.

We'd already broken the news to my twin and his wife, Ann. They were apprehensive but supportive. They would be the ones to carry the biggest load when a third of the partnership moved elsewhere.

"Why Pakistan?" Barry asked.

"It was like a silent voice," I explained. "It suddenly took up residence within me. I'm one hundred per cent sure that Pakistan is where God wants us to be."

The following spring my family and I were at the Adelaide airport, about to fly to "half way across Asia". The farewells were almost done when a person I never expected to see emerged from the back of the small group. It was Dad. I was amazed. I was starting to feel special. I moved forward to greet him.

"Dad, you've really come?"

He stood in front of me, clenching and unclenching his hands.

"Look, Grant, someone has to tell you."

"Tell me what, Dad?"

"You just go to Pakistan and have a good look around. Find out what you're going to do, then come back home. I'll personally pay for a Pakistani to do it instead of you."

My shoulders dropped. He still didn't understand. Perhaps he didn't want to.

"Dad, they don't have Pakistanis to do it. They need to be trained, and that takes time." I gave him a hug but his body was unresponsive. "Goodbye, Dad."

"Goodbye, Son. Just remember what I've said."

He turned and left the terminal. I would never see him again. Before we returned from our first three-year term, he had succumbed to a massive heart attack.

*

The Pakistani officer's pen hovers impatiently over the well-worn, important-looking ledger. His job is to register our family with his government. "Well, Sir, what is your good name?"

"Lock," I repeat.

He is mystified. *Lock? What kind of name is that? Lock! It's amazing. These foreigners have some very pedestrian names—but no one could have a name as short as that.* Moomkin nahee—*It's just not possible.*

Puzzled, he leans forward for repeated clarification. The paraphernalia on his uniform is perfectly polished and his black moustache is faultlessly symmetrical. He still cannot comprehend the ridiculous brevity of my family name. He raises his voice: "What is your name?" His ears seem to fold forward like an elephant's, waiting to hear a correct name, a respectable name, a name with more than one-and-a-half miserable little syllables. Preferably, a name with special meaning such as *Noorallah*, Light of God, or *Shaherallah*, Lion of God.

His intense gaze is making me uncomfortable. I thought I'd articulated clearly, but I'll try again. "Lock," I repeat slowly.

He still looks disdainfully puzzled. Suddenly a light of descriptive genius flashes in my brain. I rotate my hand as though I'm turning a key. "Lock! You know! Lock, as in door!"

His face changes. He gives a satisfied sigh, as though his lips have just sampled the rich blend of spices in a superior mutton *karahi*. "Ah yes, that is a good name, Sahib. That is to be a very good name." Under Matthew's watchful gaze he completes the entry with meticulous care. Then he looks up and addresses me warmly: "Welcome to Pakistan, Mr Lokazindore."

*

We leave the airport with my wife and daughters drawing the stares of scores of moustached Pakistani males. I had better get used to it—if I can.

THREE

WE THE BEGGARS

The following week Janna and I spend a morning searching for furniture in a crowded Karachi bazaar. We're famished. Our busy Aussie host has given us directions to a food place and assured us we'll be okay.

"No, no!" Janna says very slowly and clearly. "We. Don't. Want. Money. We. Are. Not. Beggars." She rubs her stomach and continues, "But. We. Are. Hungry. Where. Is. The. Food. Shop?" To me she mutters, "John said there was a place to eat near the furniture bazaar. I wish he was here right now!"

The Karachi shopkeeper stares vacantly across his grubby desk. He doesn't understand a word of English, and the only Urdu we know is *shukria*—thank you.

A clutch of men attired in baggy cotton *shalwar kamiz* rapidly gathers round the two foreigners. The culture-shocked Australians also wear *shalwar kamiz*, albeit awkwardly. The clutch oozes into the confines of the dusty Singer Sewing Machine shop. The tallest slouches to avoid decapitation by the ceiling fan, which pushes stifling hot air from one oppressive corner to another. Inquisitive and rude, the men press in on us.

"If only one of them knew a bit of English."

"If only it weren't so swelteringly hot."

"If only there were some women around."

"If only we had taken more careful note of John's directions."

"If only John were here."

Janna breathes in deeply and exhales quietly, then starts again. "Sir, we are hungry." She rubs her stomach. "We need to eat." She points to her open mouth. "Food. Where is the food shop?" And in frustrated indignation, "We. Are. Not. Beggars."

A light switches on in the shopkeeper's turbaned head. He mightn't understand English, but he's not stupid. *It's very unusual for foreigners to be beggars. Well-dressed foreigners, too, except the guy doesn't have the seams of his shalwar kamiz straight. And the woman, well, at least she has her head respectfully covered. But she shouldn't be wearing red. Don't they know that red is for new brides? But these two have obviously been married a long time.*

One thing is certain, though: they are very accomplished beggars. They've learnt to rub their stomachs and point to their mouths just like the locals do when they plead for bread. It's also clear they're unhappy with what I've given them. The Red Woman is very upset with my offering. If only they understood a bit of Urdu. After all, I've given her two rupees. That's double what the local scavengers get. Two rupees is enough for four pieces of flat tandoori bread. Well, so be it. They are guests in Pakistan, and our ancient custom is to give honour to our guests.

Yes, my generosity is sure to be recorded by the angel on my right shoulder. A good thing too. Yesterday down at the Customs Office I had to pay large bribes to an equally large, glassy-eyed Customs officer. My new sewing machines had to be released somehow. The fat man didn't care that my customers might take their business elsewhere. Mmm, I'd like my son to have a job in that Customs office. "Paanch ungliaa ghi mei hai—*Five fingers in the butter pot." If only I could afford to buy him a place. Well, the angel on my left shoulder will certainly have recorded those bribes, but everyone does it. Everyone has to do it, even if it is against our religion.*

The shopkeeper breaks out of his reverie, withdraws the two rupees and fossicks in his money drawer. *I'll give them five rupees instead. That should earn some real merit. At least they didn't throw my first offering on the ground and stomp out in disgust. That would have been really shameful for me.*

Unfortunately, our relief at sighting the English sign on the Singer Sewing Machine shop's exterior has not been rewarded by hearing a similar vernacular in the interior. That's when Janna articulates her slowest, clearest English, to ask, again, the location of the food shop.

The seemingly enlightened shopkeeper returns the grubby five rupees to his money drawer. With his gappy grin amply displaying the ruthless handiwork of the local roadside dentists, he confidently thrusts a ten-rupee note toward us. "*Bahoot, bahoot khana kayleeay*—That will buy you a lot of food."

He is secretly pleased on several counts. Firstly, he has really impressed the crowd. "He's a good man," they all murmur. Secondly, he's scored some extra merit points to balance the heavenly Judgment Day scales. Thirdly, he's shown these strange foreigners a real dose of genuine Pakistani generosity.

The Red Woman's shriek demolishes his smugness. "He *still* thinks we're beggars, Grant! We are not beggars! Can't anybody understand simple English around here?" She bursts into tears and runs into the street, hurling the generous note onto the dirty cement floor. The mystified shopkeeper's jaw sags.

Around the corner, Janna looks for a place away from all the staring black moustaches. Haven't these men ever seen a woman before? Even though appropriately covered from head to toe, she feels so vulnerable, exposed and out-of-place.

The demoralised shopkeeper looks at me in baffled silence. I feel useless. I feel embarrassed. I don't know what to do. He's been so generous and well-meaning. I frantically search the English-saturated recesses of my cranium for the one Urdu word I know. Serious language study can't come quick enough. "*Shukria!* Thank you!" I blurt out, and rush after Janna.

Around the corner she's weeping and pointing at the lost "hotel", with its promises of *roti* bread, tea and Coke.

Janna chooses a not-so-dirty table in the back corner. With a swipe of his grubby cloth, the young male attendant adds another smear to the table. Janna grimaces. The place is full of flies, unintelligible conversation, stale Peter Stuyvesant smoke and men. Not a woman in sight.

In unison, as if choreographed for a Bollywood movie, the male eyes all rise from chipped cups of sugar-laden, milky chai. They all focus on the Western bride weeping in the corner.

"What was her family thinking?" they mutter.

"They should have arranged her marriage years ago."

"Perhaps her mother is a widow and couldn't afford the electric fan and string bed and refrigerator that go with the wedding."

"Well then, where are her uncles? They've surely failed in their responsibilities."

"I know why she weeps, *Bhai Jhi*. Her new mother-in-law must be very *sukht*, a hard woman to live with."

"And where's their driver? All the foreigners have big cars and a driver."

We point to the food on an adjacent table. The attendant understands and scoops a couple of ladles of oily yellow lentils from one of a row of simmering pots. Two plates are delivered with a practised flourish, along with great-smelling, freshly baked slabs of *naan*. But he's forgotten the customary offering of water. He's embarrassed. That won't augur well for a big "Amreecan" tip. Unknown to him, he's actually dealing with tight-fisted, tipping-illiterate Australians. Full of apologies, he reappears bearing a dented metal jug brimming with invisible amoeba. With the aplomb of a French wine waiter, he fills two stainless steel beakers and meticulously places them before us.

We decline. I point to the ubiquitous Coke sign.

The flies settle on the table, the grey cigarette smoke swirls, the Bollywood eyes continue to focus. I continue to feel useless, and Janna continues to weep.

"I'm never coming back to this bazaar, Grant," she sobs, covering her face. "Never!"

I am in full agreement. Thus far I'm not impressed with alternative-language bazaars. But two hundred miles away, in a more rural marketplace, charming Akhter is going to help remedy that.

FOUR

PERFUME AND PUNCHES

MIRPURKHAS, SOUTH-EAST PAKISTAN, 1984

Janna and I have settled in dusty Rattanabad village, five irrigated miles west of Mirpurkhas in the province of Sindh. We don't have our own vehicle yet, so I often ride into town on a horse-drawn *taanga*. As we clip-clop past the mango trees and fretting tombs, I mull over the words of Sir Charles Napier, a British commander in India in the 1800s: "The best way to quiet a country is a good thrashing, followed by great kindness afterwards. Even the wildest chaps are thus tamed."

Perhaps that's why the British built the railways and canals I'm clopping past now.

The pages of history relentlessly turn and the lessons are soon forgotten. Could it be that the United States has never read Napier's advice? After they "thrashed" the Afghan Taliban, instead of concentrating on the great kindness follow up, George W. Bush rushed off to another war.

When a delegation of Hindu locals complained to Napier about the British prohibition of their custom of *suttee*, he replied: "You say that it is your custom to burn widows. Very well. We also have a custom: when men burn a woman alive, we tie a rope around their necks and we hang them. Build your funeral pyre; beside it, my carpenters will build a gallows. You may follow your custom. And then we will follow ours."

I don't know if Sir Charles studied Urdu, but we certainly have to if we are to serve these people well. Every day Janna and I slog away at it with tapes, textbooks and teachers. For Urdu practice I do the shopping. That's the cultural thing for a male to do here anyway, particularly if you want to keep your wife domestically cloistered. That's not my motive, though. I just want language practice. So I join the other, mainly male, shoppers and chit-chat with the shopkeepers. Many happily offer me a seat and a cup of chai. If a Pakistani offers you tea, he really means it; in fact he will often dispatch a boy to the tea house even before you reply.

In the Mirpurkhas bazaar I drink a lot of tea, practise a lot of Urdu and make a lot of friends. One of them is Akhter.

Akhter is a leader in the local business community and a particularly congenial proprietor. His general store is not large but it's stacked to the ceiling. If he doesn't have everything on Janna's list, he sends one of his assistants out to find it.

"You really must come to my home for a meal, Lock Sahib," he insists, "and please bring your good wife."

So on a Friday afternoon we find his substantial house in the backstreets of Mirpurkhas. Akhter begins the formalities: "This is my wife, Shaneela."

"*Salaam alekoom,* Shaneela," Janna and I chime in unison. "Peace be with you."

Shaneela has a dumpling face with a body to match. She's amiable and warms immediately to Janna. Unknown to me, so does Akhter. "Grant Jhi," he says, "this is Sohail, my oldest son. He's sixteen." His chest expands like a show pigeon. "And these are my other sons." The other sons add up to eight. "And these are my three daughters." The oldest, Nadia, is an attractive twelve-year-old. Like her mother she looks a little weary. Vestiges of tiredness seep through the cracks of their Sindhi hospitality—after all, they have just prepared a feast for fourteen mouths.

Janna and I are now used to the absence of knives and forks. Pieces of fresh *chapatti* bread scoop up the coriander-laced curry just fine. Akhter assures us that metal cutlery spoils the taste of a good curry. In keeping with Sindhi tradition he compels us to eat more and more: "*Khaao! Khaao!* Eat! Eat!" We feel like force-fed French geese. Then come the succulent mangoes. "Mirpurkhas produces the world's best mangoes," Akhter brags.

We don't see much of Shaneela during the meal. She's busy in the kitchen. Our suave host presides over the banquet and is more intent on plying us with food than on eating. Tall, black hair, cultured moustache: he is the perfect model of mature Sindhi manhood, except that the pupil of his right eye is totally opaque. He is blind in that eye.

After the meal, panting Shaneela sits with Janna and they are instant friends. The weather is warm. The small talk continues. We fight off post-feast drowsiness.

"Sister Janna, you look so tired," remarks our charming host. "You must take some rest."

Janna politely declines, but under pressure agrees it would be a good idea. Shaneela leads her to their bedroom, and as the ceiling fan picks up speed over the giant double bed, she leaves her drowsy guest and closes the door. I am engrossed in discussing international cricket with Sohail and his brothers. Unnoticed, Akhter leaves us and drifts back into the bedroom.

There is a hissing noise. Janna stirs from her slumber. Akhter gently pushes her shoulder back. "*Fikr na kaaro*—Do not worry, Sister Janna. This is our custom." He continues to spray her with perfume, from top to toe. Then he leaves. It's warmly intoxicating and she dozes again.

Then someone takes her hand. Foggy Janna stirs. "Oooh, what are you doing with that … that syringe?"

"This is henna," Nadia answers. She gently opens Janna's palm. "My father says you are an honoured guest, Sister Janna. We paint special designs on the hands of our honoured guests. It is our custom."

When we are saying our farewells, Akhter strides to a wall cupboard and returns with a bolt of silk cloth. "Lock Sahib, you are our honourable guests, and Sister Janna, this is especially for you. I can recommend an excellent tailor. He'll make a perfect *shalwar kamiz* suit for you." We've been told this is not an unusual thing to do for special guests. I think nothing more of the gift except that it looks like an extremely expensive piece of cloth.

"You must come and visit again soon," Akhter says, directing his one-eyed gaze at Janna.

"But first we insist that you come out to visit us at Rattanabad village," Janna replies. Shaneela visibly brightens and Akhter is equally keen. We set a time for next Friday, when Akhter's shop will be closed.

❋

Accompanied by four of their children, Akhter and Shaneela cheerily arrive an hour-and-a-half later than our appointed time. We try not to show our in-bred Western irritation. After the curry, which is not up to Shaneela's practised standard, Janna produces a roly-poly pudding. "We have enjoyed your Pakistani food so much, I thought you might like to try a traditional Australian dessert," she says, and cheerfully serves the syrupy pudding with thick cream.

My mouth waters. The guests are unmoved. They impassively study their bowls.

"We are not familiar with this kind of food," announces Akhter.

"Just have a try, Akhter Jhi. You will find it very nice." No response. They continue to gaze blankly at the nefarious foreign fare. The hot pudding is growing cold. Etiquette prevents me from starting on my favourite dessert. Finally courageous Shaneela samples the uncultural contribution. She likes it. I pick up my spoon and join her.

Akhter and the kids continue to emulate Easter Island statues.

Chubby Shaneela finishes her plate. Then she finishes Akhter's. Then she progressively demolishes two more bowls removed from before a pair of the smaller statues. She leans back, folding her hands beneath her ample bosom. "*Bahoot mazeedar*, Sister Janna—very tasty."

We serve chai. It's a familiar substance, so there are no problems here.

Janna and Shaneela retire to a corner. Despite the language limitations it's clear they enjoy being together. "My dear Shaneela," Janna says, "may I visit you to practise my Urdu? And you must teach me how to cook a really *pukka* Sindhi curry."

Shaneela looks at her husband. Akhter effusively supports the suggestion. "A splendid idea, Sister Janna. You are always welcome in our humble house. Our home is your home." Shaneela nods enthusiastically.

"She's a lovely woman," Janna confides later, "but really, really lonely." Then she smirks. "At least someone enjoyed the roly-poly pudding. I'm not sure what to make of Akhter, though. Sometimes he gives me the creeps, and it's not just that white eye."

*

The following week Janna visits the shopkeeper's home. Shaneela hugs her profusely and goes straight to the telephone. She talks briefly to Akhter who is over at the shop. She's unsettled. Something is not right.

"Akhter will be here in ten minutes," she explains. Then she lowers her voice. "He makes me ring him. If I don't he gets very angry."

Janna is disappointed she can't have Shaneela to herself. "What is that on your face, Shaneela?" Janna draws back the obligatory *dupatta* head shawl. There is a huge purple bruise on the woman's cheek.

"He beats me, Janna!" She stoically rolls up her long sleeve. There are ugly black bruises all the way up her arm. Janna's jaw drops. "He has another woman in Karachi," Shaneela whispers. "He takes gifts to her, and cloth. Please pray for me, Dear Sister."

Janna nods. She has already learnt that troubled Muslims readily seek the blessings of intercession from anyone they consider spiritual. She gives the wounded Sindhi woman a long, consoling hug, which is unceremoniously interrupted by the master of the house.

Akhter oils his way in. "*Salaam alekoom,* Sister Janna. We are truly honoured by your presence."

Janna ignores the smooth talk. She's incensed. "Tell me, Akhter, what are these marks?" She points to embarrassed Shaneela's face.

Akhter falters with only the faintest trace of guilt. "Oh ... er, one of the boys threw a ball. He threw it very hard."

Janna looks him squarely in the eye. "Well, Akhter, you must beat that boy very hard, and tell him never to do it again."

The remaining time is stilted. Janna joins Shaneela in the kitchen, but Akhter hovers around exuding unwanted charm. Nevertheless, lonesome Shaneela enjoys Janna's company immensely and pleads for her return. Akhter enthusiastically adds his support. Janna hesitates. She's not too sure about this smooth, perfume-spraying wife-beater. "Thank you, but our children will be home next week on holidays from boarding school in Rawalpindi and I will have no time, no time at all."

But that's before her encounter with the black shroud.

FIVE

THE UNWANTED WOMAN

The kids have arrived home, and the girls go with Janna to the bustling food bazaar. Yellow wasps sip on over-ripe grapes. Flies congregate in open meat shops. The pungent odour of fresh horse manure blends with the exotic tang of chilli and spices.

Maria moves closer to Janna. "Mum, tell this woman to stop pulling on my sleeve."

Angela joins in. "Just tell her to go away, Mum."

Janna is haggling over the price of the "world's best mangoes". Behind the fruit barrow, the turbaned *dukandar* is not budging. Janna's annoyed. She has just seen a local pay much less, and now the girls are getting upset. *It's enough that the men ogle my daughters without this woman pestering them. I've already given out today's quota to beggars.* She turns on the black-shrouded woman. *Whoa! This one's plump.* She *shouldn't be begging.*

"Move on, woman. *Chelo! Chelo!*"

The black-shrouded dumpling leans forward and whispers, "Janna! Janna!"

Janna gasps. "Shaneela! What are *you* doing here? Does Akhter know you're out in the bazaar?"

"Bah! He is in Karachi, with that other one. I can't stand it. I bribed the driver to get me out of the house. Please, please come and visit me, Sister Janna, and bring your lovely girls."

Janna hands the cash to the triumphant shopkeeper and turns back to Shaneela, but the black shroud has gone. Did she see a male relative or a son? They would surely report the prison-break to her one-eyed jailer. That would mean more bruises: big, black bruises.

*

Next time I'm in his shop things are a bit stony, but Akhter insists we arrange another meal at his house. "For the benefit of your language,

Grant Jhi, and Shaneela would really like to see Sister Janna again. And your children must be home on *chooti*. You must bring them along too."

So the five of us arrive, all dressed in our best *shalwar kamiz*. We warn the kids to take only small servings to start with so they can handle the delicious force feeding. This time we finish with *kheer*, custard with pistachios, followed by small bowls of mouth-freshening aniseed.

Akhter gets on well with Matthew and with his one good eye sizes up Angela and Maria. It's hard going for the kids as they have very little Urdu. Maria would prefer to be writing to her globally scattered school friends. Matthew would like to be flying kites or chopping down thorn bushes with his new-found village mates. Angela would prefer to be reading *Where There Is No Doctor*, a health education book for developing countries that has inspired her to consider a future career in nursing. Overall it is a good time, which the kids bear with goodwill.

But a week later, Janna and I are alone again.

It's hard enough for me to see them leave, but it's soul-wrenching for Janna. We have our family hugs at home. Janna can't handle public goodbyes. I leave to take the kids to Hyderabad Railway Station and Janna throws herself on the bed. Between sobs she remonstrates with God on issues of family separation and the meaning of sacrifice. God always wins in the end, for he has experienced the deep hurt of such things. But it's maternally painful for Janna.

At the bustling station the kids join their group for the dusty trip north to Rawalpindi on the Tez Gam Express. Red-jacketed coolies, with our children's trunks on their heads, weave through the throng shouting, "*Bachaao! Bachaao!* Watch out! Save yourself!" They thrust their loads through the open windows of the carriages, then turn to dispute the already-agreed remuneration rate.

Finally the metal monster's belly is full. Whistles and flags provoke the beast into action. It shakes itself then launches northward for twenty-four hours of dust and rattle. As soon as the forlorn parents have shrunk out of sight, the kids start catching up with their much-missed school friends. The train trip and return to boarding school is always an adventure.

*

Ten days later Akhter is plying me with tea in his cornucopian shop. "Grant Jhi, now that the children are gone, Sister Janna will be lonely. I absolutely insist that you both come for another meal." For the sake of brow-beaten Shaneela, I accept. She is always delighted to see Janna.

On the agreed day we are served delicious mutton *karahi* and fresh *naan*, then move to the sitting room. There are plenty of seating choices, but Akhter skilfully manoeuvres himself so he's sitting next to Janna on one end of the settee while I am on the other. That's a huge cultural no-no. *Hey, Akhter, you know better than that. Or are you pretending we're now all like family?*

Janna edges up hard against me. Shaneela fusses in and pours the chai and pretends not to notice. My grip tightens on the arm of the settee. Akhter carries on as though he's merely sitting next to a daughter. Seemingly oblivious to the rising tension, he points to a photograph on the wall. "You remind me of my dear mother, Sister Janna. I loved her so very much." While speaking he slips his free arm around Janna's shoulder and doesn't remove it.

That's the equivalent of an Australian guy slipping his hand into my wife's blouse. Janna stiffens. I bristle. I can't believe it. This guy is trying to seduce my wife right in front of my eyes. If he tried this on a fellow Sindhi, blood would be spilt without delay. Totally embarrassed, Shaneela averts her eyes.

There's a pause in time, as though all the clocks have stopped.

Then Janna takes our host's arm and pushes it from her body. We rise in unison. I'm forcing platitudes through gritted teeth. "Excuse me, Mr Akhter, it's time for us to go."

Akhter gives a smooth smile and responds with all the normal formalities while Shaneela has tears in her eyes. She knows this will be the last hug from her dear friend Janna. Her well-furnished prison will be lonelier than ever.

SIX

THE ARRANGEMENT

For several weeks I avoid visiting Akhter's shop, even though I have to walk right past it. But today he intercepts me in the narrow street and drags me into a tea house.

With feigned innocence he remonstrates with me. "Where have you been, Grant Jhi? Is my little shop not worthy of your presence? Have I done something to offend you?"

I remain silent.

Then, as though to re-establish his credibility, he raves on about the respect his Memon clan engenders in the community. "From ancient times we have been businessmen, serving the people. I am the chairman of our group. And, Lock Sahib, have you not heard of Abdul Sattar Edhi? He has set up a huge fleet of ambulances all across the country. He is a Memon." I hear tones of approval from nearby tables.

I happen to know about this fine charity initiative and I've even read Edhi's book. Edhi I respect, but not Akhter. Not any more. Is he speaking loudly for my benefit, or is it for the other male patrons? Without doubt Akhter is milking his association with a foreigner to the maximum. I'm feeling more and more uncomfortable, but I'm cornered. Once again Akhter has engineered the seating arrangements and has me stuck between him and the wall.

We are on our second cup of spiced Kashmiri chai, the best drink in the house, when my host reaches across the grubby table and takes my hand. I cringe. He lowers his voice. "I have something special to talk to you about, my dear friend."

"*Voh kia hai?*—What is that?"

"Lock Sahib, you have three very fine children."

"Yes, Akhter," I nod in agreement. I'm very proud of our kids.

"Your daughters are very attractive."

"*Beeshuk*—Without doubt."

"And Allah has blessed me with nine fine sons." Akhter's chest expands. In this culture it's a point of great respect to have many sons. I note a calculating gleam in his one good eye. "Grant Jhi, you are a good man, a very good man. We must come to an arrangement."

He leans closer. Now he's holding both of my hands in his. "Grant Jhi, I am thinking that our families should be united. Your oldest daughter, Angela, should marry my oldest son, Sohail."

I try not to let my hands betray my absolute resistance.

But Akhter has more. "And sweet Maria will marry my second boy, Nadeem."

I gulp. I'm doubly flabbergasted. Akhter is looking at me intensely, expectantly. I have to say something. I hope my mouth will not convey what my brain is shouting.

My mouth: "Akhter Jhi, I am truly honoured that you should make this suggestion."

My brain: *What!* You'd have to be joking, mate.

Akhter: "And then my sons could live with your daughters in Australia."

More stunned silence.

My mouth: "That's very interesting, Akhter Jhi ... er, very interesting."

My brain: Now I get it, Akhter. This is the big forward plan to marry your sons into the West, then get a sponsorship and end up there yourself. Very clever.

Akhter: "Grant Jhi, all my boys are very intelligent. Why, even now Sohail is almost managing my other shop. You know, the shoe store across the road."

My mouth: "Yes, I know your other shop, Akhter."

My brain: It wouldn't matter if he managed Adidas International. And yes, I know about your other store. It's the typical shoe store with a hole in the ceiling. As numbers are shouted up to the concrete sauna, some sweating kid tosses the boxes down.

Akhter: "Well, my dearest friend, what do you say?"

My mouth: "Akhter Jhi, again, I am greatly honoured by your proposal, but this is not the way we do things in my country. Our girls are very young. Angela is only thirteen and Maria is just eleven."

Akhter: "That's no problem, Lock Sahib. Here we arrange

engagements for our daughters when they are much younger. After your girls complete their university education, we will have a great wedding party, here in Mirpurkhas."

My mouth: "But it's different in our culture, Akhter Jhi. We allow our daughters to decide for themselves who they will marry."

My brain: You sly fox, Akhter. How many months have you been cooking this up? Well, I've got news for you. It's not going to happen.

Akhter: "But Grant Jhi, females cannot decide for themselves. That is the responsibility of the men. Surely you yourself will find a good family and then choose the groom."

My mouth: "We will offer some guidance, Akhter, but only in the background. I'm sorry, my friend, but all this is just not possible. They are from the West and in fact they will probably go out with a number of young men before they decide."

My brain: Ha, I see that's given you a nasty cultural jolt. For sure there are lots of successful arranged marriages, possibly more than Western love-based relationships, but neither of my daughters will be in one.

Silence.

Akhter: "But Grant Jhi, we have spent so much time together, your family and mine. We have shared many meals, and have I not given you great help with your language learning? It is only reasonable that you consider my proposal."

My mouth: "I'm very sorry, Akhter. I know this is a totally unworthy response, but it's just not possible."

More silence.

Akhter: "But Grant Jhi, what about … what about our friendship?"

My brain: Our friendship? Right from the start you've been cooking up this plan. You two-time your wife. You beat her up and head to Karachi with gifts. In between times you make passes at my wife. If that's being a friend, you know what you can do with it!

My mouth: "Once again I ask you to excuse me, Akhter Jhi, but it's not possible. It's just not going to happen."

The tea's gone cold, and so has our "friendship". As I clip-clop home, I wonder what Angela and Maria will say when I tell them about their first marriage proposal.

SEVEN

IT'S IN OUR BLOOD

HYDERABAD, SINDH PROVINCE, 1985

Bishop Sahib is running late. In the meantime Janna and I are getting to know the Church of Pakistan's Thar Desert team.

"Hey, did you hear about the lion?" Sam's Aussie drawl catches everyone's attention.

"What lion?" says Don.

"Well, you know how thousands go to the Tando Allahyar fair every year. It was on again last week. Some of the Sindhi Christians were running their stall selling books and song cassettes. A bunch of local toughs turned up and abused them for deserting the true path of Hinduism. These guys were about to beat the Christians up. Then a lion comes and saves them."

"Yeah?" Joan rolls her eyes. "I reckon this is another one of your tall stories, Sam."

"No, no." The lanky development worker shakes his head. "It's fair dinkum. This huge lion appears and the tough guys all take off."

Janna blows air through her lips. "That couldn't be true!"

"Too right it is. It's in the paper. Well, just then," and he pauses for effect, "the circus guys turn up, grab their runaway lion and take it back to the cage!" Sam rolls his head back and guffaws. We all join in.

Janet, his equally tall, curly-haired wife, turns to Sheena. "Sorry to hear about your mother, Sheena."

The eyes of the slim Scottish midwife well up. "I hate to leave you guys, but Mum really needs me now."

To break the painful silence, long-serving Joan Smedley wraps a supportive arm around her working partner. The feisty Australian has a Member of the British Empire medal in her drawer, plus a serviette from the annual afternoon tea in Buckingham Palace.

Hundreds of mothers from the Thar Desert are thankful that the two midwives have made regular visits to the desert crossroads town of Mithi. They've also assisted the three local male doctors. Fearing revenge from outraged husbands, the Doctor Sahibs do not examine women, before, during or after labour.

Up until now the plan has been for the four of us—Sheena, Joan, Janna and me—to establish a permanent project base in Mithi. It would also support Dr Don and Nancy Curry at Ghori, a remote sandhill village two hours beyond. Bishop Sahib sent them out there when a delegation of elders came and pleaded for help.

The Canadian doctor is talking to us about a major problem in the desert. "If only they'd finish the course," he complains. "They take the medication for a couple of months and then drop the treatment when they start feeling better."

"Or because there's a wedding or a funeral to pay for," contributes Nancy, his fine-boned bride of two years.

"The tuberculosis invariably returns with a vengeance." The doctor thrusts his palms in the air. "I've got to work out something or we're just propagating resistant strains of TB out there."

Meanwhile Nancy is sharing with Janna. "I decided to go all the way and really identify with the women. You can't imagine how excited they were. They fitted me out with an entire tribal outfit, including white bangles all the way up both arms."

"What kind of bangles, Nancy?"

"They used to be made of camel bone, but now they use hard white plastic."

"I guess I should do the same when we join you out there," says Sam's wife, Janet. She's a trained speech therapist with immaculate diction.

Janna and Nancy are discussing language study and I'm talking to Don about the brakes of his well-travelled Land Rover by the time Bishop Bashir Jhivan arrives from another meeting. His congenial twenty-year-old son, John, accompanies him. Affectionately known as "Baba", John has been supporting the desert team in all sorts of ways.

He addresses the group in his quiet voice. "Please excuse me, everyone, but Keemo has just arrived from the desert and we have to go and organise another truckload of wheat for next week's distribution."

Bishop Sahib joins us with a cup of chai. He sits, and the conversation halts. "Janna and Grant, we are so glad that you have joined us," he says. "Welcome to the Thar Aid Program team." Affirmations come from all sides. This is what we came to Pakistan for, and I feel warm inside.

I note that the bishop is slightly stooped, perhaps a physical manifestation of the heavy load he carries. He's always had a special concern for the desert dwellers. Now that Sheena is returning to Scotland, his plans to set up a permanent team in Mithi, the main desert town, have come unstuck.

He turns to Joan. "I'm afraid the visits will have to go on hold, Joan. I can't send you out without another midwife."

Joan opens her mouth to complain but the bishop raises his hand. "I'm sorry, Joan, but without another midwife you'd burn yourself out in weeks." His eyebrows sag in sympathy with his shoulders. "And now, Grant and Janna, I don't know what to do with you. I cannot send you out to set up a base on your own. You're too new."

My mind starts to race with counter arguments. *Hold on, Bishop Sahib. Don't you realise you're talking to a couple from rural Australia who personally know the tyrannies of drought and distance? Our forebears were all pioneers in the harsh Flinders Ranges, and we still carry a bit of that stuff in our blood! My Great Uncle Ted checked the government dog fence from the back of a camel. My Great Uncle Bennet dug for gold at Arltunga in the Northern Territory. John Hamp, my great-great-grandfather, had a run-in with the Aborigines and they cut off his head and left it roasting in the camp oven. Janna's grandmother's family, the Keys, ran donkey teams from Beltana to Innamincka. Her grandfather, Toby Rankin, worked for the Cattle King, Sir Sydney Kidman. Even now my sister Gaynor and her husband, Tom, manage a cattle station at the top end of the Simpson Desert.*

Janna and I look at each other. I see a cocktail of determination and uncertainty in her eyes. I turn and address the chairman.

"Bishop Jhivan, we're not sure how we'd go on our own, but don't you think someone should take us out for a look?"

The bishop ponders for a moment and his shoulders elevate a little. "Well, Baba is going out to plan next week's famine distribution. He'll be taking Keemo back with him. Keemo is a semi-retired truck driver from Mithi who's helped us a lot. Perhaps you could do the trip with them."

"When are they going out, Bishop Sahib?"

"They leave at dawn tomorrow."

EIGHT

A WINDOW IN THE DESERT

The next morning Baba picks us up before first light, with Keemo as his passenger. Several hours later the green, irrigated fields abruptly give way to the rising, white dunes of the Thar.

We're ten miles into the desert and I am fascinated by the soft tar road. "What sort of road is this, Baba?"

"The government's building a quick and cheap road to Mithi so that buses can come out." He waves a descriptive hand. "They're working about two miles up ahead of us."

I'm scanning for a major road-building plant. All I see is one undersized tractor with a grader blade, five labourers and a small cement mixer. The toiling workers mix tar with sand and add it to the black ribbon snaking its way through the sandhills. Strategically placed tar barrels are visible as far as the eye can see.

"No foundations and no gravel. It sure is making the most of the materials at hand." I pucker my lips. "Mmm. Let's hope it lasts."

Keemo has hopped out and switched the hubs to four-wheel drive. We press on over the deeply rutted sand track. He's more animated now. Mithi is his home and the desert is his backyard.

"Five hundred years ago," he proudly announces, "Akbar, the greatest of all the Mughal emperors, was born out here."

We slow down to pass through a sepia desert village. Monotone thatch roofs, on monotone stick houses, in monotone surroundings.

Janna surveys the passing settlement. "It looks like things haven't changed much since Akbar's time, Keemo." Some desert women appear, and Janna studies each one. "I love the colours in their long skirts. Look! They're wearing the white bangles Nancy told us about."

"Unmarried girls wear them to the elbow," volunteers Keemo, "and the married ones wear them all the way up their arms. If a woman becomes a widow, she loses them all."

We roll past another string of statuesque village women, each carrying two perfectly balanced waterpots on her head. "They look so elegant," says Janna. "Keemo, do the different coloured skirts mean anything?"

"*Beeshuk*—Definitely. You can identify any Hindu tribal group by the women's skirts. Bhils, Megwars, Kholis, they are all different."

We pick up speed and I turn to Baba. "How come there are so many Hindus in this corner of Pakistan?"

Amiable Baba is not an academic like his older brother, Peter. Bishop Jhivan has realised his younger son loves to be out doing something, and he's seen John grow to love the outdoors and the desert.

"Back in 1947, Grant Jhi, India gained its independence from *Englistan*. The Muslim minority figured it would be impossible for them to live with the Hindu majority. The British finally had to give in to Muslim demands and mapped out a new country. The Muslims named it Pakistan, 'Land of the Pure.'"

"Is it correct that Pakistan has about two per cent Christians and two per cent Hindus?" I ask.

"Yes, that's right."

"Well, why do most of the Hindus live in this corner of the country?"

"When Independence Day came, millions of Hindus had to move out and they headed east to India. At the same time millions of Muslims left India and moved west to settle here. Over twelve million people were on the move. As the masses passed, mutual hatred boiled over and they slaughtered each other." Baba grimaces. "A million died, mainly up north in the Punjab. Islam is more moderate here in the Sindh, so many Hindus either didn't leave or crept back soon afterwards."

I'm mulling over the huge loss of life and the implications of a separate Islamic country when Baba adds a bit more history. "Originally Pakistan was in two parts, one on each side of India. Then in 1971 there was a civil war and the eastern part became Bangladesh. Some say another million died in that process."

More big numbers to add to my mulling. "Then do you think the Muslims are better off for insisting on a separate state, Baba?"

He shrugs. "That's very debatable. There are nearly as many Muslims living in India as there are in Pakistan."

"So there were lots who just stayed put."

"That's right, Grant Jhi."

We're crawling up white dunes and passing occasional donkeys and camels. In the loam flats, rough furrows bear testimony to the agricultural activity of better years gone by. I scan each side of the road but there is no sign of any dry stockfeed between the thorn bushes and the occasional drought-defying trees.

"They say the Thar is the heaviest populated desert in the world, Keemo. What do they live on out here?"

He answers my question obliquely. "Mr Laark, when the monsoon rains are good, this place is like *Eden ka Bagh* (the Garden of Eden). There is grass up to your waist. The people from Hyderabad come out here for picnics."

We pass a skinny shepherd with his flock of equally bony goats. "And when was the last time that happened?"

Keemo doesn't answer but Baba does. "It was five years ago."

"I'm sure it will happen this year," Keemo adds. He gazes at the shimmering horizon as though the dark monsoon clouds were already dropping their bounty. "Yes, the desert will bloom this year." The desert truckie displays the universal optimism of dry-land farmers everywhere. It's what keeps them going. I should know—for twenty-five years I farmed in the driest state of the driest continent on earth.

"So, Keemo," I say, "what do people do when the grass runs out?"

"Well, gradually they drive out most of the livestock. First the sheep, then the cattle, then the goats. But not the camels; most of them stay. They sell the bulk of the animals and try to graze the rest in the irrigated area. They work for the big landlords, cutting sugarcane and picking cotton and chillies and mangoes. As soon as it rains out here, they rush back. Some have to leave a son working for the landlords as a surety for the money they've had to borrow."

Baba dodges a desiccated carcase on the side of the track. "It's getting really serious now," he says. "Not all of them can go to the irrigated areas. That's why we've been distributing truckloads of food aid, and Don and Nancy are doing their medical work further out, and Joan and Sheena have been running women's clinics at Mithi." His voice carries a tone of quiet resolve. "Bishop Sahib really wants to get a permanent base set up at Mithi. It's a strategic place for all sorts of programs like eye-camps, TB treatment, women's health and animal husbandry—there are so many needs."

We crawl to the top of another high ridge and Baba pulls up. "Well, there's Mithi," he announces.

We all get out to enjoy the panorama. Wedged between the white dunes is a khaki collection of flat-roofed houses, mud walls and occasional trees. A web of winding alleys networks the homes of sixteen thousand souls. It just seems right to pray for this crossroads town, so we pray.

Then we wind down the slope into a world of underweight cattle, roaring desert trucks, braying donkeys and villagers arriving on undulating camels. We pass bustling bazaars and block-printed cloth drying on the sand. There are mosques, temples, graveyards and holy men's shrines. We hear the Sindhi alphabet chanted from spartan classrooms and inhale the aroma of hot, fresh flat bread. We see brightly coloured saris and graceful tribal skirts, and every man wears a baggy *shalwar kamiz* and sports the mandatory moustache.

*

"Welcome to Mithi," Keemo announces proudly as we pull up in the sand outside his home. Plump Mirran serves chai and roasted pumpkin seeds and we are proudly introduced to the six sons. Then Baba takes us for a visit to the government offices. The Punjabi Deputy Commissioner feels as much like an outsider as we do. He effusively greets us and addresses Baba.

"Baba Jhi, we appreciate so much the help of the Church of Pakistan. Tell Bishop Sahib I keenly wait for his next visit. And Baba, do you think he will soon set up a project base in Mithi?"

Baba glances at us and replies with an Islamic phrase: "*Enshallah*—God willing."

Mirran lunches us on heavy millet bread and potato curry. It's midday and getting really hot, so we all rest for a while.

An hour later Baba rises from his string bed. "Grant Jhi, in case you move out here, Bishop Sahib suggested that Keemo show you some houses that might be rented. It will give you an idea of what's here. I've got to go and talk to the government people about food distribution. We're bringing out another truckload of wheat next Wednesday."

Janna has excused herself and returns from the courtyard hot and obviously agitated. "Whew! These Mithi toilets are something else," she pronounces. "You get microwaved by the sun because there's no roof. You squat on a couple of blocks and everything goes on the floor. And when you're about to leave, it's all being scraped into the street through a hole in the wall."

Keemo slowly changes weight from one embarrassed foot to the other. "*Muaf kaaro*, Sister Janna—excuse us. The woman with her bucket picked a bad time to come today."

"So where does it go after that, Keemo?"

"You know how the women and children collect cow manure and then use it for cooking." We nod in unison. "Well, on the edge of Mithi there are people so poor that they use human dung. When it's burning"—he contorts his face—"it makes the cow stuff smell like incense. " As if to erase even the thought of the obnoxious stench, he lights another cheap cigarette and draws in deeply. "*Chelay?*—Shall we go?"

We step outside and, through impotent sunglasses, squint into the painful glare of the sun and hot white sand. Keemo, unfazed by the brightness, leads us through an endless maze of sandy, mud-walled lanes. It seems incongruous that in this wide-skyed desert we are now restricted by tall, windowless walls in twisting, boa-constricting alleys. We tread carefully around globs of fresh goat dung, and Keemo frequently pauses to chastise a gaggle of small boys who follow us shouting, "*Engrez, Engrez!* Vot is your name? Vot is your father's name?" It seems those phrases amply satisfy the curriculum for primary school English classes in Mithi—not surprisingly since they give priority to the study of Sindhi, their provincial language, Urdu, their national language, and Arabic, their religious language. Many speak a tribal tongue as well.

Behind the ubiquitous high walls we inspect several run-down houses, each with copious amounts of sand and dust inside. Janna is not impressed. "There's nothing to keep it out," she mumbles to me. "Look at the windows. Just rough wooden shutters with bars behind."

"Most of these are far too expensive," Keemo explains, "but of course we would bargain them down. The trouble is, although the starving villagers desperately need help, the greedy town people are out for all they can get."

Finally in exasperation Janna turns to our guide. "Keemo Jhi, can't you show me at least one place that has glass in the windows?"

He looks at her nonplussed, "Glass, Sister Janna? Glass? Why would anyone want glass in their windows?" My specialist homemaker stares at him for a moment, then turns away to hide the tears in her eyes.

*

Our desert host farewells us at his gate and Baba points the Toyota back towards Hyderabad. It's late afternoon and the intense heat of the day has receded. The villages are coming to life again and colourful tribal women are heading for the wells. Janna catches the eye of one of them who faintly returns her smile. I detect that an unspoken bond is forming between my compassionate wife and these resilient desert women.

We crawl past two men driving bony cattle along the road. I give a hearty Western wave to my fellow cattlemen. They could do with a bit of encouragement.

Baba frowns and quickly reproves me. "Don't wave like that, Grant Jhi! Put your hand across your chest instead."

Taken aback, I blurt out, "Well, what did my wave mean, John?"

"It meant, 'I never want to see you again.'"

I give an embarrassed laugh. "Well, I certainly won't be doing that again."

*

Next morning we're reporting back in Bishop Jhivan's office. He listens carefully and then sums things up.

"We don't know how long before we can find another midwife to partner Sister Joan. Until then she will have to work in our hospital at Kunri. I'm putting a Pakistani team together for Mithi, but that takes time. Right now we desperately need someone out there to get things moving." He leans forward. "Over the past year you've both worked very hard on your language. John was impressed with your use of Urdu yesterday." He pauses. "Would you consider going to Mithi alone? Keemo will be there to help you settle in."

I respond first. "I'm ready, Bishop, but only if Janna is prepared to go. I know she was really counting on working in a team."

"You'd be the only foreign woman living in Mithi, Janna," Bishop Sahib cautions.

Janna hesitates, then turns and looks me squarely in the eye. "I'll go, Grant, as long as you build me a decent toilet."

God, I love this gutsy woman.

NINE

BHOPA ANYONE?

MITHI 1986

An agonising scream shatters the silence of the desert night. "Grant! GRANT! Wake up. HELP!"

Drugged by yesterday's hard work in the desert heat, I am so exhausted that the shriek only just pierces the fog that cocoons my delicious sleep. I'm slipping back into oblivion when I hear it again.

"GRANT! HELP! Where ARE you?"

My outstretched arm confirms that Janna is not beside me. I climb out of bed. Now my racing brain is ahead of my body. Only last month the Commissioner Sahib was kidnapped. As the only foreigners living in Mithi we could be targets, though I haven't felt threatened yet.

"GRANT! I've been BITTEN!"

I run toward the scream, along the veranda and into the kitchen. Fear begins to pump through my frame. Has she been struck by one of those snakes that come out in the cool of the night? In tears of pain, she's sitting on the flagstone floor holding her right foot. Her instep is changing colour.

I drop to her side. "What happened?"

"It was a scorpion," she sobs. "I came out for a drink. I had my sandals on too. I must have trod on it and its tail curled over my sandal. It's agony! It's worse than after a caesarean." She points. "Just kill the thing, Grant! It went under that plastic bucket."

I search for the attacker. Scorpions are nocturnal. Usually before we see them we hear them quietly tap-dancing along the rough flagstone floor. They often hide under things and even in shoes and boots. We've found them inside buckets when they drop down from the ancient thatch ceiling in the kitchen. That's why we always slip sandals on when we walk around at night.

I grab Janna's loose sandal. Yes, it's a scorpion all right, five inches long. I smash it repeatedly, verbalising with every blow.

"As if settling here …"

SMASH.

"Isn't hard enough …"

SMASH.

"Without you …"

SMASH.

"You ugly black brute!"

SMASH. SMASH.

I help Janna back to the bedroom. She writhes on the bed. "Oooh! I think I'm going to die. Do something, Grant!"

I'm reading part of our essential equipment: our copy of *Where There Is No Doctor.* My hands are shaking. I'm not very good when Janna is sick. There are three doctors somewhere in town, but we're new and have no idea what they are like. Anyone with a white coat can be called "doctor" in this country. Furthermore, it's the middle of the night and Janna needs answers right now.

I exhale loudly. "Good news! It says here: 'Scorpions can kill small children but it's very rare for adults to die.'"

She rolls her pain-filled eyes. "Well, that's something, isn't it? Come on, what's the treatment? There has to be some kind of treatment!"

"It says painkillers, rest and ice."

"Well, don't just stand there, get me some ice. Quick!"

Fortunately we have a refrigerator, and the government has recently run electricity poles across the dunes. Neighbours even knock on the gate and ask for ice when they have guests. The ice and the painkillers help a bit. We pray and Janna moans continuously until Keemo reports for work early in the morning.

"Did you kill the *bichoo*, Lock Sahib? The pain won't stop if you haven't killed it."

It's not logical, but I reply, "Yes, I killed it."

He heads for the door. "I will bring the *bhopa*. He will draw the pain out."

I call him back. I've heard about these *bhopas*. They are a specialised group of Hindu holy men. In Africa they would be called witchdoctors.

"The *bhopa* will come and sing and stroke the MemSahib's foot and he will draw out the pain. They never fail," says Keemo proudly.

Janna and I look at each other. "Thank you, Keemo, but there'll be no incantations for me," moans Janna. "We've already prayed."

Keemo is a kindly man but his Hindu eyes tell me he's not impressed with the efficacy of our Christian prayers. He shrugs slowly. "Anyway, because you killed the *bichoo*, the pain will leave in twenty-four hours." I give him a couple of tasks and he shuffles off in his plastic flip-flop sandals. Deep cracks gutter his calloused heels and it occurs to me that a scorpion would have a hard time puncturing them.

Janna is helped by the constant ice and regular Disprin, but the red-hot-poker pain remains intense. At lunchtime she sits up. "I've had enough of lying here. If I do something I won't notice the pain so much." She's a great housekeeper and working with the washing machine always gives her a certain amount of therapy. She springs out of bed and strides across the rough flagstone floor.

She doesn't even make it to the door. There is an explosive shriek and she hurls herself back onto the bed and alternately weeps and groans.

By midnight, just as Keemo predicted, the pain has slowly left Janna's exhausted body. Next morning Keemo makes an announcement. "One of the neighbour's girls has been bitten by a *bichoo*."

"Poor girl! Take us there right away, Keemo," Janna the compassionate demands. "We'll take some ice. That helped me a bit."

We enter the nearby mud-walled compound. "Where is the poor girl?" Janna asks a woman peeling well-travelled potatoes. "I've brought some ice."

"There she is, playing with the others." Her mother nonchalantly points to the dusty courtyard half full of kids.

Keemo calls the girl over. She shows us the black spot where the scorpion struck her finger. Then she runs off, laughing. Janna's jaw drops. "But why isn't she in pain like I was? It was awful."

Keemo gives a knowing look. "They did what you wouldn't do, MemSahib. They called for the *bhopa*."

TEN

SON OF THE PROSTITUTE

Lali is a prostitute. Well, that's what they say. The destitute young widow with the dull, dark eyes is now Janna's part-time helper. Keemo couldn't find anyone else.

"I don't care what they say about her, Grant," Janna declares. "Providing she does a good job, she can work for me. If she's a prostitute it's because she has no male relatives and she's desperate. Do you know what happened to her husband?"

"Apparently he died of tuberculosis a couple of years ago. Keemo tells me Hindu women aren't allowed to marry again because they're the cause of their husband's death."

"That's ludicrous!" says Janna, and I nod.

*

Lali has insisted we come and have chai at her tiny mud house on the edge of town. We're sitting on a string bed in the one-room home while she is outside feeding twigs to the fire, and tea leaves and sugar to the blackened kettle. The tethered goat supplies the milk. Aromatic smoke from the *Kehjra* wood drifts through the doorway.

Suddenly, Janna whispers and points at the little rack on the wall. "Look, Grant! See those three spoons up there? They're my dessert spoons, from the set I brought from Australia. I've been wondering where they got to."

"You'd better speak to her about it."

"No, I'm not going to say anything. She has so little, and compared with her I have so much."

Lali enters with the tea. She's delighted that we're visiting her tiny abode. "Thank you so much for giving me work, Sister Janna. You know, I have no family—only my old mother-in-law and she's also a widow, and can hardly see." She brightens. "When does your eye-camp come,

Grant Jhi? Maybe they can do something. They do treat the poor for free, don't they?"

"Yes, Lali, they do. They come next month."

"Ah yes, when winter is here."

Winter in the Thar Desert is like summer in England: if you sleep in, you might miss it. Only yesterday my neighbour proudly announced he had put on his winter shoes and it was still 39°C in our veranda! Definitely cooler than 50, though.

Lali is chortling on. "They always come in winter. Better for the operations."

"Better for Dr Heaton, too," I add. "He comes out from England and even the winter here is very hot for him."

Janna has brought some home-made biscuits and Lali's two children demolish them with speed. "How old is Rani now?" inquires Janna.

"She's five."

"And Ranji?"

"He's twelve, and he's a big problem. He refuses to go back to school. I have no money anyway, and there's no work. All he does is get into trouble with the other young boys."

Ranji's untamed, fatherless eyes stare right through me. I make a mental note to find some part-time work for him before he's lost down the slippery slope of unemployment, no supervision and Afghan imports. There are a lot of Afghan truck drivers in Pakistan these days. Squeezed over the border by the Russian invasion, they will drive trucks for a pittance. Afghan truckies are often conduits for cheap Afghan opium. Even the remote Thar is not beyond the clutches of the zombie powder.

Two days later Lali is comfortably sitting cross-legged on top of our kitchen bench, peeling onions. In Mithi the women all work at ground level, but Lali prefers the elevated smoothness of our new-fangled bench-tops. As she weeps through the onions, she helps Janna with her Sindhi vocabulary.

I interrupt the peeling. "Good news, Lali. Keemo and I have found work for Ranji."

She beams and the black streaks on her teeth can't obscure her delight. Mithi's well water is overloaded with natural fluorine. It produces black marks on very tough teeth. That's why the recently arrived dentist is having trouble making a living.

"He can start tomorrow, at the carpet weaver's house in the next street."

"Sometimes he gives me much trouble, Grant Jhi,"—and she sets her jaw—"but he will be there."

⁂

A month later I check in to see how Ranji's weaving is going. Six boys squat before two rough wooden looms. Sixty fingers fashion numberless knots. The crescent trimming knives flash. The Master Weaver pronounces the necessary numbers, and the exquisite patterns morph into life. Ranji's fingers are not included in the sixty.

"If he can't come every day, he's finished," declares the Master.

I'm angry. Ungrateful kid! He'd rather hang out with the other layabouts than earn some money for his mother. I'm fuming along when who should I see but the lazy absentee, lounging in a side street with his mates.

"Ranji," I call, "I want a word with you."

He rises to his feet and stalks off in the other direction. I'm walking fast. "Hey Ranji, I want a word with you." *I'm going to follow this through, Lali. I'll stand in for your dead husband. I'll get this kid back to work, whatever it takes.*

Ranji jogs. I jog. Ranji runs. I run.

The Church of Pakistan's eye-camp team is working at Mithi's spartan District Hospital. That's where my recalcitrant truant is heading. Supportive families crowd outside the compound door, waiting for a number to be called. Ranji snakes through the throng, evades the watchman's staff and dashes into the hospital compound. I'm right behind him. The astonished watchman gawps as the crazy foreigner races past. *I don't care where you're going, kid. I'm going to nab you and get you back to work. It's the least I can do for your frustrated mother.*

"Hey!" a loud voice shouts. "You can't go in there! That's the women's compound."

Neither Ranji nor I take any notice. *Ha! I've got you cornered now, Ranji my boy.*

Lali's son may be slothful but he's not stupid. Somewhere among the forty string beds in the open-air compound his grandmother is recovering. Both her eyes are bandaged. Ranji radars in on the far corner and makes a final dash, shouting, "Grandma! Grandma!" I'm closing in. *This is it, Ranji. I'll grab you and march you out of here real quick, before all hell breaks loose.*

Behind me angry voices are shouting. "Hey, *Engrez*! You can't go in there! That's the women's compound."

Alarmed female patients, their eyes covered by the opaque bindings of their eye bandages, rise up from their beds like reincarnated mummies. "What's going on? Who is it? Who is it?"

A swarm of jabbering female relatives are pouring in from the ant's nest I've disturbed. The other doorway frames a collage of angry turbans and twisted black moustaches.

I'm about to apprehend him when desperate Ranji dives under Grandma's sheet and disappears from view. A little voice within me speaks up. *Grant, you might want to help this kid, but he's got you culturally snookered. If you lay one hand on that woman's sheets they'll run you out of town, even if she is a geriatric. Just back off. And quick about it, before you get in too deep.*

Emulating the style of Basil from *Fawlty Towers*, I depart from the females' compound as though pursuing wayward boys through a Sindhi women's ward is part of my daily routine. In the phenyl-fumed corridor Dr Heaton approaches in gown and surgical gloves. He's unaware that I'm the one responsible for the uproar.

I suppress my panting. "How's it going, Ralph?"

"It's going well, Grant. What's all that ruckus about?"

I shrug my shoulders. "Whatever it is, it'll settle down soon."

"I've done another sixty cataracts today," he continues. "There'll be a lot of happy people when those bandages come off. Thanks for helping to organise the camp this year."

"That's okay. When you give up your holidays to come out and lead the team, it's the least I can do."

Later that day I tell Janna about Ranji's escape. She listens, then grins. "Looks like you'd better drop the surrogate father routine, Grant, and stick with organising projects." I nod in agreement.

*

Next day dark-eyed Lali is all smiles. "Thanks for getting Ranji back to work, Lock Sahib. He started again this morning."

I'm surprised. I'm dumbfounded. I'm pleased. "You're welcome, Lali. Let's hope he sticks with it this time."

ELEVEN

ROCKY RIP-OFF

MITHI 1987

Keemo, Matt and I are taking a break from a check on the work at our project's new plot.

"The well is down to one hundred feet, Janna, but I've got big problems. I don't know if Nali Mittoo is ripping me off or not. Whew, it sure is hot out there."

Matt waves a half-eaten scone in the air. "The bottom of the well is the coolest spot, Mum."

Janna stabs an accusing glance in my direction and an inquiring finger at Matt. "Have you been down that well again, Matthew?"

"Er ... only after Dad's been down. Then the men give me a turn."

Janna visualises her eleven-year-old son swinging in a rope basket 100 feet above the bottom of the new well. "You go down if you have to, Grant, but Matt, you won't be going down there again." And with another arrow glance at me: "Understand?"

"But Mum, it's not very deep. Keemo says they go down four times that deep at Umerkot."

"Never again, Matthew, and that's final. I don't want you going back to school with a broken leg, or something worse!"

"Looks like you've done your last inspection, Matt," I mumble in deference to Janna's maternal concern.

Lali brings out a tray with more bottles of cold water and I take one gratefully. "As I was saying, Janna, I'm suspicious about those well diggers. I've ordered them to stop until I can work out what's going on."

My wife offers me some common sense advice. "Then you'd better find someone who can tell you."

*

Last month in this shady veranda, Keemo and I discussed the newly acquired plot and the need for water. The diocese's land is near the edge of town and it is five acres of undulating sand with a few thorny ber bushes. I have a vision of it becoming a desert oasis with many shady trees. I can see buildings for staff and for training in TB prevention, mother and child health care, community development, animal husbandry and agriculture. I can see Sindhi villagers sitting and talking in the shade of those trees, with a new look of hope in their eyes. They're learning new skills, gaining knowledge and planning together.

To get those big shady trees we have to start with seedlings. For the babies I plant, it will be a daily fight against drifting sand, desiccating winds and hungry animals. I'm already applying my fencing experience to build a stock-proof barrier to prevent every goat, sheep, cow, camel, donkey and horse from accessing the plot.

But to start my trees I need water, and that's not easy to find, as my desert assistant is explaining.

"Water has a mind of its own, Mr Laark, and there are a lot of dry wells in the Thar."

"I'm amazed that so many people live here considering the problems finding water."

"It's not just finding water, Laark Jhi. The problem is that it's usually too salty for livestock, let alone people."

"But Mithi has plenty of wells."

"That's the reason the town is here. *Mithi* means sweet, but of the two hundred wells only twenty are sweet, just like the water Khanjhi brings to your house every day."

As if on some theatrical cue for *The Arabian Nights*, turbaned Khanjhi bowlegs his way through our wooden gate. He grips a rope, and on the end of the rope is a haughty camel carrying two bulging black bags. The complaining animal perambulates into our courtyard. Khanjhi gets five rupees for every fifty-gallon load.

We watch the water vendor manoeuvre the growling beast up to the small tank, then untie his rubber spouts. Later I'll pump the water to a tank I've installed on the flat roof. It's all part of the promise I made to

Janna before she came out to be the first foreign woman to set up a permanent home in Mithi. I've piped water to the bathroom, laundry and kitchen and installed a flush toilet with a septic tank. My basic plumbing has impressed the locals, who were totally convinced I was a top engineer when they saw me using a spirit level.

Khanjhi empties his water bags and leaves for another undulating load. "Okay, Keemo," I say, "what's the first step for us to get water?"

"I'll call Nali Mittoo. He's from the well-digging caste. He's the one to talk to." My right-hand man lights another cigarette and is on his way. Keemo used to drive a truck all over the Thar and he knows just about everyone worth knowing.

There's an irate yelp from Janna. "He's done it *again*, Grant," she remonstrates loudly as she carries away another dustpan full of warm camel manure. "And I'll have to wash away that yellow camel pee *again*. Why does that animal always do it all in *our* yard?"

"I guess he hears the water running into the tank and it sets him off."

"Well, I wish he'd pick someone else's place for a change." She calls out, "Angela, this is going to be your job while you're home on holidays."

Keemo returns with a toothy grin. "We're in luck, Mr Laark. Nali Mittoo is digging a well right here in town. He'll be around at five o'clock."

*

It's still toasting hot at five. Nali Mittoo arrives with three colleagues. They're small, muscular Hindu tribesmen sporting black moustaches and grubby white *lungis*. The three remain silent, but Nali Mittoo has the gift of the gab. I ask him to explain his method of digging a well.

"Well, Sahib, we choose a likely site and then we start at the top." I resist telling the old joke that well digging is one of the few jobs in the world where you do start at the top; I can't trust my Urdu to get it across. Nali Mittoo continues, "We make the well about four-and-a-half feet wide."

I interrupt. "There's a lot of sand down there. What do you do to stop the well from caving in?"

"We dig about three feet at a time, Sahib. Then the men at the top wind up the buckets of sand and send down bricks and sticky mud. We use the clay mortar to set the wedge-shaped bricks in place and then we repeat the process. If we hit rock we dig straight through that. No need for bricks then."

"Okay. So approximately how far will you have to go down?"

"Not far. About 140 feet."

"Seems like a long way to me."

"Not really, Laark Jhi," my ex-desert truck driver chimes in. "I've seen donkey teams pull water from over 500 feet in the northern Thar."

Pulling water from that depth boggles my mind, let alone sending diggers down that deep.

"And if you find sweet water," the digger chief points out, "it's floating in a four-foot layer above the heavier salty water. It seeps in slowly and you can pull it out twice a day."

Keemo cuts in again."That's where it doesn't pay to be greedy. If you dig just a bit too far you hit the salt water and the well is finished."

Nali Mittoo nods."Only last month I dug a well out Diplo way. The water was really sweet. The big land-owner waters a lot of stock and he insisted he wanted a bigger reservoir to pull from. I told him not to do it, but he compelled me to dig another foot. We hit the salt water and it ruined everything. Now he won't pay me." His three colleagues grunt and roll their eyes in unison.

"And how long will it take to dig, Nali Mittoo?"

"Could be three or four weeks." He rises to go. "It all depends on how much rock is down there. Tomorrow you can show me where you want it."

I nod and see the diggers to the gate. Janna emerges from the kitchen and is pleased to see the veranda has been vacated. "Help me roll out these mats, Grant. We'll be starting our girls' craft group in ten minutes." A gaggle of excited ten-year-olds are already at the gate. For once they are the ones getting the attention, not the boys.

Next day Nali Mittoo checks the site and we settle on a price. The first week they set up their simple pulley and start digging. Progress is slow. I have to go to Hyderabad for four days to get more fencing gear and report to Bishop Jhivan and the Thar Aid committee. I take Matt with me, and when we arrive back, we are keen to get out and see how the well is going.

Keemo is all smiles. “They’ve made very good progress, Laark Sahib. They’re down to one hundred feet.”

I’m amazed. It took more than a week to dig the first thirty-five feet. Then when I’m away for four days they dig twice that far. It sounds fishy to me. At the plot Nali Mittoo is smirking like a Cheshire cat: “Lock Sahib, the gods have been good to us.” I’m feeling suspicious and vulnerable. I suspect that I’m seen as the ignorant foreigner whose wallet needs lightening. In fact, I have to account for every penny, and I want to give donors, big or small, value for their support.

“That’s great, Nali Mittoo. Really impressive. But I’m just wondering how you’ve dug it so fast.”

“You see, Lock Sahib, we bricked down to thirty-five feet then we struck rock and picked up speed.”

“That doesn’t make sense. How come you hit rock and go faster?”

He waves at a big heap of whitish chunks. “Because the rock is not very hard, and because we don’t have to stop every three feet to brick up the wall.”

I apprehensively select a chunk of what looks like white solidified sand. Matt picks up a piece. “If that’s rock, Dad, it’s the softest rock I’ve ever seen.” I’m inclined to agree with him.

Nali Mittoo is reading my thoughts. “Put it in a bucket of water overnight, Lock Jhi, and if it doesn’t go soft, it’s okay. Try it for yourself.”

Next morning I’m looking at it when Khanjhi arrives with his bad-mannered camel. He studies the results with me. The rock hasn’t dissolved and appears to have passed Nali Mittoo’s test.

Khanjhi disagrees. “That’s too soft. See, if you press really hard with your thumbs it breaks up. That means it will collapse in time. Watch those well diggers, Sahib. They have a reputation for cheating people.”

Yes, I’m thinking, *especially unsuspecting engrez with deep pockets.*

Keemo turns up and disagrees with Khanjhi. Angela comes out, groans and cleans up the camel’s mess, again.

“Okay,” I announce, “I’m going down the well to have a look.” Actually, apart from applying common sense, I know absolutely nothing about hand-dug wells. I’m hoping that if I go down regularly they’ll think I do know what to look for and won’t take short cuts. My strategy seems to be coming unstuck.

Inside the well I poke the rock walls with my pocket knife. I'm not impressed. It just seems too soft to me. "I'm sorry, Nali Mittoo, I'm not happy. I want you to brick it up all the way down. Otherwise I'm afraid it will cave in."

The digger's face goes black. "That's not what we agreed."

"But what if the well collapses?"

"All right, if you really insist, but it will cost you double!"

At the well-mouth Keemo sides with Nali Mittoo. Now it's getting messy. I don't want to doubt Keemo, but I know the propensity of human beings to dupe each other. They even tried to take down Bishop Jhivan when he first came out to buy a plot. It was almost a done deal when he found out the guy selling the land didn't even own it.

Khanjhi's comment rings in my ears: "Watch those well diggers, Sahib." How am I going to decide? I want this well to last but I haven't the funds to pay double. I'm feeling frustrated, confused and isolated. "Well, Nali Mittoo," I announce, "you'll have to stop work till I sort this out."

The digger fumes and marches off with his colleagues. Keemo turns and gives me a sour look.

*

I can't sleep, and it's not because the power has gone off again, taking the fan with it. For the umpteenth time I verbalise my dilemma to Janna. She's a supportive listener, even when only half awake.

"Grant," she says, "there must be someone who can tell you if Nali Mittoo is taking you down or not." As she rolls over she adds, "I only wish Khanjhi would house-train that camel of his."

A name drops into my brain: Akram, the Muslim school teacher. I recall he said his father is a big landowner and has a lot of wells. I'll talk to him tomorrow.

Mohammad Akram is positive. "Bring some of the rock, Lock Jhi, and we'll go and visit my father. He'll put you straight. He digs a lot of wells, and he's always wanted to meet you."

I respect Akram. He's a quiet, well-educated thinker. We've discussed many things including our views on what God is like. His father,

Mohammad Hassan, owns a big tract of country about an hour east, toward the Indian border.

We leave early and hit the rutted, sandy track in our four-wheel drive Hilux. The countryside is bare. A lot of families are walking their drought-weary cattle out. As we crawl up another steep dune, a six-wheel-drive *keekra* truck waits at the crest for us to pull through. The informal desert rule is that the vehicle about to come down waits for the one struggling up.

"That's what I used to drive," says Keemo proudly as he studies the Second World War relic. "*Keekra* means sand-crab."

Akram points ahead. "My father's land starts over the next ridge."

The terrain starts to flatten and there are more trees. I can even see some *roheros* with their orange trumpet flowers. Famous for their light-weight hardwood, they were protected in the days of the Raj. As soon as the British left, the axes came out. I decide I'm going to grow some *roheros* after I get my well dug—if we find water, and if the water is sweet enough, and if the well doesn't cave in. Why do things have to be so complicated?

Akram's turbaned, white-bearded dad comes out to meet us. Distinguished and self-assured, he serves us chai in the village *ootaaq*, the circular male-only guest building. Built on a sand ridge, its open stick structure allows any breeze to filter through to its shaded beneficiaries.

Mohammad Hassan wants to show us around. We walk past a nearby village where the native peacocks adorn the trees. "These are my Bhils. They plant the *bajara* (millet) when it rains." Adjacent is another small Hindu village. "And these Kholis look after my livestock and camels."

I don't ask, but I assume these tribal peoples have a serf-like relationship with the big landlord. I really want to get back to the shady *ootaaq* and talk about my well. "Is that all there is to see, Mohammad Hassan?"

He waves his hand in an absent gesture. "Well, there are the *jangli janvars*—the wild jungle animals."

Matthew and I look at each other. That could be interesting. Perhaps we'll see some rare chinkara deer.

"Dad, do you think he has some houbara bustards?" Matt asks with anticipation. "I've read how they breed in Mongolia and migrate down here, but the Saudi princes come over and hunt them out with their falcons. I'd love to see one." He addresses our host: "What do these *jangli janvars* look like, Sir?"

"Well, they're black animals with black hair."

My mind immediately goes to black buck. "You mean there are still black buck in the Thar?"

"No, no, Lock Sahib. I mean people." He grimaces. "You know, those black people with black curly hair." He points to a cluster of thatched huts and we can clearly see the disdained *jangli janvars* going about their daily lives. "We think their forebears came as African slaves with the early Islamic invaders."

I share the disappointment in Matt's eyes. We really thought we were going to see something special. Perhaps we did.

We head back to the *ootaaq*. Mohammad Hassan sends a boy to bring more chai and then studies the bucketfull of rock. "What do you think?" I ask. He takes a piece and puts it through a close visual inspection, then a scratch test, and then a crumble test. Finally he gives the verdict. "This is okay, Lock Sahib. No problems here. Nali Mittoo is right; your well doesn't need bricking up."

I lean back, feeling greatly relieved by his arbitration. As we say our farewells, Mohammad Hassam asks if we could take three villagers into Mithi. I readily agree. By the time we leave, the three have cloned themselves into six. I don't mind. I'm driving back a much happier man, despite the I-told-you-so look in Keemo's eyes.

*

"Let's see if Nali Mittoo is at the hotel," Keemo suggests as we approach Mithi. "He told me he'd probably be there in the late afternoon."

The "hotels" are actually rough tea houses clustered around the sandy square where the six-wheeled *keekras* load and unload. They're not the kind of hotels that sell alcohol—at least not openly.

"Uh-oh," says Akram, "looks like there's trouble."

A group of irate men are pushing a neatly dressed guy out of the hotel. One is holding a cup high in the air, as though it contains a virus. He smashes it on the non-existent footpath. "And make sure you go to your own hotel next time. Don't you know your place?"

"What's going on, Keemo? Didn't he pay his bill? And what's the cup smashing thing all about?"

"Each Hindu group has its own hotel. That's Sondro. He's trying to do some social climbing. But it doesn't matter if he's wealthy or not; he has to go to his own hotel. They destroyed the cup because a higher class person would never drink from it after he has used it. Ah look, there's Nali Mittoo."

Nali Mittoo is black and silent but his verbosity rapidly revives when Keemo takes him aside for a chat in the local Dhatki language. They return and well digger berates me. "I told you my work was good. I've been digging wells for thirty years, and my father before me, and his father before him."

"*Muaf keejeeay*, Nali Mittoo—please forgive me. I want to apologise to you. I really am just an ignorant foreigner and you were right all the time." I am genuinely sorry, but I lay it on extra thick to help restore his wounded pride. "Please continue tomorrow, my respected brother. I can see that you are a very good man and that you really know what you are doing." The digger's body relaxes. We are all relieved.

When Khanjhi delivers his next load of water, I tell him of my decision. He takes his five rupees, scowls and walks away. I can't help but wonder if there is some long-standing rivalry between him and the well diggers.

*

Next morning Keemo greets me. "Mr Laark, I have found some camel owners who want to pull the water at the plot."

"That's *if* we find water, Keemo."

"Don't worry, Jhi. I've already made offerings to the god of good fortune."

I'm quite familiar with Ganesh. His over-fed elephant figure appears on posters in almost every local Hindu store and he stares vacantly at me from the gaudy bazaar temple. I can't explain it, but whenever I pass that temple, or the Hindu graveyard, my spirit stirs within and I find my tongue moving in prayer.

"Keemo, my friend, I'm not going to hire a camel."

Keemo raises an eyebrow. "But Laark Sahib, donkeys tire very quickly. It's much better to hire a camel."

"No, I'm going to do it for free," I boast.

"Ah," says Keemo knowingly, "you will buy your own camel, Jhi."

"No, that's not my plan either."

His black eyes take on a baffled sheen. "*Moomkin nahee*—Then it's just not possible."

"It is possible, Keemo. I promise to explain after my next trip to Karachi."

TWELVE

A CRACK IN THE CASTE

"Where's Raja, Keemo? He should be here levelling sand on the plot. Good grief, he only lives up on top of that sandy hill." Keemo looks apologetic but says nothing. "He's been gone three days now. Has there been a death in the clan, or a wedding? If only these guys would tell us before they take off. Look, I'm going to the bazaar; I have to get the banking done. If he's not back today you can find someone else, and that shouldn't be hard."

The bank manager rises from his large, plain desk. "Welcome, Grant Lock Sahib, it's so good to see you again. Please sit down. I've been wanting to talk with you."

I'm always treated well at Mithi's local bank. It's probably because we are the only foreigners in town and possibly because Mr Khanrimo belongs to a very low Hindu caste. He is just about as amazed as I am that he was appointed manager.

"I have worked long and hard, Mr Lock, and I've passed all the exams. Now that I have this position I plan to keep it. It's a great honour for our Megwah caste."

As usual I've been ushered directly into Khanrimo's office at the rear of the building. He immediately dispatches the old *chaparasi* for chai and calls in the teller to deal with my paperwork. Then he settles back for a good gripe session.

"I am continually watching my back, Lock Sahib. All the time they're sending rumours to head office." He leans forward and makes his distinctive, air-gulping cough. "Those high castes want my job. They always want to keep us down."

"But Keemo says the Brahmins all ran to India at partition and never came back."

"That's true, but it's the Vanias, the business and trader class—they are the top caste here now."

"Isn't Pakistan's constitution supposed to give everyone a fair go?"

The funny cough again, and a wry smile. "You are very new in this country, Lock Jhi. Maybe you haven't heard of the Hudood ordinance and the blasphemy laws. They have been added by our military president, General Zia ul-Haq. Now it's even tougher for the small Hindu and Christian minorities. You should know that."

I stand rebuked. I need to do more research on the current situation.

The teller returns with my paperwork. Khanrimo draws the obligatory stamp from his unlocked drawer and, like one setting the seal on the Magna Carta, authenticates my mundane monthly statement with a rubbery thump and a flourish of his fountain pen.

He coughs, lowers his voice and confides, "But the biggest problem for the Hindus is with the Hindus themselves. Everyone must stay in their place or there is big trouble. That's why it's so difficult for me to keep my position."

I've started my second cup of sweet chai as the fan does battle with the hot air and droves of schoolboys prattle past the window. Desert six-wheelers overloaded with villagers belch their fumes into the dust-laden air.

"Well, Khanrimo, I'm actually surprised that more lower-caste Hindus don't convert to the majority religion. It would make it much easier for them to get jobs."

"No! Oh, no!" The Hindu manager draws back as though I've just placed a beef steak on his dinner plate. "And I can tell you why."

"Please do."

"Well, firstly, the Muslims would insist that our womenfolk wear *shalwar kamiz*. But we are proud of their traditional *goghara* skirts. Each group has its own distinctive cloth, you know."

I was expecting a more theological reason. "And …?"

"Muslims always marry their cousins. We don't like that. It's not our custom. But Mr Lock, what do you think about these things?"

At this point we are joined by the manager's two sons, just released from the rote-learning classes in primary school. They sit on the floor, pull out their books and slates, and begin their homework.

"I think the rule-keepers have missed the point, Khanrimo," I respond. "The important thing is to learn to enjoy God."

"And how does a Christian do that?"

"Well, it's no secret. It's all written down in our holy book, and if—"

I'm forcefully interrupted by the Hindu teller who has just rejoined us. "Lock Sahib, my Bible is much more powerful than yours!"

I'm taken aback. "You have a Bible? But you're a Hindu."

"Oh yes, it's on my prayer-shelf with the other gods. It is very old, very powerful. It gives us much more protection than yours."

I'm still a bit stunned. "Protection from what?"

"From bad and dirty spirits, of course."

I'm starting to realise how much these people live in daily fear of the spirits of darkness. There are places in this town where even my spirit, albeit dulled by a blinkered, Western worldview, warns me of their presence. "My friend, the Bible is not for magic spells. It's for reading. It's all about what the cosmic God has done for us. He is the one who delivers us from the fear of death and the power of the *djinns* (evil spirits). You should read it some time."

*

My next stop is the barbershop. On the way I pass the mosque, then the Hindu temple with gaudy Ganesh and his divine colleagues staring out at me. I pause at the silversmith's to watch the artisan at work. With blowpipe and simple tools, he's fashioning delicate ankle chains, all done at ground level. I must buy a pair of those for Janna—she'd love that, and so would the locals.

The barbershop is five feet wide. There are several in Mithi, all close together. They vie for my custom, but Sim Jhi is my favourite. A heap of schoolboys gawp through the entrance while Sim Jhi revels in the status of his shop. *Why drive them away? It may be good for business.*

I'm relaxed and chat on with the congenial hair man. Where else on the face of the globe could I get a good haircut, a cup of chai and a head massage, all for the equivalent of thirty cents? However, there is one serious downside: the dreaded towel. At the end of the process, Sim Jhi proudly surveys his workmanship and reaches for the abominable cloth. He's about to throw it over my face to massage my brow, wipe out my eye sockets, clean out my ears and remove all unwanted hair particles.

The towel is almost black. For how many unwashed aeons has it been wiping perspiring ears, sweaty faces and black beards? By its stale, acrid smell, I'd say at least fifteen or twenty.

But I'm prepared. With practised timing, and at the last possible moment, I grip the worn armrests and draw a very deep breath. The dreaded cloth descends; all is in darkness. The Sindhi precursor to water-boarding has begun.

Sim Jhi starts with the brow massage, then the ears. *Hurry up, man! Stop talking to the other customers.* Now the eye sockets. I'm exhaling slowly. I yearn for the lung capacity of an Italian glassblower or an Indonesian clam diver. My body demands oxygen. I can't hold out much longer. At last the barber completes the ritual, removes the detestable cloth and nonchalantly flicks a few fragments of hair from my shoulders. I inhale deeply, hopefully in a discreet sort of fashion. Desert air never smelt so good.

Then I notice a rather expansive paunch right next to my face. It's Keemo.

"Raja is back, Laark Sahib," he says. "He's back at work."

"Good. What was the problem?"

"He had to buy a camel."

"But he already has a camel. Why does he want two?"

"He doesn't want two, Grant Jhi."

"Well, did the other one die?"

"Not really. Come on, you can ask him yourself."

We leave the barber, and as we're walking through the bazaar, Keemo says, "We should buy some sweet-meats, Laark Jhi."

"Why's that, Keemo?"

"Because Nali Mittoo has reached water."

"Hey, that's wonderful!" We pause in the middle of the narrow market. "Why didn't you tell me?"

"Well, I knew it would happen. I told you I gave offerings to Ganesh." His eye wanders to the temple further up the busy lane.

I'm wondering why my right-hand man isn't a little more excited. "Okay then, Keemo, what's the bad news?"

"It's … it's at about 140 feet."

"Well, that's where Nali Mittoo said it would be. So …?"

"I'm sorry, Laark Jhi, but it's not sweet. It's no good for drinking."

I'm disappointed. I was hoping we'd strike a nice sweet stream, but I always knew there was only a ten per cent chance of that, providing we struck water at all. "But Keemo, will it be okay for my tree planting program and for building project offices and training rooms?"

He brightens. "*Koee baat nahee*, Laark Sahib—no problem. It will be fine for all that."

I breathe a sigh of relief and slap him on the shoulder. "Then we really can celebrate. That's heaps better than a dry well. Let's pick out a few things."

The range in the desert bakery is very limited. I select a variety of small cakes and Keemo chooses the biscuits with currants on top. The shopkeeper shovels the biscuits onto the battered scales and the currants produce wings and begin to buzz around our heads. From the scales the biscuits are poured into a packet made from newspaper.

The front of the packet informs me that "The South East Asia Trade Conference is to be held in historic Raffles Hotel." The back clearly mentions the *Straits Times* and gives me a date. It's a bit incongruent having newspapers come all the way from Singapore to be handmade into paper bags in the back end of this Pakistani desert, and it only took them five years to get here.

We're in luck. Out on the sandy footpath the baker's son is deep frying golden *jelaabees*. He drizzles a mixture of honey and chickpea flour into the bubbling oil. The end result is a sweet, crunchy pinwheel. Several go into another *Straights Times* packet before the winged currants can settle. We grab some bottles of Coke and head out to the plot.

Raja is swinging a shovel and not looking happy. "Welcome back, Raja," I say. "Come up to the well and we'll celebrate."

Nali Mittoo greets us with smiles. Our geological disagreements are well behind us now. "*Paani moobarak*, Lock Sahib—Congratulations, you have water."

"Thank-you, *Bhai Jhi*. Keemo's just told me."

Then the lines of his weather-beaten face sag to match the drooping moustache. *Bahoot afsohs*—I'm very sorry." His voice drops. "It's no good for drinking."

"Let me try for myself, Mittoo." I reach for his bucket. I cup my hand and take a sip, spit it out and nod in agreement.

"But," he adds more cheerfully, "it's okay for everything else."

The barren sand and the prickly ber bushes look just the same, but my vision of a shady desert oasis is a giant step closer to reality. "That's good. That's very good, Mittoo. So let's thank God for what he's given us."

We pause and I give thanks for the water and for these Sindhi men who are fulfilling the oasis vision with me. As we share out the goodies, I turn my attention to my prodigal worker. I'm puzzled about his camel purchase.

Raja is small, lean and muscular, and sports the typical black moustache and mirrored Sindhi cap. He lives on the nearby sandhill in a circular, thatched stick house. Several weeks ago Janna and I paid his family a visit. For late afternoon exercise we walked out from town carrying a bag of oranges. Raja's bare-foot, raggedy kids were euphoric when they received the treat. The sun was sinking low as we sat outside on a string bed and drank chai. The glowing orb disappeared behind the distant sandhills, the ridge picked up the first evening breeze, and a hundred threads of smoke wisped upwards from the distant township. As the first stars appeared, Janna and I felt privileged to be the guests of this little sandhill family.

As we departed, young Mrs Raja, in her full-length tribal skirt, gathered all the orange peel and fed it to the tethered goats. Nearby, Raja's hobbled camel impassively chewed its cud. The family depends on that camel. At first light every morning Raja walks the beast into town and pulls water for several hours. Mrs Raja's last delivery was very difficult. Fortunately, Joan and Sheena were in town for a three-week woman's clinic. That was eighteen months ago, before Sheena had to return to Scotland. Neither mother nor child would have survived if Raja hadn't taken them to the dedicated foreign midwives. It was after that evening ridge-top visit that I decided to offer Raja some day-work on the plot. He accepted immediately.

Raja has obviously enjoyed the biscuits and cakes, but he is still not himself. I want to find out about his camel deal. "Raja, take these spare *jelaabees* and give them to your children." I hand him a half-full *Straights Times* paper bag.

"Thank you, Lock Sahib. You are too kind."

"Raja Jhi, Keemo tells me you bought a new camel. What happened to the old one?"

Raja's countenance returns to its fallen state. "Someone stole it, Sahib. They untied it in the middle of the night."

"Did you know who took it?"

"No Jhi, not at first, but I found out."

"How, Raja?"

My sand-shoveller's muscular arms hang limp at his side. "I followed the tracks all the way to the edge of the desert. At Naukot I checked if anyone had seen it."

"And ...?"

"There was a man at the tea house on the road into town. It was as though he was waiting for me. He asked me what my camel looked like. I told him and he gave a funny laugh. 'Seems to be very similar to the one my boss has in his compound. Come and I'll show you,' he said."

"And ...?"

"He took me to the compound of Mohammad Jawan. He's a big landlord with three wives, a Toyota Land Cruiser and eight sons. Last year his eldest son put me on to cut sugarcane and pick mangoes. Hard work and not much pay, but we needed the money, particularly when the Thar missed out on the monsoon rains again."

"Was your camel there?"

"Tell him the bad news," says Keemo, giving a wry smirk. It's funny how the misfortune of others can be such a source of amusement.

"Yes, Sahib, it was there. I recognised it straight away, and my camel recognised me. Then a man with a gun appeared, and then Mohammad Jawan and a heap of other men. 'This is definitely my camel,' I told them. 'See these marks on his shoulders? That's where he's been pulling water.'

"Fat Mohammad Jawan just laughed. 'A lot of camels pull water, my desert friend,' he said. 'If you want this camel, you'll have to pay for it.'

"'Sir, I'm very poor,' I told him.

"'Then I'll be generous,' he said., 'and I'll sell it cheap. Instead of 7000 rupees you can give me just 5000.'

"I pleaded with him. 'Please have mercy, *Janaab* (respected Sir). I worked hard for you all last year and I didn't steal a thing, not even one stick of cane and not one mango.'

"'All right, Raja', he said. 'I'll be really generous. You can have it for just 4000 rupees, but I need the money right now, before the sun goes down. My men will take you down to see the money lenders.'

"So I had to borrow money, Lock Sahib, to buy back my own camel." He raises his arms in a gesture of hopelessness. "What else could I do with all those men with their big moustaches and guns? And without my camel I can't pull water. I'll have to sell most of my goats and I'll have to visit my brothers and cousins and ask for their help."

I visualise Mrs Raja and her raggedy kids. How will they manage without the goats?

A pall has fallen on our well-side celebration. Empathy replaces levity. We're all silent, all feeling Raja's pain. Inside I'm angry. I'm all the more determined to get this program going so the little people can be served and respected. It's no wonder the Nazarene got stuck into the proud and arrogant, and showed compassion to their powerless prey.

Keemo scowls. "That's what these big landlords do. If they need extra cash they just send one of their henchmen out to steal a camel." He spits into the sand. "I can't stand them."

"Well," I ask, "why didn't you go to the police, Raja?"

They all stare at each other and then burst into laughter. Keemo, Nali Mittoo and his helpers, they're all laughing. They look at me as though I'm an ignorant imbecile. Nali Mittoo turns to Raja, waves his head and mimics my question in a sing song voice. Now even Raja is laughing.

Keemo is suddenly embarrassed that they're making fun of the boss so he starts to explain.

"Mr Laark, if Raja had gone to the police they would have demanded another 3000 rupees to go and arrest the big landlord. Then Mohammad Jawan would have just paid them off. They wouldn't have done a thing. They only work for the big people. If you are small you don't have a chance." He waves his palms in the air. "You are nothing. The government only pays a pittance to the police, so they top up wherever they can."

"Well then, Keemo, why doesn't the government pay them a decent wage? Then they wouldn't have to take bribes."

They all look at each other. For a moment I foolishly think I've offered a sensible solution. Then they all crack up again. The tone of their laughter tells me what they are thinking: *We can't believe it. Who is this guy? Are all* engrez *as ignorant as this?* Finally Keemo draws a breath and sighs in resignation. "That would never work, Laark Jhi. If the government paid them a good wage, they would still go on taking bribes. So it's better not to pay them a good wage in the first place."

The party is over. Heading back to town, we pull in behind a mob of big-horned cattle. They are white Thar Parkars. The Indian sub-continent produces different strains of cattle just as Australia produces different strains of kangaroos. The Thar Parkars are native to this area, like the graceful peacocks we see occasionally. Keemo nods toward the turbaned owner who trails behind the cattle on his skinny horse. "It's too dry out here now. He's taking them into the irrigated area. He'll sell most of them to the Muslims. We Hindus don't touch beef."

Being a fellow cattle breeder I engage the desert herdsman as he comes alongside. He's pleased I appreciate his stock. I ask him, "Where do you go to get a really good bull to keep up the standard of your herd?" He appears baffled, then looking me straight in the eye, he responds with a question of his own. "And why would I want a really good bull, Sahib?"

Once again I'm getting the "Who is this dummy?" treatment. As the mystified horseman rides on, he calls back over his shoulder, "I don't want a really good bull, Sahib. If I had a really good bull, someone would only come and steal it!"

I still have a lot to learn.

THIRTEEN

TOO FAT FOR MUJH

KARACHI, 1987

They're lounging on large stacks of Afghan carpets. Lethargic, well fed and secreting the odour of success—the kind that comes at the expense of others.

The languid carpet sellers rouse themselves from their afternoon torpor and beckon us to check out the bountiful layers on which they recline. "Afghan carpets, Sahib, Afghan carpets. *Bahoot susta!*—Very cheap!"

We're in Karachi's amazing Lighthouse Bazaar, one of the world's biggest destinations for second-hand clothing. Apart from what's sold right here, thousands of bales of the West's unwanted wardrobe is trucked out to every corner of the country.

"Why do they call it Lighthouse Bazaar, Dad?" pipes up eight year-old Matthew. "I don't see any lighthouses."

"Well, the street-signs are of no use to many Karachi taxi drivers because they can't read. So they use the big cinemas as landmarks. Lighthouse Bazaar is named after the Lighthouse Cinema. See? It's just over there."

This being our first visit, we're almost lost in the huge conglomeration of narrow-waisted shops disgorging their pre-owned wares onto the footpaths. Shopkeepers vigorously beckon us into their stores—after all, everyone knows you can squeeze more from foreigners. It's called "skin tax". The less you know about the Eastern art of haggling, the more you pay.

We walk past a street full of second-hand socks, then a street full of men's coats, and here is a street swinging full of suspended, second-hand bras. An unabashed male customer somehow conveys his wife's size to the bearded shopkeeper and chooses a bright green model to take home to his cloistered spouse.

At last we reach a street full of blue jeans. Angela and Maria need some of the winter-weight variety. During next semester, snow will start whitening their mountain school. We rummage through the stacks and find some possible starters. Janna casts a searching look around. "Where's the try room?" she ruefully asks, realising a decent changing room would take up half the shop.

Even though his body odour permeates every corner of his claustrophobic premises, the shopkeeper is not stupid. He's visited his relatives in *Englistan* and has seen rows of try rooms in Manchester's huge stores. Although none of the locals would ever ask for a try room, the innovative *dukandar* knows what the foreign woman wants, and he's not going to miss out on a sale. He points to the obligatory large shawl on Janna's head. "*Idhar racko*—Put it here."

Janna and I stretch the versatile cloth across the eight-foot-wide shop. The girls try on the jeans. A pair of laggards sidle by, eyes crab-stalking from turbaned heads.

"*Chelo! Budmaashi mut karo*—Push off! Don't do bad mannered things," shouts the shopkeeper.

Haggling completed and jeans procured, we also "push off" and wander into Carpet Street. The indolent carpet seller repeats his call. "Afghan carpets, Sahib. Very cheap! Very cheap!"

My mind transports me back to the colourless refugee camps I visited in Pakistan's North-West Frontier Province last summer. There I saw vultures just like these waddling through the unpaved lanes, attending to their carpet weaving business. They target fatherless families who have left all to flee from the death-dealing Soviet gunships.

They say, "We'll provide the loom and the wool, and we'll buy the completed carpet back from you." It sounds too good to be true, and the family has to eat. So the kids set to work. Tiny fingers tie off myriads of knots and the trimming knives flash. Several months later the intricate three-by-four-metre piece is finished. That's when Mr Indolent and his brothers turn up again. "Of course, we can't pay you very much," they moan. "Did we not supply the loom? Did we not supply the wool? And here is more wool for the next carpet."

The iron teeth of the vice tighten. The widow has no escape. Of course, she could sell a daughter as a child-bride to a polygamous, grey-haired suitor, but what mother would want to do that? They are trapped, and very hungry. Mr Indolent's smirking brothers carry away the completed piece and pay only a pittance for the labour. Yes, I despise these parasites who grow fat off the misfortune of their fellow countrymen. Later I will be involved in a project which gives small loans to families to buy their own loom and material. They repay the loan with their first two or three carpets and after that things start to look up. They earn money to educate the kids and pay off the food and medical debts.

With some effort Mr Indolent swaggers to his feet and, with a well-practised flick, unfurls a rich red piece before us. "Afghan carpet, Jhi! Cheap carpet!" Then, in an attempt to impress his potential customers, he thrusts his chest out like a show pigeon. "We are Afghan mujahidin," he brags, as if he had personally taken out twenty Russian soldiers with a rocket launcher. "We are brave freedom fighters."

I picture his family securely tucked away, enjoying mountains of mutton kebabs in some fancy house near Karachi Beach. I see his menfolk gathering in the mosque to thank Allah for their well-being and prosperity. I look Mr Indolent straight in the eye and, with uncontainable contempt, spit out my response.

"You? Mujahidin? Nah! You're too fat."

I shouldn't have done it. It was bad manners, and Afghans are extremely jealous of their honour. There could be Kalashnikovs under those blankets. Like a granite monolith, his face turns to stone. His eyes blaze at me. Then slowly they soften and he starts to laugh. In a chain reaction, his brothers' iron-hardness slowly vaporises and they join in.

It's a perceptive, companionable sort of laughter, as if we are comrades. They are not just laughing at my boldness, but also at the mutually understood truth. They have read my unspoken thoughts and have perceived the reason for my uncharitable outburst. They know, and I know. There's a strange instant of recognition that we all share in the weakness, frailty and darkness of this thing called humanity. I feel a spark of respect for their unspoken honesty. It's a moment of mutual connection. I start to laugh too. Briefly, we are brothers.

In this transitory moment of unlikely connectedness, I'm given a fleeting insight into the nature of my God. Amazingly, while knowing every flaw, every weakness, every dark corner of our humanity, his desire is to connect with us, to laugh with us and to share our company. Remarkably, he has found a way to do it.

I look down at my puzzled children. "Let's go, kids. It's time to let the brave mujahidin sell their carpets."

FOURTEEN

PUTTING OFF OR PUTTING ON

MITHI, 1987

At the gate of our tiny Mithi compound, a black cobra sways and flicks its tongue. The tatty-turbaned old charmer lays aside his flute, takes the snake in both hands and, to convey his hunger, puts it in his mouth. Janna finds it repulsive. Partly out of compassion, and partly to get rid of the revolting reptile, she calls for Lali to bring some *roti*. The white-whiskered performer shuffles away with the bread and his shabby basket.

Maya, our Hindu neighbour, is watching from her gate. "You are such a good Muslim, MemSahib."

"Maya, I've told you before, I'm not a Muslim," Janna says. "I am a *Masih*—a Christian. Why do you keep calling me a Muslim?"

The neighbour raises her hands in the air, mystified by the abject ignorance of this foreign woman. "MemSahib Janna, you are wearing a *shalwar kamiz*. All Muslim women wear *shalwar kamiz*. Therefore, you are a Muslim."

"But Pakistani Christians also wear the *shalwar kamiz*."

Again Maya thrusts her palms in the air. "I don't even know what a Christian is." She flicks the skirt of her orange sari as she closes her gate. "But I do know about Muslims."

Janna is frustrated. "What can I do, Grant? If I wear a shalwar, I'm a Muslim. If I wear tribal skirts, I'm a low-caste Hindu. If I wear a sari, I'm a high caste Hindu."

"Why don't you talk to Joan next time you see her?"

*

Joan suggests that Janna wear Western "maxi" dresses, with full length skirts. "Just make sure you wear a *dupatta* scarf with them, preferably a big one."

Taking her advice, we pick up several virtually new linen bridesmaid dresses with Californian labels in Karachi's Lighthouse market.

*

A month later, over a cup of morning tea, I raise the dress-code subject. "So how are the 'maxis' working out, Janna?"

"Great. All the women love them. Now they don't label me as anything, so they all talk to me."

A four-wheel drive pulls up outside. Blacky, our dog, announces that we have guests. It's the English woman Wendy with her driver and translator. She works with another relief agency. A chatty forty-year-old, she often drops in on her way to villages further out in the desert.

Wendy stirs sugar into her tea. "I really think I'm making an impression on the villages, particularly with the women."

"How's that?" Janna asks.

"Well, you know how the women have no rights and no self-esteem around here." We nod. "I've come up with a way to help them out."

"What's that?"

"While I'm doing community development work, I show them they can be liberated and can make their own choices. Hey, these oatmeal Anzacs taste just as good as ever, Janna."

"Thanks. So what are you doing?"

"Well, I make a point of not wearing my *dupatta* on my head or around my neck. I just leave it off altogether."

Janna gulps. "But every woman in Sindh, Muslim, Hindu or Christian, wears a *dupatta*."

"Yes, and every one of them is under the bondage of males."

"But Wendy, they use the *dupatta* for practical things too. They use it to carry ber berries, wipe babies' faces, keep the sun off and all sorts of things. It's not just a cultural adornment; it's a useful piece of equipment as well."

"I'm just trying to show them they can be free. They don't have to wear that thing. It's a symbol of their bondage."

"Do you really think they're ready for that? This isn't Karachi, you know, and even there very few would be without a *dupatta*."

The gate opens and Janna's helper arrives. "*Khoosh ayo?*—Are you well?" Janna greets her and then directs her to her first task.

Wendy is impressed. "I didn't know you spoke Sindhi, Janna."

"Only the basics, but it was a matter of have to."

"What do you mean 'have to'?"

"The women don't know any Urdu because they just don't get out like the men. So I'm learning a bit of Sindhi. It's made a huge difference. In fact, I have about a dozen women coming with their daughters to my afternoon girls' group. I think they're just glad to get out of their walled compounds."

"Good for you." Wendy's lip curls a little. "But I don't have time for that language stuff. I'm only here for an eighteen-month contract and I want to get into it and make a difference. Leaving that piece of rag off is the fastest way for me to show the women they can have a life of their own." She rises confidently. "I haven't had one objection, not even from the men. I really think they're getting the message. Thanks for the cuppa, Janna."

"You're welcome. Remember to drop in on the way back."

The Land Cruiser roars off. We look at each other and roll our eyes. "Of course they're not going to complain about her not wearing a *dupatta*, Grant. She's their guest, and guests must be respected. How embarrassing for them. And it won't do anything for Wendy's credibility either."

I nod. "I can just hear that translator talking to the villagers. 'Look, you lot, don't get upset. I can't help it if this foreign woman is half crazy and goes around undressed. Just remember she's the one with the money for sewing machines and wells and health programs. So just jolly her along. She won't be here much longer.'"

We separately ponder the dangers of not recognising our own ethnocentric views, then my wife rises.

"Hey, Janna, did I tell you the story about Don Curry and old Kumbo from Vinjeera?"

"No."

"Don was in his Land Rover following a desert truck. Old Kumbo's riding on top of the truck with a heap of villagers and a few of Mithi's Vanias, the upper-class trading caste. The truck stops at a village and Kumbo shouts out to Don, 'Eh, Doctor Sahib, can I travel with you?'

The Vania traders get cranky with him. 'You'd rather travel with that unbeliever than with us? Aren't we your Hindu brothers? Aren't we the ones who help you?'"

Janna is stacking the empty cups. "So what did old Kumbo say?"

"He really got stuck into them. 'Oh yes,' he said, 'you say you help us, but you take us down whenever you can. And you say you're our brothers but you wouldn't even drink tea with us. Doctor Don and MemSahib Nancy actually come and live with us. They eat with us, wear our clothes, learn our language and treat our sicknesses.' Then he climbed down from the truck and told them, 'Doctor Don is the one who is a real brother. I'm going with him.'"

Janna looks at me. "You know, I think that's the way God is. He doesn't sit up there writing us off. He came and lived on our sandhill, put on our clothes and talked our language."

I smile and reach for my hat. "And he offers us a seat in his Land Rover. Well, I'm off to the post office. I'm waiting for an important letter."

*

Janna closes the gate and wipes the sweat from her brow. "Grant, I've just been back to Khanjhi's to see that baby camel. It's really soft and cute, even if it is so big."

I look up from my desk. "Well, I might be putting one of his humpy uncles out of a job soon."

"How's that?"

"After I talked to BP Solar in Karachi, I sent off a proposal for funding a solar-powered pump for the well."

"And ...?"

I wave a letter in the air. "It just got approval. Once it's installed I'll be using free sunlight. That means I won't have to hire a camel every day."

Success, innovation and saving money all feel good to me. But Janna looks sceptical. "What about that defunct Southern Cross windmill in the middle of town? And there's another one out in Islamkot that's just the same."

"What about them?"

"I'll bet they haven't worked for years."

"Yeah, I asked around and no one knows much except that they came from Australia about forty years ago. I reckon it was probably some Aussie aid program when Pakistan was just getting going. Keemo says people were trained to look after them."

"So what happened?"

"He reckons the trainees put the money in their pockets, and when things went wrong they weren't fixed." I close the lid of my laptop and cover it with dust-proof fabric. "Windmills look simple enough, but I know from experience that they won't keep going without regular attention."

"I can remember you fuming because you had to wait for parts," Janna smirks, "or getting cranky because there wasn't enough wind."

"Ah yes, but that's where solar power comes in. There's sun every day—too much, usually." I mop my brow and turn the ceiling fan up a notch.

"So what happens when your solar system breaks down?"

"There are a lot fewer moving parts in solar equipment and I can get anything I need sent up from Karachi."

"And what about when you're not here, Grant Lock?"

I squirm. "I'll train Keemo to do it."

She laughs. "As if Keemo could understand a technical manual. It would end up just like the windmill in town. In the end a camel would be pulling the water, so you might as well use a camel right from the start."

I'm grasping at straws, but I still want to win some points for my scheme.

"What if the camel gets sick?"

"Don't be silly. There are plenty of camels round here. You just hire another one. No waiting for the wrong part from Karachi."

I sigh. She's right and I know it. "Looks like I won't be doing business with BP Solar after all." I study my empty tea mug and mumble, "It's really hard to introduce change and not overlook local culture and resources."

Janna finds a rag and starts removing dust from the top of my filing cabinet. "Yes, but Sam's well pulleys are a success story. Keemo says all the villagers are bringing their wooden pulleys into the bazaar and getting old truck bearings fitted into them. It's cheap and makes a huge difference every day. Particularly if you don't have a donkey or camel and you and your wife have to pull it yourselves."

I really had intended to impress Keemo and the rest of the locals with my free water. I thought the idea might change things for a lot of wells at Mithi. But what one thinks and what will really work are two different things.

I fossick around for my recently moved sunglasses. "Well, I'm off to tell Keemo to hire a camel."

FIFTEEN

ALMOST ORANGE MARMALADE

SINDH PROVINCE, 1987

Around the bend up ahead, the gaudy bus has pulled off the narrow black ribbon. It's packed. From a quarter of a mile away I see it disgorging some of its sardines. I immediately start braking and leaning on the horn.

In Australia, if you use your horn, you feel like a criminal. In Pakistan, if you don't use your horn, you *are* a criminal. If the horn fails here, you are driving naked. Wanderers on the road won't move to the side unless they hear a horn behind them. As soon as we got our vehicle, I fitted extra horns for just this kind of situation: to warn anyone thinking about moving out from behind a bus.

Soon after we arrived in Pakistan I opened an official-looking letter. It was from my life insurance company.

> Dear Mr Lock
>
> It has come to our attention that you are currently residing in Pakistan. Our statistics department has shown that driving in Pakistan involves a much higher risk of accident and death than driving in Australia.
>
> Due to the increased risk borne by this company we are obliged to notify you that your annual insurance premium will be increased accordingly.
>
> Yours sincerely, etc.

I was really upset and promptly wrote back with passion.

Dear Sir

As you are aware, I have been living in Kimba in rural South Australia. The next town is 70 km away and it is a 1000 km round trip to visit our accountant in Adelaide. We have clients and stud cattle colleagues in every state of the country. For twenty-five years I've been driving countless hours on long empty roads. Your statistics department will tell you that the greatest risk in such monotonous situations is driver drowsiness. All over rural Australia newspapers regularly report on single driver accidents caused by sleepy drivers.

Driving on Pakistani roads is different. One never goes to sleep. Apart from the unruly cars, undisciplined trucks and unpredictable buses on the road, there are people, push-bike and motorbikes. There are all manner of animals, from goats to unswerving buffaloes and strings of camels. There are deaf old men and there are boys chasing cricket balls.

Sir, I strongly disagree with your premise that, for me, the risk of driving in this country is greater than in Australia. Therefore I am not inclined to pay any extra premium.

Yours sincerely, etc.

The statistics department must have accepted my logic as the company did not reply, nor did they increase my premium.

*

We've just left the desert and have picked up speed on the flat Indus plains, the biggest single irrigated area in the world. Tomorrow we'll put the kids on the train, and the day after that they'll be in the foothills of the Pakistani Himalayas, boarding in Murree Christian School. They can't wait to get back with their friends, but it's a tough time for us, particularly Janna.

I'm braking hard and still leaning on the horn. If someone steps out from behind that bus they'll be right in my path. The road is only one-vehicle wide and slopes away dangerously on each side.

Oh no! An unhearing tribal woman in her colourful skirts strides out single-mindedly from behind the bus. She's carrying something in her arms. My adrenaline is pumping. The brakes are full on, but I've still got too much momentum. The sound I fear most is the thump of flesh colliding with my sturdy bull-bar. Now it's going to happen. "Go back, woman! Go back!"

She comes out of her reverie, looks our way and springs back behind the bus, dropping some of the contents of her bundle. Whew! Relief.

But now she's back on the road, reaching for something. I can't believe it. She's right in the middle of this narrow road, chasing the oranges she dropped. She's obviously poor. Perhaps she's spent her last *paisa* on something special for her family or a sick grandchild. The brakes are full on again but I'm going to hit her.

I jerk the wheel, swerve and spear the vehicle down the embankment. The girls are screaming, but I can't hear them—I'm fully occupied. If I turn harder I'll roll; if I don't I'll hit that wall.

We hit the wall. The vehicle rocks back and settles in a cloud of powdery dust. There is a moment of silence as we teleport back from the vacuum of shock. "Is everyone okay?" I ask. Four voices shakily reply in the affirmative. The seat belts have done their job. We look at each other with thankfulness, and at the same time I'm thinking the weirdest thought: "So that's what it's like to be a stunt driver."

I look back. The bus has gone, the village woman has gone, and all the oranges have gone. Thankfully I haven't heard the dreaded thud of flesh on moving metal—but in a few more years, I will.

*

A decade later Matthew discusses the accident with me. "That crash had a big effect on me, Dad. I'd always viewed seat belts as a pain, especially since the local Pakistanis never wore them. They said that if Allah ordains that you're going to die that day, you're going to die. But without that seat belt I would've been a goner. I know I was only eleven but it made me think. Before that, I figured there was plenty of time to get serious about life, and about God. It was then I realised that you just never know when your time is up."

SIXTEEN

THE WAITING ROOM

KARACHI, DECEMBER 1987

It's been three long years. There have been many difficulties, many blessings, and it has never been boring, except for some of the slog of language learning. Now we're due for our first home assignment. After snake charmers at the door, fears of being kidnapped in the Kirthar National Park, long hours on dangerous roads, late nights on book work and budgeting in the oversized oven called the Sindh, we're both totally bushed. It's time to head back to Australia for three months, take a break in our original culture, catch up with family and supporters, and have complete medical checkups.

Last year Bishop Jhivan met with us. "Grant, I want you to take on the leadership of the Thar Aid Program. That means you keep an eye on the team, handle the project proposals and financial accounting, and liaise with the government departments."

He kept going. "In the next twelve months I want you to work with the team and produce a ten-year strategy for our role in rural development in the Thar Desert. I want you to consult with Don and Sam and design our project buildings for our plot outside Mithi. Then you'll need to produce fully costed project proposals and budgets to present to potential donors."

He turned to Janna. "Apart from supporting Grant, Janna, I want you to keep up your afternoon programs for the girls and women, and to encourage Joan, Nancy and Janet wherever you can."

Whew! I thought. *That's going to keep us really busy.*

Since then it has been a solid twelve months but the deadlines have been met. The planning, proposals, audits, tree-planting and visits to government offices have all been done. Now we are totally exhausted. The kids will join us in Singapore after we have had a week's recovery time and they have finished their semester.

A week before we are due to fly out from Karachi, Janna develops some leg pains. Fortunately Don and Nancy call in on their way out to Gordi. "You'll have to get them checked in Karachi," Dr Don says. "If it's blood clots you won't be flying."

*

So here I am in the waiting room of one of Karachi's best hospitals. A helpful doctor has seen Janna. "Mrs Lock, we'll pump dye into your veins on the left side and follow the flow through your left leg. Then we'll do the same on the right side. If there are clots they will show up. We should be able to fit you in soon." He turns to me. "Nurse will guide you to the waiting room, Mr Lock."

Waiting rooms are for waiting. They are well named. I've been waiting and waiting for nearly three hours. I start asking questions.

"Sorry, Mr Lock, we've had some technical difficulties. I think that Mrs Lock is being checked right now."

More waiting. I'm hopeful Janna will soon come back smiling and say, "All is well, Grant. We can fly." When she finally does appear, it's a different story. She's in a flimsy hospital gown, shivering and almost in tears.

"They couldn't get a needle into a vein, Grant. That air-conditioned room was so cold and I was there so long, my veins all contracted. They took turns at digging around with the needle in my arm, in my wrist, in my ankle."

The weepy description of multiple jabs and pokes is tipping me over the edge. Needles ... digging ... veins ... The words penetrate the core of my vulnerable psyche and I'm feeling woozy. I'm not good with needles and blood, at least not when it's related to humans. I've slashed open huge abscesses on bulls, spent hours on difficult calf deliveries, even fixed a cow's inverted uterus, but I can't handle this.

Janna's distressed voice sounds like it's coming down a hollow pipe. "Finally the fourth doctor found a vein and they pumped the dye in and checked the left leg."

I'm getting woozier. I'd better sit down. The pipe is getting longer; Janna's voice is coming from the stratosphere.

"Then they couldn't get the needle into my right arm, and they're all taking turns at poking around again. Grant, it was horrible! Then someone said the machine had stopped working again, so they brought me out here."

"I'm going to faint," I mumble from fuzzy-land.

I looked up my aversions once. Fear of blood is haemophobia. Fear of sharp objects, which includes needles, is belonephobia. It's this nasty combination that causes people like me to faint.

"Quick, bring the oxygen!" shouts the young Pakistani doctor. "Sit down here, Sir. Put your head low."

In my fuzziness I'm surrounded by white-coated medics flapping around, giving orders to each other and anyone else who might be listening. *Hey, it's only a bit of fainting. It's not a cardiac arrest.*

Down the corridor an old peon, the only one who was taking any notice, is pushing a large oxygen cylinder. It rolls up and halts directly before my blurry eyes. *Is that a badly tangled hose wrapped around the gauges or is it Medusa's head?* I'm fading out. The last thing I hear is Janna's voice: "He'll be all right. He does that sort of thing."

The fog is lifting. I hear Pakistani medical voices coming from around the oxygen cylinder.

"Hurry! Get that hose untangled!"

"There it is—put the mask on him."

"Hey, he's coming around."

"Turn it on."

"Have you turned it on?"

"There's no oxygen coming."

"The cylinder must be empty."

"Quick, get another one. He may need it."

Janna, in her hospital gown, is sitting beside me, holding my hand. She's the one who has suffered. I should be holding *her* hand.

"I told them you'd be okay," she says.

Another cylinder appears—the non-Medusa model. I slowly wave a leaden hand. "I don't need it. I'm all right."

Having gone to all the trouble to prove the hospital can deliver oxygen, albeit a little late, they jam the mask over my face and compel me to take some draughts.

Janna and I look at each other. Neither of us is in very good shape. I'm trying to evaluate the situation without mentioning needles. "So they only checked one leg?"

"Yes, and that was fine."

"And they couldn't check the other one?"

"No, I told you they couldn't get the—"

I cut her off. I don't want to hear the n-word. "Well, the question is, can we fly out at midnight tomorrow night?"

"They're saying it will be okay."

"Then let's get out of here."

We both stagger out of the hospital. I can't wait to be on that plane. But throwing a six to get out of Pakistan is going to be harder than we think.

SEVENTEEN

SWISSAIR SCARE

"You cannot leave Pakistan," the stone-faced immigration officer at the airport announces. "Your papers are not in order."

"I beg your pardon, *Janaab*. Our passports are all up-to-date, and we have not overstayed our visas."

The officer takes the police papers from our passports and waves them in my face. "You did not give these departure documents to the police."

"I most certainly did, Sir! I visited the Mirpurkhas Police Station and did all the required paperwork and they put those pieces of paper back in our passports."

The officer is not convinced. "Stand over there," he orders, and stalks off to find his superior.

I'm breaking out in a cold sweat. *Lord, just get us on that plane. We don't need all this.*

"How was I to know the police should have kept those papers?" I complain to Janna. "They must have had a new chum doing it or something."

We wait and wait. The Swissair plane is out on the tarmac, but until we get the nod it might as well be circling Lake Geneva. Finally the immigration officer reappears with his imperious supervisor. The superior officer's uniform bristles with insignias and he looks like he won't stand for any funny business.

*

The trip from the guesthouse to the airport wasn't simple. At nine at night I was out scanning the streets. It seemed that every taxi was either full or had gone home to bed. Finally I saw one parked at a nearby service station. It wasn't going anywhere, though. It was jacked up and the driver was on his hands and knees looking at the tyre.

I spoke to him. "We need to get to the airport quickly. Where can I find a taxi, Jhi?"

He jumped to his feet. "That would be me," he stated promptly. *I can't knock back a foreigner just because there's a flap of rubber coming off the tyre. There should be a good tip in this, particularly since he's in a hurry.*

Before I could object to the obvious immobility of his vehicle, he clicked down the jack, threw it in the back and stood tall, ready for business. We negotiated a healthy but essential fare and were off to pick up Janna and the suitcases.

"What was wrong with the tyre?" I asked from the back seat.

"Nothing, *Janaab*. Absolutely nothing. We'll be there in twenty-five minutes."

I was relieved. Getting a taxi had taken longer than I thought and we were cutting it fine. He pointed the ancient rust-bucket in the direction of the airport and rapidly picked up speed. Only one word of my instructions was present in his cognisance, and that word was "quickly."

Over the noise of regular Karachi rattles, a thumping began and got louder and louder. Janna was alarmed. "What's that noise?"

"*Kooch nahee*, MemSahib—it's nothing." He spurred his metallic steed on through the night.

It was not a comforting sound for people who had to catch a plane. It was coming from his suspect tyre and I deduced he had a flap of rubber lifting, and the faster he went the more it tore and banged against the mudguard.

"*Ahista! Ahista!* Slow down! Slow down!" I commanded. "We do want to *get* to the airport."

That was the part of the original instruction he had overlooked, the getting there. He eased off on the accelerator, but like a Formula One driver who's been ordered back to the pits, he was totally deflated. Before long, however, that word "quickly" overrode the cerebral controls and the foot went down again. Each segment of the Karachi Grand Prix then played out like this:

Driver increased speed.

Noise sensor on rear mudguard alerted team to a component failure.

Angry sponsors ordered reduction of acceleration.

Driver reduced forward movement of vehicle, temporarily.

Cycle repeated.

Finally the sponsors heaved a sigh of relief as the driver cleared the chequered flag. He was all grins. The lack of champagne was obviated by a healthy tip.

Pushing the loaded trolley through the terminal door, I looked back. Michael Noisemaker had his machine up on the jack once more and was inspecting the offending rubber. Perhaps the team needed to match the tyres better with the conditions next time.

*

"You cannot leave Pakistan," the bristly uniform confirms. "You failed to observe our laws."

I'm flabbergasted. I explain again that I did all that was required and the Mirpurkhas police are the ones who failed in their duty, not Janna and me. We're both praying hard.

"Then you must go to the police station here and hand in the documents."

Oh good, they've got a police station here at the International Airport.

"Sir, please tell me where it is."

"In Shahrah-e-Faisal Road."

"And which part of the airport is that, Sir?"

"It's not in the airport. It's in downtown Karachi."

Oh no, not downtown. Hold on, Karachi is a mega-city. That central police station will be open all night. If I score a decent taxi, I can be in there, hand over the documents and back in fifty minutes. We might make it yet.

Then the officer adds, "They open at eight o'clock in the morning."

All my optimistic avenues have evaporated. I feel like I, too, have been ordered back to the pits.

The senior officer moves closer. "Sir, you are not cooperating with us," and he extends his hand. "I will have to confiscate your passports. Give them to me."

Exasperation, deflation and now despair.

Reluctantly I obey orders, but Janna clutches hers with an iron grip. "No, I will not let you have my passport. We've done nothing wrong."

I just want to get Janna out of here.

She looks at me in alarm. "Grant, did you hear that? They're calling our names to board. It's the last call. What can we do?"

Lord, we've both had enough. We need to get out of here. We can't face going back, and now our plane is leaving.

Immediately a thought flashes into my brain: we are guests, and this society operates on hospitality, shame and honour.

I look the officer squarely in the eye. "So, Sir, this is the way you treat your guests in the Land of the Pure? This is how you treat those who come to serve your people? This is how you show hospitality to visitors who come to help suffering Pakistanis in remote places like the Thar Desert?" I see the uniforms wilting in the desiccating winds of dishonour. They look at each other. Their posture slowly changes. The taller thrusts my passport at me. "Go! Just go! And do not let this happen again."

⁕

The Swissair 747 lifts off. Clunk! Clunk! The wheels fold into their cavities. I breathe a sigh of relief and take Janna's hand. "That was the sweetest sound I've heard in a long, long time."

"Do you think they were squeezing us for a bribe, Grant?"

"How ignorant of me! I never even thought of that."

"Just as well you didn't. You wouldn't have paid it anyway."

EIGHTEEN

FRIES YOUR BRAINS

MITHI, MARCH 1988

We've returned from Australia for our second three-year term in the Thar Desert. It's summer and the plains are an oven. I leave my family in a rented apartment in the cool Murree hills. The kids will attend school and Janna will spend three months grappling with yet more language at the Sindhi summer school.

In Australia some folks eye-balled us. "Look! It really is too dangerous over there."

We found that interesting. While we were gone a local farmer went spear-fishing with his wife. There was a splash and a scream, and as he watched a great white shark took her. And some young men from our district were flying to an agricultural conference when they flew into fog, and a mountain. Danger and death can be anywhere.

On the way back to the desert I call in on the head of police in Hyderabad. His uniform is immaculate; a crease would not dare enter these precincts. He barks an order to his *chaparasi:* "Bring the very best chai for Mr Lock. *Jeldi!*—Quickly!"

I thank him for his consideration and explain my visit. "Sir, I have a problem."

"*Janaab,* you are an honoured guest in our country and we appreciate what you are doing for our people. I am at your service."

"Sir, you have a regulation here in Hyderabad that the windows of vehicles cannot have dark antiglare paper on the glass."

"That is right, Mr Lock. In this city we must be able to see into vehicles to apprehend any criminals. The dacoits have more weapons than ever these days, and kidnappings and robberies are on the rise. It's for your own protection."

"But Sir, when my family travels with me and we stop in some of the towns on the way to the desert, the men all crowd round the windows, like animals, to stare at my wife and teenage daughters. It's terrifying for them, even though they wear culturally appropriate clothes. That's why we have antiglare paper. If we have to remove it from the windows while we're here, it will be even worse for them."

Tea arrives and, as the *chaparasi* pours me a cup, I make my request. "Sir, if you can kindly give written permission for us to keep the dark film on the windows, it would be greatly appreciated."

The Head of Police clears his throat. "Hmm, I'm afraid that is not possible, Mr Lock, but there is an alternative."

"Please tell me, Sir."

"When you are driving in the city you can simply wind the windows down."

"But Sir, we would still have the same problem, and it would be extremely hot. The air conditioner would be useless with the windows down."

He slowly rubs his chin. "There *is* another, more traditional, solution."

I lean forward. "Yes?"

"Instead of winding the windows down you could install curtains. That way you will not be breaking the law, and your lady folk will not be visible and will feel protected."

Wait a minute, Mr Chief of Police, that doesn't make any sense. If there were bad people inside my vehicle, wouldn't a curtain be more difficult for your officers to see through than dark film? Your countrymen have a saying about the Pakistani summer: "It's so hot the sun fries your brains." I wonder if you've been reviewing too many police parades out in the heat of the sun.

I grapple to find a polite way to raise this commonsense objection. In the end I refrain. I'm learning that sometimes the seemingly illogical is totally logical. In this case it's just the modern application of a man's age-old rights of *purdah* for his women. Too bad if the dacoits kidnap someone and cheerfully flee away with the curtains drawn. At least they are not breaking the no-dark-film-on-glass law.

I thank the chief and leave his crease-proof, air-conditioned office. Shaking my head in bewilderment, I step out into the blowtorch of the Sindhi sun.

*

In Mithi I'm having trouble sleeping. Daytime temperatures are reaching 50°C—that's over 120°F. I now know what the four-and-twenty blackbirds felt like. After soaking my sheet in water I lie directly under the ceiling fan. When the power fails, which is often, I stretch out my sleep-deprived body on a string bed in the courtyard. The high, hot walls are like Manchester United's top defenders, not letting much through. Ironically, no one sleeps on the flat roofs where the breeze is unrestricted. It's too risky. The neighbour might look across and see your wife and daughters. He might allege that you saw his womenfolk. Better to perspire in the heat than risk your family's reputation, and a possible feud.

Then there's the night watchman. I question Keemo, who is elated that I'm back.

"Keemo, how much do we pay that night *chaokidaar* (watchman)?"

"Laark Jhi, all the households pay him 30 rupees a month to patrol the streets and lanes in this part of town."

"Well, why should I pay him to keep me awake at night?" *I wish I knew the Urdu word for "masochist".*

"What do you mean 'keep you awake', Laark Sahib?" He scratches his head. "Because of him, you can sleep peacefully."

"No I can't, Keemo. Every hour he comes past, and every second step he takes he thumps that big staff on the road. Thump. Thump. Thump. You can hear it coming two hundred yards away."

"But Laark Sahib, he is obliged to make that noise."

"Obliged?"

He spreads his hand out in bewilderment at my unbelievable density. "That way everyone knows he is working and not sleeping."

"Well, what about the robbers, Keemo? You wouldn't have to be a very smart thief to listen until he has gone past and then make your break-in."

Keemo frowns. "But Jhi, it's most important to know the watchman is on patrol and not sleeping. You wouldn't want to pay him to sleep would you, Laark Sahib?"

Something about a circular argument crawls through the dunes of my heat-fuddled head, but then, "the sun fries your brains". I give up.

NINETEEN

GOOD NEWS, BAD NEWS

AUGUST 17, 1988

The grass is knee high and everyone is in high spirits. After seven years of cheating the desert, the monsoon clouds have finally released their bounty. Back in the flat irrigated areas there have been massive floods. In Karachi, two million items of water-damaged mail have been burned. I wonder if any was meant for us.

Bishop Jhivan has sent out a small team of Sindhi singers and I'm taking them out to Gordi village, where Dr Don and Nancy Curry are based. Just out of Mithi we drive past our five-acre plot and I can see the trusty dromedary pulling water from the well. I'm pleased that our trees have grown up to six feet in twelve months.

I turn to my grinning assistant. "You were right, Keemo. It does look like the Garden of Eden."

With the rains the desert dwellers rushed back from the irrigated areas. They increased their debts by buying expensive grain to fuel their skinny camels and cows to pull simple stick-ploughs. They scratched the loam flats and planted millet seed. As we scoot along the rain-compacted desert tracks, I note numerous platforms erected above the now head-high millet. A few men, and many boys, crack whips and re-load their slingshots to drive off hordes of frustrated birds from the ripening heads. After all, millet is also known as "bird-seed".

Gordi village appears in the distance. Sharing the sandhill with forty cone-shaped thatched dwellings are two flat-roofed brick buildings. The headman lives in one and the Canadian doctor in the other.

A crowd of men and boys welcomes us. It's common to use religious phrases in Muslim, Hindu and Christian greetings. Padre Raj, a popular local singer, greets the crowd: "*Yesoo ki jaai*—Jesus be praised."

One of the men steps forward. His face contorts with anger. He begins to remonstrate and shout. Trance-like, he waves a box of matches in the air, and then slowly and dramatically crushes it under his heel. The Padre starts to speak with him but he strides off, cursing and waving his arms.

"He has an evil spirit," Padre Raj announces. "I offered to pray for him. Maybe he will come back later."

The headman and Dr Don emerge from the group and we exchange lengthy greetings. Don leads me to his home while the villagers look after my passengers.

I greet Nancy in her arm-length bangles and colourful tribal skirt and we all exchange news over tea.

"How are things going out here, Don?"

"Do you want the good news or the bad news, Grant?"

"Good news first."

He smiles. "Well, I've finally come up with a way to get TB sufferers to finish their course of treatment."

"That's good."

"I stopped the pay-as-you-go monthly treatment system."

"You're doing it for free then?"

"That doesn't work either," Nancy says, pouring the chai. "They still stop half way when they feel better and think they're cured."

"So what did you do, Don?"

"I told them that if they are serious, they have to pay everything up front. Usually they have to sell a goat to do it. But then they keep coming back for what they've paid for. And I give them a guarantee that if at the end they are not cured, I will pay for a course of the more expensive medicine to knock it out. The plan seems to be working."

"Good thinking."

"And of course," adds Nancy, "they really appreciate having a general practitioner out here in the middle of nowhere."

There's a faint call at the gate. "That will be Kumbi," announces Nancy as she rises. "I'll take her inside."

The young woman moves slowly past our chairs on the veranda. She carries a small baby in one arm and holds her *dupatta* to shield her face from us with the other. Her movements indicate a deep heaviness.

"The poor girl is not well," Don explains. "She's very depressed."

"Post-natal depression?" I tentatively suggest.

"No, it started last year. She hadn't produced a child so her husband took her to a particular *pir* (holy man). The *pir* promised her a baby, but they had to sacrifice a goat and go through a lot of rituals while he called up the spirits."

"I see she has a baby."

"Yes, but at what cost, Grant? She used to be a cheerful girl, but she came back from that *pir* dull and heavy. It doesn't pay to do business with those spirits. They are real, and they are evil."

I pour myself another cup of tea. "So what's the bad news, Don?"

"It was really a cultural slip-up on my part." The Canadian looks visibly upset. "They nearly threw us out of the village."

"What happened?"

"Well, the neighbour's ten-year-old boy kept coming into our yard whenever he pleased. He intrudes on Nancy when she's talking with the village women and he bosses their kids around."

I adjust my chair to avoid the moving sun. "Sounds like a real nuisance."

Don nods. "I warned him several times and talked to his father, but none of that worked."

"So what did you do?"

"One day, after more warnings, I grabbed him and put him over my knee and spanked him on the backside, just like my dad used to do to me every now and then. Well, all hell broke loose." The Rocky Mountain-bred doctor groans. "It didn't help that the kid is the headman's favourite nephew."

Nancy has seen Kumbi to the gate and she gives the village girl a farewell hug.

"So what happened?"

"All the men came round and they were very angry. They said it wasn't their custom."

Nancy sits and her finely chiselled face shares the pain. "I wish Don had just screwed his ear, really hard, like the locals do. That would have been all right, but not a North American paddling."

"I apologised profusely," Don says, "and I promised not to do it again. It was very embarrassing all round."

Nancy stirs her second cup. "We're still here," she goes on, "but we might have to leave anyway."

"What do you mean? Is the village still upset?"

"No, that's all settled. This is another matter. It's political, and it's with the church."

"Well," I comment, "there's always some group in the diocese pushing for their man to be the next bishop. I guess where you have people, you have politics."

"No, Grant, this is to do with the government and India."

I'm puzzled. "India?"

"You know how Pakistan and India never get along and have frequent border scraps?" I nod. I'm well aware of Pakistan's paranoia about its eastern neighbour. "Well, there are certain people who are saying Bishop Jhivan has foreign spies living in the desert."

"That's you, I suppose," I say, smirking.

"And you too," grins Don. "You're not exempt. They're accusing the bishop of sending us all out to spy for the Indian government."

My jaw drops. "How ridiculous!"

Don passes the aniseed biscuits. "It's getting serious. The bishop is under pressure to pull us all out. We'll be first to go, of course—we're only an hour's drive from the Indian border."

I can't believe it. Here we are toughing it out in the desert, doing things Pakistan's government can't or won't do: TB treatment, eye-camps, women's health, community development. And now someone is labelling us Indian spies. They're saying we're enemies of the very government and people we have come to serve. It makes me angry. We're just pawns in a political power struggle. With elections coming up, I'll bet some conniving group wants to look good by playing the old patriotism card: "Watch out for India. India is to blame for everything! And watch out for those foreign agents the bishop has planted in the desert." So who misses out again? The desert people.

A tabla drum tuning up in the distance brings me out of my irate reverie as Don goes on. "It's all politics. Who knows who's behind it? There mightn't even be an election yet, if President Zia changes his mind again. He knows he's unpopular, for many reasons."

"Including pushing for stronger Islamisation," interrupts Nancy. "For eleven years he's put off holding full general elections, and he just might do it again."

"It's possible," I say, "but it looks like the people are really behind Benazir Bhutto, and she is demanding elections."

My host holds up his glasses, scowls at the snail tracks of dried perspiration on the lenses and slowly wipes them clean. "It's not surprising she wants to topple Zia. He was the one who lead the coup against her father, President Bhutto, and then had him hung."

"Benazir is a pretty smart cookie," Nancy says with feminine pride. "She was a top debater in Oxford, and if she wins she'll be the first woman to lead an Islamic country. That would really upset Zia and the fundamentalists."

Don draws us back to local realities. "Anyway, the bishop says there's a lot going on, and he's caught in the middle of it. He says he'll let us know if and when we have to move. I only hope he gives me time to finish training my TB workers."

There's a respectful cough at the door. It's Akhibo, a gentle young man with compassionate eyes and one of Don's trainees.

"What is it, Akhibo?"

"The men are gathering in the *ootaaq* and they're all waiting for you, Doctor Sahib."

We rise and leave the veranda together. On the edge of the village, the *ootaaq*, with its thatched cone roof, looks like something the second little pig would have constructed from sticks.

The circular guest room is full of Hindu tribal men. It's a mystery to me how they can sit cross-legged on the sand for hours without moving. I carefully choose a post to lean on. Outside the door is an array of fifty pairs of identical, village-made leather shoes. I wonder if they all go home on the same feet they came on. Sandals are no good out here; this is snake country.

The harmonium and the drum are tuning up. Sindhis love listening to their singers. The singer plays the small boxlike harmonium with one hand and pumps its built-in bellows with the other.

The headman welcomes the visitors and everyone settles back for the entertainment. As the sun's orange orb dips behind the distant sandhills, the Padre introduces a song about the marvels of God's creation.

Then old Shanka is invited to speak. "I used to be afraid of evil spirits," he says. "And I thought I had no hope for the future. I'm just an old desert shepherd. What chance is there for me to go through all those reincarnations to be accepted by the gods? Then Yesu (Jesus) appeared to me in a vision. Now I follow him." Shanka's leathery face radiates confidence. "I even graze my goats in the graveyard at night."

Low gasps and murmurs pass through the gathering as the musicians begin the next song. It is not completed. Sporting a mere shadow of a moustache, a young villager bursts into the crowded men's room and waves his battered transistor radio at the real moustaches. "General Zia is gone!" he shouts. "The President is gone!"

The drummer freezes. The singer's hand stops pumping the harmonium. All eyes fall on the bad-mannered intruder.

The white-turbaned elders make indignant noises. "How dare this upstart interrupt?"

"The younger generation and their gadgets! They've lost all sense of respect."

Other voices rise above the white-beards' grumbles. "Gone? Where has the President gone?"

The centre of attention holds the radio to his ear: "*Soono! Soono!* Listen! Listen!" He turns the receiver's volume to maximum and holds it aloft.

The crackling voice comes from Islamabad, the national capital, a thousand miles away.

"... there are no survivors. It is the worst aeroplane crash in Pakistan's history. All thirty on board the Army's C130 died instantly when the aircraft exploded shortly after takeoff. I repeat: it has just been confirmed that today, the seventeenth of August 1988, our beloved and honourable leader, President Mohammad Zia ul-Haq, is dead. The US Ambassador and top military leaders have also perished."

I look around at the assembled faces. Some are totally unmoved, some look a bit shocked and some show a faint smile of relief. After all, the Sindh is the heartland of Benazir Bhutto and her People's Party.

The *ootaaq* begins to hum with speculation. Don turns to me. "Wow! Do you think it's an assassination?"

I'm about to reply when just outside the stick walls, a panting camel growls as it is forced to kneel. Political suppositions take a back seat as an ashen-faced visitor enters. He offers the briefest of greetings then jabbers to the headman in the Dhatki dialect. The headman approaches us. "Get your Land Rover out, Doctor Sahib. There's been an accident. This man has travelled ten miles. His brother is in trouble."

Don greets the distraught visitor and they have a short discussion in Dhatki.

He turns to me. "Bad news, Grant. This guy's brother was waiting for a desert truck, and he went to sleep on the sandy track. Then the truck comes over the ridge and runs over him—both legs." Don grimaces and shakes his head. "Apparently he's in a really bad way. I'll do what I can, but I'll have to take him to Mithi tonight, or even on to Hyderabad."

Don leaves with some of the men. The remainder now have two tragedies to speculate about. The local event takes precedence.

"Sleeping on the track—he must have been crazy."

"Maybe he was fighting the birds all day and was really tired."

"Or out in the heat too long and the sun fried his brains."

A better-dressed villager speaks up. "I wonder who fried the brains of President Zia?" He smirks cynically. "One thing is for sure, it wasn't the sun!"

TWENTY

GARDENING THE TALIBAN

SEPTEMBER 1988

After General Zia sent his boss to the gallows and set himself up as a military dictator, things changed. For over a decade he irrevocably altered the tone of Islam in Pakistan, with critical spin-offs for the rest of the world. Many people ask me, "Where did the Taliban come from?" It's not the whole story, but it's helpful if you understand the legacies of General Zia ul-Haq.

The General was the champion of greater Islamisation and the proponent of the blasphemy laws. That's why the desert Hindus are not overcome with remorse that his plane never landed. Like the Christians, they too are a vulnerable two per cent minority in the Islamic Republic of Pakistan.

For example, three Christians have been sentenced to death by a Sessions Court. Their alleged crime: they wrote blasphemous remarks against Islam on the wall of a mosque. Amnesty International reported that, prior to the alleged graffiti incident, Salamat Masih had argued with a neighbourhood boy over pet pigeons. The boy went to the village elders and claimed that he had seen Salamat write on the mosque wall.

"What were the blasphemous remarks?" the judge asked the Maulvi (the local Muslim prayer leader).

The Maulvi would not repeat them "because they were so offensive".

"But others must have seen them."

The man replied in the negative. He claimed he scrubbed them off as soon as he saw them.

The three Christians were then accused of scattering leaflets that defamed Islam, but no copies could be produced for the court. Nevertheless, they were declared guilty.

Now the convicted "blasphemers" have appealed to the High Court in Lahore. Salamat is only fourteen years old. All three are poor and cannot read or write. The Islamists are incensed that the "unbelievers" have actually appealed. "Surely they are guilty. The Muslim brothers would not lie. President Zia was right to introduce the blasphemy laws to protect the holy faith of Islam."

When the hearing is over, the High Court judges are safely whisked away from the noisy demonstrations outside. The Christians wait for things to settle down, until it's safe enough to return to their lodgings. They quickly walk clear of the court precincts and are well away from the outraged demonstrators, who declare that regardless of what the judges decide, these *kafirs* must be punished. "Islam" means "submit". The honour of Islam is at stake; all must submit to Allah.

Sure that no one is following them, the Christians breathe a little easier. But they are not safe. Several gunmen on motorcycles roar out of the traffic and open fire with automatic weapons.

As the motorbikes accelerate away, Manzoor Masih lies dying on the footpath. Rahemat and Salamat are injured but survive to re-appear in the appeal court dock. Ultimately declared innocent, they will have to start a new life away from the Muslim avengers in their village.

Within days one of the senior judges is found dead. It looks like murder.

*

In Mithi everyone is speculating about the cause of President Zia's plane crash. I've sought out my Muslim school teacher friend, Mohammad Akram. His uncle used to be a Member of Parliament, so I'm sure he'll have some perspectives to share.

"So what do you think, Akram? Was it an accident or was it wholesale assassination?"

Akram pours two cups of milky chai. "Well, Grant Jhi, President Zia has been around for a long time and made many enemies. India is being blamed."

"That's normal though. What about Russia? They must be angry that Zia supports the mujahidin resistance against the Soviet invasion of Afghanistan."

"Maybe," Akram says, "and it's ironic, but I'm sure Zia thanked the Russians for keeping him in power."

"How did Russia keep him in power?"

Akram reaches for the switch and turns the ceiling fan up another notch. "After his military coup Zia was internationally shunned. Then Islamic fundamentalists attacked the US embassy in Islamabad. The US was very angry and stopped all its aid programs. Zia was finished."

"And then?"

"In the nick of time, the Soviets marched into neighbouring Afghanistan. That was December '79, nine years ago. The US desperately needed a partner to fight their proxy war against the communists, and guess who was there with his hand up?"

"Self-preservation all round." I lean back to enjoy the fan. "Blind Freddy could see that Pakistan would be next as Russia pushed south to get a warm-water port, and that would have affected the whole balance of power in the world. The USA was naturally threatened by that."

Akram reaches for his pencil. "Who is this person Blind Freddy?" Apart from being a thinker, the teacher is also a keen student of English. It's his fifth language.

I explain the saying and continue. "So Zia had a political resurrection?"

"Absolutely! The international bad guy became the hero of the non-communist world. America has channelled billions of dollars in armaments to the Afghan freedom fighters. Pakistan has done very well out of it. Now the mujahidin, with their American Stinger missiles, are taking out the Soviet helicopters and turning the war around. *Jiski laati ooski bhains.*"

"Now it's your turn to explain a proverb, Akram. What's a buffalo got to do with it?"

He smiles. "'He who has the big stick gets the buffalo.' And in this case, the one with the strongest weapons gets Afghanistan."

"Okay, so Zia comes back from the political graveyard to implement a stricter form of Islamisation, and to push Islamic sharia law. But it seems that his blasphemy legislation is being used unfairly against people, particularly minorities like Christians, Hindus and lesser Islamic groups."

Akram offers me a hot samosa. "The problem is, Grant Jhi, the judges and magistrates are often afraid to pass a 'not guilty' sentence."

The samosa is tasty, albeit greasy. "Not even if it's a very clear case?"

"The powerful Islamist groups come out on the streets and everyone is afraid of them. They take the law into their own hands because they claim they are protecting the honour of Islam." The electricity goes off suddenly and the chopping ceiling fan slows. "Zia also introduced the terrible Zina ordinance."

"Doesn't that shackle Pakistani women more than ever?"

Akram lowers his voice. "We had a typical case recently. A girl, not yet married, was gang raped by three young men. She bravely complained to the police. They asked her if she had the required four reliable male witnesses to verify her claims that it actually was rape."

"She was supposed to provide four male witnesses? I can't believe that's part of sharia law."

"It is, and of course she didn't have them, so instead of taking up her case, the police charged her with fornication and locked her up." He lowers his voice even more. "And while she is in prison they help themselves."

"What happened to the men?"

"Nothing! They walked away."

"That's not a fair go."

"The Zina law can also be used by husbands, like a big stick, to keep their women under their control. If a woman wants to divorce her husband—and that's almost impossible anyway—he can threaten to accuse her of adultery, even if it's not true. At the minimum it would mean jail for her. According to Islamic sharia law, a female's testimony is worth only half of a male's, so her word would count for nothing against his. She is trapped."

There is silence for a moment. I ask about the girl in prison. "Can't the family do something to get her out?"

"One day her case will be heard. If she was married, according to sharia law she could be stoned. But more likely she will be jailed for life. Since she's single, after a time in jail she could be whipped and released. By then her family may not want her back. Although innocent, she has brought much shame on them, and that makes it hard to arrange marriages for her sisters." He averts his eyes and sighs. "They say it's just a part of sharia law, but until it's revised, countless women will suffer."

Perspiration trickles down the inside of my shirt. I stare at my cup and give silent thanks I'm not a Muslim woman. It's no wonder Janna has such a burden for them. It just doesn't add up. Back in the West some Muslim leaders claim that sharia law is the best thing for women since sliced bread. But from what I see here most of the time, females don't really count.

Not that the West has all the answers. I'm embarrassed by some of the sleazy Western-produced videos the men take home from the video shops here. I cringe. I know what they are thinking; I can read it in their eyes. "The entire West is like this. All the women are easy. It is a disgrace the men allow their women to be like that. They need good Islamic values." But their lofty condemnations do not stop them heading for the door clutching their dubious movies, reflecting the same expectant look in their eyes as their Western peers.

The silence is broken by the ceiling fan's motor kicking in. The artificial breeze helps me think. "But Akram, you're a Muslim. Aren't you supposed to be in favour of sharia law?"

"We Muslims in the Sindh have a lot of Sufi influence, Grant Jhi. We are more restrained. There are a lot of moderates in the country. Just wait till we have a proper election. You will see, the fundamentalist parties will lose ground."

"Then how has Zia been able to survive so long?"

"Firstly, he is head of the army. Secondly, he has the support of the vocal fundamentalists. And thirdly, somehow he's been able to keep one step ahead of all his political opponents. He manipulated a referendum and appointed himself President. That upset a lot of people, but they couldn't do anything about it." My host offers me another samosa. "And Zia has also upset the Shias."

"Most Pakistanis are Sunnis, right?"

"Yes, eighty per cent. Zia made life unbearable for the Shias. It's not good that we Muslims fight each other, but these days there are more and more Sunnis throwing grenades into Shia mosques and vice versa."

"But hold on," I say, putting in a word for the General. "Zia has allowed over three million Afghan refugees into Pakistan. Surely that deserves some credit."

"Yes, it does, but there are some negatives about that, too."

"Like what?"

"The number of *madrassars* (mosque schools) in the Afghan refugee camps has increased hugely, with tacit support from Zia. My uncle tells me many of them are training grounds for militant jihadis to fight in Afghanistan."

*

Akram's uncle is right. "Taliban" means "students", and half a decade after my conversation with Akram, many Taliban jihadis, young and old, will emerge from *madrassars* in refugee camps and join their Afghan Pashtun brothers to deliver their "perfect and pure" brand of Islam to Afghanistan. And it happens with the clear support of Pakistan. While Zia did not initiate the Taliban, he provided fertile soil and ready fertiliser for fostering their aspirations.

Not all the Taliban will return to Afghanistan. Some will remain in Pakistan to sow a legacy of violent thorns in the fields of the gardener.

Meanwhile, the Locks' time in the Thar Desert, like sand in a Sindhi hourglass, is slowly running out. When the last grain falls, where will Janna and I be?

TWENTY-ONE

THE SPIES GO NORTH

OCTOBER 1989

"I'm sorry, but you have to leave the desert before the end of the month." Bishop Jhivan heaves a sigh and folds his hands on his office desk. "Political factions are still spreading accusations."

"That we're spying for India? It's so bizarre," Janna scoffs.

We don't know whether to laugh or cry at the absurdity of it all. But it's real. "Is your Pakistani team ready, Bishop Sahib?" I ask.

His ageing shoulders are stooped more than ever, but his eyes are sound and his tone positive. "Thanks be to God, yes, including a female doctor and midwives. One of our best administrators will lead the project." He gives a wry smile. "It won't be easy for them. Most Pakistani Christians are urban, and for them Mithi is like the end of the earth. Grant," he continues, "you and Janna have kept the vision of our desert work alive. And Sister Janna, if you had not gone out it would not have happened."

Janna's tired face flushes. "I haven't done much, Bishop Sahib. I just supported Grant, and tried to survive, and ..."

The old man raises a silencing hand. "Because of your perseverance, Janna, the foundation has been laid. And I know all about your programs for the girls and the women." His tone becomes more paternal. "It's been a tough assignment, and I've seen how the stress has affected your health."

Absolutely right, Bishop, I say to myself. *Janna has been amazing, living in Mithi without the team support she was originally counting on. With no female colleagues to join for coffee and a chat, it's been lonely and demanding. She hasn't even been able to talk on the phone to the kids in boarding school. With all those exchange operators listening in to the strange foreign voices, the signal gets so weak it won't even reach the edge of the desert, let alone the top end of the country. Because our living allowance is so stretched, when we've come into Hyderabad City I've really limited her calls to the school. I'm ashamed about that. It has really hurt Janna. We should have gone without something else and made the calls. It's one of those life rewinds I'd like to do. And now, the mineralised Mithi water is causing my dear life companion's hair to fall out in distressing handfuls. Yes, it's time to hand over. Well done, Janna. I've given it my all, but you've given more.*

Bishop Jhivan is still speaking. "I sometimes wonder how you managed to keep on going."

"I've wondered that too," says Janna, then her face lights up. "I think it's been the singing."

"The singing?"

"Every evening we sing a couple of praise songs. We've worked our way through a whole pile of song books."

The old man nods knowingly. "Your next assignment must be closer to better facilities, and to other foreign friends." He smiles, "We all need a bit of support from our own tribe now and then."

Janna's eyes stare beyond the room. "I'll miss the desert women, and the Sindhi girls, and the big sky."

I interrupt her musing. "Well, Bishop Sahib, what do we do next?"

"Grant, I have some openings I want you to consider, but you are free to check out the needs in other parts of Pakistan. Just remember you are always most welcome in my diocese."

*

With mixed emotions we drive back to Mithi. There is something poignant and sad in seeing things for the last time. The camels are more imperious, the well women more statuesque, the sunsets a richer colour. It's fulfilling to know we have paved the way for a local team to serve their fellow countrymen.

With a tray on her lap, Lali hums a Sindhi song as she meticulously checks the rice for small, tooth-shattering stones. Janna studies the ping-pong ball sized potatoes and wonders how they could be the same genus as those that produce the big potato chips in the Farhan Hotel in Hyderabad. She brews a pot of tea and joins me in my office.

"I don't think Bishop Jhivan's jobs are quite right for us, Grant," she says. "What do you think?"

I'm absorbed in balancing the project accounts for auditing and hand-over. She places the mug in front of me and repeats the question. I lean back and stretch. "I agree, and the positions in Karachi and Lahore don't seem right either."

We gaze out of the glassless window as Khanjhi tops up the water tank and leads his camel out of the yard.

Janna springs from her chair and peers through the bars. "Hallelujah! For once that camel hasn't left a calling card. Nice time to reform, just when we're leaving."

"I think you'll really miss the camels."

"Absolutely, but not that one!"

I wrap my arm around her shoulder. "It's going to be hard to leave the desert people."

"I know I have to let go. But where to from here?"

We mull in joint silence. Suddenly her pensive face clears. "Peshawar! That's it! We should check out Peshawar!"

"Peshawar!" My head jerks up. "Good grief! It might be a thousand miles north, but when we visited years ago, we absolutely roasted. No desert breeze at night—it's an oven! And what about the bombs in the bazaar? No thanks."

"Look, Grant. We could drive up and visit the kids at Murree and then drive over to Peshawar, and we could stay with the Cawthornes." Mike and Mary Cawthorne work in development for the Diocese of Peshawar.

"Well, I suppose we could go up and check it out. If we find what seems right, I'll come back on the train and hire a truck to move our gear."

"Aren't you worried they'd steal it on the way?"

"Absolutely. That's why I'd travel back with them. I'd be my own *chaokidaar*."

❋

Janna farewells long-faced Keemo and weeping Lali. "I will always remember you, Sister Janna," the dark-eyed ex-prostitute sobs. "*Mehrbaani*—Thank you for your kindness."

Janna gives her another hug. "God be with you, Lali. And keep singing those songs I've taught you."

*

In Peshawar there are many opportunities for service. The communists have retreated from Afghanistan and some of the three million Afghan refugees in Pakistan are returning to their decimated country. Near the Afghan border in the north-west of the country, Peshawar has become the hub of refugee and rehabilitation work.

"Grant, can you supervise our road building project in Afghanistan?"

"Refugees returning to their fields are being blown up every day. Can you come and supervise our de-mining teams?"

"You've worked with cattle and sheep, Grant. Can you come and run our livestock improvement program in Northern Afghanistan?"

Despite the Afghan needs, Janna and I feel committed to Pakistan. Not a problem: there are plenty of openings here in the North-West Frontier Province.

"Our simple solar oven is the answer for the poor who can't afford wood. Can you help?"

"Can you co-ordinate our vocational training program for unemployed young men?"

"Janna, we need a head mistress for our Peshawar girl's school. Can you come?"

We talk it all over with our hosts, Mike and Mary Cawthorne. Tall and with ex-Royal Navy bearing, Mike strokes his clipped white beard. "We're retiring soon and the Diocese of Peshawar needs replacements for us. You could take over from me, Grant. I supervise all sorts of development work up and down the province, from the mountains to the desert."

Mary's English accent is beautifully correct. "And Janna, with your teaching background, you would be a wonderful mentor to support Talat, the Pakistani woman I'm training to take over as director of our five schools."

Several days later, aging Bishop Khairuddin welcomes our offer to serve under him. With Mike's help we locate a suitable house to rent.

Then I head to the railway station and catch the Khyber Mail. Thirty rattly hours later, I'm back in Hyderabad, looking for a truck to move our gear from one end of Pakistan to the other.

TWENTY-TWO

MIDNIGHT MOVEMENTS

Pakistanis do unique things with their trucks. They can make an old Bedford look like Cinderella. The oil change may be long overdue and the brake pads calamitously thin, but the high-sided, beautifully decorated exterior will be kept meticulously clean. Perhaps it's a commentary on Pakistan; perhaps a commentary on mankind. Truck-art is big business. There will be large paintings of politicians, or tribal leaders, or maybe seductive, well-covered women. Mountain scenes, jet planes and horses are also favourites. Bad spirits are everywhere, so you need a pair of large eyes painted on the back to ward them off. Black rags, and even an old shoe, help to deflect the unwanted evil eye.

In Hyderabad the truck stand is a big mobile art show. After a few false starts I come across the three drivers of the Khattak Trucking Company. Yes, they will happily run out to the desert and take our household belongings up to Peshawar. They come from up that way. All are fine upstanding Pashtun men. With plumes in their hats and rapiers in their hands they could be the Three Musketeers, and no doubt they have plenty of muskets tucked away in that cabin.

I play the usual game of haggling and posturing with the Three Trucketeers and we strike a deal.

"Sahib, we will be in Mithi at ten o'clock tomorrow morning." We shake hands and I head to the Mithi bus stand. Confound it! There is one just pulling out. It looks full, but the vociferous assistant hanging out of the open door enthusiastically beckons me to run. He grabs me as I leap onto the running board, just as the driver changes into second gear. Fortunately there is always room for one more on a Pakistani bus.

I worm my way into a non-existent space among the perspiring men in the aisle. The air is hot and fetid but it gets better as we pick up speed. There is one seat left. Too bad it's next to a woman. The men are all coveting that space, but it would be a scandal to sit beside her unless you were closely related.

An hour later, as the bus empties, I score a seat next to a university student with a large box of mangoes on his lap. Surprisingly, he's studying anthropology. He is disillusioned. "I thought anthropology would give me answers to the meaning of life, but it hasn't." We discuss the subject until he gets off at Naukot, on the edge of the desert.

*

Keemo and I pack late into the night. Next morning we've just carried all the gear into the courtyard when we hear the Khattak truck arrive outside. I send Keemo to the gate, and when I emerge from the storeroom the Three Trucketeers are standing akimbo, staring at our gear.

First Trucketeer: "You won't fit that onto my truck. You should have got two trucks."

Second Trucketeer: "You won't fit that onto our truck. You'll have to leave half of it behind."

Third Trucketeer, looking at the five steel wardrobes: "You won't fit all that onto this truck. *Moomkin hee nahee*—Absolutely impossible."

I stare back at our three unhelpful heroes and feel my blood pressure rising. I've seen Pakistani truckers at work. They're not packers. They're not even stackers. They're just "tosser-inners" and "let's-get-going-ers".

I'm about to retort, "So you think it's impossible, eh? Well, just you watch," when Keemo, sensing the need for Eastern diplomacy, pipes up. "Laark Sahib is from Australia, and Australians are world famous packers. We will help him."

Thanks, Keemo, you've saved me again.

The sceptics reluctantly join in, and after a number of rehydrating tea breaks we're ready to close the painted tailgate. There's still room for a couple of potted plants, the only garden we've had in Mithi. The last thing is our foam double-bed mattress, which fits nicely into the big box over the Bedford's cabin.

Keemo and I hug goodbye. We both struggle to hold back tears. This kindly Hindu with his plastic sandal shuffle and salt and pepper stubble has been a desert mentor and proxy father to me. Tearfully I look him in the eye. "Faithful friend, thank you for your care for me. Now you must support the Pakistani team when they come out. *Khuda aap kay saat ho*—May God always be with you."

Keemo's cocker-spaniel eyes glaze up and I can feel deep emotion in the strength of his long hug. Choked up, he only just manages to return my blessing. "*Khuda hafez*, Laark Sahib—goodbye."

The truck grinds slowly through the sandy streets of Mithi. From my open-air box on top of the cabin, I feel like the desert-born emperor, Akbar the Great, perched high on his decorated elephant. I wave to the street ruffians, salute turbaned Khanjhi and his reformed camel, and admire the elegant posture of the bangled women bearing water from the wells. Inwardly I thank God for the opportunity to serve the desert people. I think of all those with whom I've rubbed shoulders, from the provincial deputy commissioner and the bank manager to the garbage collectors on their donkey carts and the watchman who kept me awake at night.

From Mithi's sandy escarpment I look back and offer a prayer for the town, and for a safe journey.

*

Finally we're on our way. The adrenaline slows and I realise how desperately tired I am. The mattress beckons me.

But the Third Trucketeer wants to talk. Joining me on the foam, he inquires about my family and what I think of wonderful Pakistan.

With a thousand miles ahead of us, it's time I learnt his name. "Jhi, kindly tell me your good name."

"My name is Khushal Khan Khattak, son of Arif Khan Khattak."

"And what is the meaning of your honourable name?"

He puffs out his chest. "It is the same name as our great warrior poet. We are a sub-group of the Pashtuns and we originally came from Ghazni in Afghanistan. Three hundred years ago our great warrior poet, Khushal Khan Khattak, united the Pashtun tribes and drove out the Mughal overlords. Sadly, the Mughals bought off some of the dishonourable clans with gold, and then they all started fighting each other again." He raises his hands and shrugs. "That is the nature of Pashtuns. We have a saying: 'The only time Pashtuns stop fighting is when they go to war.'"

"What about in Afghanistan right now, Khushal?"

"The ethnic groups have united and are driving out the Soviets."

"Then what will happen?"

"The tribes will fight of course, for the honour of leadership." He clears his throat. "As our great warrior poet wrote:

> Life's no life when honour has left;
> Man's a man when honour is kept.
> Nation's honour and nation's fame,
> On life they have a prior claim.
> With thoughts of these I do remain
> Unvexed with cares of loss or gain.

The rhyme is soporific and my eyelids feel like bricks. The Khattak is pleased with his recitation. He slips a quid of chewing tobacco into his mouth and waits for my commendation.

"*Wah wah!*—Amazing! Your leader truly was a great poet, Khushal." I stretch out on the heavenly mattress. "Wake me when we reach Mirpurkhas."

*

"Lock Sahib! Wake up! Climb down. Chai is ready." I groggily look over the side. The Three Trucketeers are perched on one of many string beds in the side yard of a petrol station. There's an explosive cheer from a large group of truckies who are suffocating an open-air, black and white TV set. Imran Khan, Pakistan's venerated cricket captain, has just sent another Englishman to the pavilion. It seems that this country's obsession with cricket is only eclipsed by its paranoid suspicion of neighbouring India.

I climb down and share the truckies' meal, scooping my *roti* bread into the common bowl of curried lentils. "What is the plan, men? Where will we stop for the night?"

"Probably Hyderabad, Jhi," the First Trucketeer replies. "It's too dangerous to travel further in the dark. We always stop at night. Too many bandits around these days." He folds some *roti* and wipes the dish clean. "We'll stop at a place like this, with plenty of string beds."

I visit the indescribable toilet, wash my hands under the outside tap and rejoin Khushal Khan Khattak on top of the Bedford.

As we pull back onto the road, I notice a man vigorously hammering at the fallen trunk of a tree. It's the "tooth-log". Large nails protrude from every part of its surface. For a fee, the "holy man" writes a sacred Arabic verse and then the paper is folded. The toothache sufferer nails the paper to the log. The efficacy of the process is in doubt because a sidewalk dentist, with his pliers and a display box of previously extracted molars, sits expectantly nearby.

Passing by the central Mirpurkhas bazaar, I spare a thought for lonely Shaneela and her one-eyed, wife-beating husband.

Just out of town, squatting by heaps of large rocks, are the gravel crackers. Perspiring men and women wield hammers to convert stones into road gravel. Who said women can't go out to work in Pakistan?

The air is balmy, and, as the chugging Bedford slowly chews up the miles, the mattress calls out to me again. "*Bhai Jhi*, my brother, wake me up when you stop in Hyderabad," I say, and once again my body sinks into the luxurious Nirvana of deep sleep.

*

"Hello, Mister! At last you wake up! You sleep too long."

I don't want to wake up. *Who is that? Stop rocking the bed. Turn off the light—it's too bright. My muscles ache so much. Leave me alone. I just want more rest.*

"Hey Mister, you slept all night, even when the bandits came."

Bandits? Did someone say bandits? My body is so tired. I feel as if I've been run over by a truck. I slowly raise my head. Hey, this *is* a truck, a loaded truck, and I'm on the top of it. Ooh, that's right, yesterday we loaded up everything, and we're heading north to Pashtun country. And that voice, that's the Third Trucketeer.

Now I'm wide awake. "What's that, Khushal? Bandits? What bandits?"

"We were travelling in convoy, Lock Sahib. They robbed the first fourteen trucks, then they came to us, shouting and waving their Kalashnikovs."

"What did they take?"

"Nothing, Sahib."

"Nothing?"

"Allah be praised, right then a police patrol drove up and the bandits took off." He grins unashamedly. "If they knew we had a foreigner sleeping up here, they would have taken you and then asked for a healthy ransom."

I'm trying to get my brain around all this. "But why didn't you stop for the night in Hyderabad? You know the Northern Sindh is bristling with armed brigands after dark."

The Pashtun is looking sheepish. He can see I'm getting upset and that I want an explanation. The Bedford diesel drums along beneath us. He doesn't reply.

Hey, you uncaring Khattak, the reason I'm on this truck is to stop you three from helping yourselves to our belongings. Now you're telling me we nearly lost them, and me, to some midnight marauders when you shouldn't have even been on the road. You rattle off your high-sounding Pashtun poem about "a man's a man when honour is kept", but what about showing a bit of honour to the guy who's paying for this little pan-Pakistan jaunt?

I repeat my question: "You said we were going to stop in Hyderabad. Why didn't we?"

Khushal is searching for words. "Well, Sahib, we were going to stop but you were asleep."

I'm not happy. I'm not getting the full story. "But you said you *always* stop at night."

"That's right, Sahib. Coming down we're fully loaded with cartons of cigarettes from Nowshera and we wouldn't want to lose them." His eyes involuntarily wander to the load behind us. "But this time we only have your old furniture. Besides, Jhi," he adds, "we really want to get home. My younger brother is getting married in two days' time."

There is silence, and then I say "Congratulations" in a bully-for-you kind of tone and terminate the discussion. Angrily staring down the tree-lined road, I finally decide to be thankful I'm not trussed up in a windowless mud room in some untraceable Sindhi village.

After a while, we see dense plumes of black smoke are billowing from the road half a mile ahead. "That means big trouble," the brother of the groom announces grimly.

Opposite a large village we reduce speed to a crawl to negotiate the newly constructed speed bump, which is a real axle breaker. Spread across the road is a row of smoke-belching tyres, and young men are rolling in more. Dozens of trucks are lined up on each side of the barrier and their drivers are shouting toe-to-toe with a big crowd of angry locals with axes in their hands.

Khushal climbs back up to the cab-top box. "They're angry because a speeding truck ran over a little boy. They know the culprit and they know he's paid off the police. They're not letting anything through till the Deputy Commissioner comes and sorts it out."

Beyond the clouds of smoke, villagers struggle to restrain the distraught mother. She's screaming in anguish and waving her fist at the assembly of truckies. It's obvious no one is going to proceed down this road in a hurry.

I turn to the Khattak. "So what are we going to do, Khushal?"

"Some of the light-loaded trucks are driving back to a detour through the fields. We can follow them." He gives half a grin. "Gotta get back for the wedding, you know."

It's getting hotter, and the First and Second Trucketeer invite me to join them in the cabin. With the windows down and shade from the huge cab-top box, it's quite bearable.

*

About every hundred miles there's a police post. This one is demanding 200 rupees. Trucketeer One is upset. "I won't pay that! I've only paid 100 at all the other posts."

I'm wondering if they've seen the foreigner in the front seat and have doubled the rate.

The greasy officer twists his moustache. "In that case, Sir, you will have to unload all your gear onto the ground and we will check everything for drugs. We're having a lot of opium smuggling these days. It's the responsibility of the Pakistani Police Force to stop it."

Trucketeer One relents and hands over the notes. The paunchy officer counts the money and slips it inside his uniform. "Sir, we are completely satisfied your load is free of drugs," he announces. He waves us past his rifle-toting subordinates. "You are free to go."

After lunch the next day we are crossing the mighty Indus River on the Attock Bridge. The Bedford halts at the toll point and I read the sign overhead: "Welcome to the North-West Frontier Province."

"Ahh, Lock Sahib. Now we are in my homeland." The Khattak puffs out his chest. "All this western side of the river was once Afghanistan, until the Sikhs, and then the British, took the plains and moved the border to the edge of the mountains."

Finally we roll into Peshawar, the ancient Silk Road trading city that is now abuzz with everything associated with the Russian–Afghan war: refugee camps, rehabilitation projects, mujahidin command centres, Afghan supplies to funnel through the Khyber Pass, and *madrassars* indoctrinating the as-yet-unknown Taliban. It's also the temporary base for a certain CIA-supported, anti-communist leader: Osama bin Laden.

*

We drive a thousand miles and we're close to the rented house, but the lane is too narrow for the truck. The unfazed Trucketeers promptly dump everything on the side of the road, take their money and head for the wedding.

What do I do now? If I leave this gear, some will certainly be stolen. There is a clip-clop sound. Three young men passing by on their horse and cart save the day. For 300 rupees they cheerfully make numerous trips over the last two hundred yards.

Only now do I notice the small plaque near the gate. The house is called "Ararat". My mind immediately turns to the great flood. Some months later our "Ararat" will also experience a flood, albeit a small one. It will build a deep friendship with our neighbours who help clean out the mud. They are Afghans from Kabul.

THE FRONTIER

NORTH-WEST PAKISTAN

1989–1998

8	1989	1990	1991	1992	1993	1994	1995	1996	1997	1998	1999	2000
A	AFGHAN CIVIL WAR								THE TALIBAN RULE AFGH			

TWENTY-THREE

FLOWER POWER

PESHAWAR, NORTH-WEST FRONTIER PROVINCE, NOVEMBER 1989

Bloodstained plates of raw meat keep appearing. "*Moobarak ho!* Congratulations!" the young couriers declare as they pass over their gifts.

I'm rather touched, almost overwhelmed. Since early morning the gate bell hasn't stopped ringing, and its only three weeks since we arrived in Peshawar. "I'm amazed that the neighbours all know it's my birthday," I confide to Janna. "It's very considerate of them. You must have told them."

"It's a birthday celebration all right, Grant, but it's not yours."

"Well, who's is it?"

"It's Eid ul-Naabi, the Prophet Muhammad's birthday. Didn't you see them butchering the goats in the street?"

A bit deflating, but it was nice of the neighbours to share. I've been so busy taking over the development work from Mike that I hardly know what day it is. I do know that Muslims don't show too much exuberance over their Prophet's birthday because it's also the anniversary of his death. They have to mix celebration with a measure of grief.

Janna changes the subject. "Grant, I want you to go over and talk to our neighbour."

"Why's that? I've seen him coming and going, but I haven't actually met him yet."

"He's making passes at me."

She now has my full attention. "What do you mean 'making passes'?"

"You know how narrow our lane is. Well, when I'm up on the balcony hanging out the clothes, he throws little bouquets of flowers at me."

I'm starting to fume. Maybe they do this in South America, but it's definitely not on in this society. You can't even look at a woman's face here without risking the ire of her husband.

"He sits there on his balcony chair and throws these things at me. Sometimes he tries to talk to me. I pretend it's not happening, but I'm getting uncomfortable about it."

"I'm on my way," I snort, and I head for the door.

Okay, neighbour. We haven't been here three weeks and you already have my wife labelled as an easy Western woman. You're lucky I'm not a local Pashtun with a big gun.

I cross the lane. Tall, don't-look-at-my-women walls rise up on each side. The gate is opened by the neighbour. I try to be pleasant.

"*Salaam alekoom,* neighbour. My name is Grant."

He shakes my hand warmly. "Welcome to Peshawar, Grant Jhi. I am Sultan. We are so honoured by your presence as our neighbour."

Well, Casanova, you are very amiable when you're not on balcony duty, but I'm not falling for your buttery charm.

"Come in and drink tea with me." He flourishes a hand. "And if there is anything I can do for you, please let me know."

Yes, there is something you can do for me, my friend, and I will let you know, very soon.

"*Shukria,* Sultan. I would like that. I do have something to talk to you about."

"Yes indeed, my neighbour," and he strokes his neat black beard. "There is much to discuss. I want to know all about your country and all about your children."

In this society, you never ask someone about a man's wife, or even mention her. That's far too forward. You always ask about the children and, somehow, the wife is included. I'm convinced he wants to know about more than just "the children".

Sultan's son runs to the kitchen to notify his mother of the tea requirements. I'm trying to be civil as I answer the questions regarding my nationality. I mustn't come on too strong, or too quick.

"Tell me about your good family, Mr Grant."

This guy is sure being very cool about it all, but now is the time for me to speak.

"Well, Sultan Jhi, I want to talk to you about that. You have been acting in a totally unacceptable way toward my wife."

His body stiffens and his hands tighten their grip on the arms of his chair. "I don't know what you are referring to."

The son brings the tea prepared by his unseen mother.

"Mr Sultan, I think you know what I mean. It's not acceptable for you to sit on your balcony and watch my wife all the time, and it's a disgrace that you are throwing flowers at her."

He scowls, then releases his grip on the arms of his chair and bursts into laughter. I'm confused and offended by his outburst. "That would be Tariq, my brother!" he says.

"Whoever it is, Mr Sultan, you or your brother, this is not a laughing matter. It's dishonouring to your family and to my wife."

Sultan leans forward. "Lock Sahib, rest assured this will not happen again. I will talk to my brother." He rises. "In fact, I will call him right now. He's never far away."

As Sultan returns I can hear him admonishing his brother in no uncertain terms.

Tariq is a mousy sort of man, partly because he is small in stature and partly because he looks like he's been in a cage for a long time. Sultan makes the introductions and I reluctantly shake the mouse-man's hand.

"*Muaf kaaro*, Mr Lock, *muaf kaaro*. Please forgive me. I promise not to do it again." He slumps into a chair. "It's because I am so bored."

Sultan re-enters the discussion. "Actually, Tariq can never leave the house."

"Can't leave the house?"

"If he does there are people who are waiting to kill him."

I'm starting to comprehend. "A blood feud?"

"Yes. Brave Tariq has avenged our clan. My mother and the old women decided who he would kill. But he had to sell his carpet shop in Islamabad because they found out it was him. Now he is safe, but only if he stays in my house."

I study the murderer slouching in his chair, impassively staring at the carpet and wishing someone else had been selected to pull the trigger. Somehow the bouquets don't seem so provocative now.

Janna continues to ignore the mouse-man sitting miserably on his veranda, but I greet him when I can. The police will never come looking for him because the crime was related to a blood feud. But there could be someone waiting, very patiently, in the tea house at the end of our lane.

It reminds me of a well-known Pashtun proverb:

> *Maa sariaam enteqaam gereftem,*
> *faqat sad saal gereft.*
>
> We avenged ourselves, and we did it quickly:
> it took one hundred years.

TWENTY-FOUR

SECRETS

JULY 1990

The fair-skinned women of the northern Chitral valley are noted for their beauty. They say that their attractiveness lures many men from the south.

*

Janna and I are busy adapting to Peshawar when school holidays come round again. The family decides to head north to do some hiking in the mountains surrounding snow-capped Tirich Mir.

Clatter, clatter, clatter. We are driving slowly across a narrow bridge near the alpine town of Chitral. Frail-looking timber planks rhythmically rattle beneath our tyres. The water below surges in a turbulent hurry to escape its incarceration in mountain glaciers and winter snow. Among the string of pedestrians moving past us, I suddenly see a face I seem to recognise.

"Janna, isn't that Mr Nazeem?"

I refer to a balding, middle-aged man who doesn't notice my reflex wave. By the time Janna refocuses, he is well behind us. I can't stop; there is a long line of assorted vehicles behind us.

"Who did you see?"

"I'd swear that was Mr Nazeem."

"You should know. He works in your office, doesn't he?"

Janna is absolutely right. Mr Nazeem works in my project office four days a week. I inherited him when I arrived, and I have not been impressed. I expected him to be more helpful as I came into the job, but getting information out of my part-time bookkeeper is harder than dragging a bogged sheep from a muddy farm dam. He leans protectively over his ledgers and his movements are slow and measured. There is something about his eyes—as if they are keeping secrets.

From the time cunning Bahram Yusuf paid my office a visit, there have been big question marks about Mr Nazeem.

Bahram Yusuf came to book one of the hill-station bungalows the diocese inherited from benevolent officers of the British Raj. We rent them to families seeking respite from the summer heat of the plains, and they produce some much-needed revenue for projects.

I'd been warned about a certain schemer who had a history of trying to take over property. "If he gets into one of the bungalows, it will be hard to get him out," Mike cautioned.

I didn't realise the effusive character who charmed his way into my office was the one to be wary of. In all the detail of the hand-over I had forgotten his name. I was new and vulnerable, and I was heavily dependent on my staff.

Bahram Yusuf pumped my hand. "Mr Lock, welcome to Peshawar. We are so glad you have come, and we wish you all the best in your work here."

For sure he was glad I had come. It gave him a chance to try out his old tricks on a new face.

In no time he had paid a month's rent for Moonrise Bungalow, taken the keys and gone happily on his way. All the while Mr Nazeem said nothing. He impassively took the money and issued a receipt. Later I learned that he knew Bahram Yusuf from past encounters, but his eyes kept the secret and he never said a word.

A month later the keys were due to come back, but they didn't arrive. Bahram Yusuf settled his family in and produced a forged document claiming his grandfather purchased the property from a certain Captain Williams in 1929. I came to the depressing realisation that I had been deceived from both inside and outside my office. This was also the time I was introduced to Pakistan's popular and perilous pastime: litigation.

*

In an Abbottabad courtroom that appears not to have been painted since the British left in 1947, our diocesan lawyer and I have just heard the magistrate's ruling. Abbottabad is the attractive mountain town where the elusive Osama bin Laden would ultimately receive his last guests: a team of US Navy SEALS.

"Congratulations, Lock Sahib!" Rahim slaps my back. "We have won the case! You will soon have the property back." We are elated. Bahram Yusuf skulks away to plan his next devious manoeuvre.

Rahim closes his overloaded briefcase. "You can collect the written statement of the ruling in a week's time."

But the written ruling is slow in coming. On my third frustrating trip to the offices of the Abbottabad courts, I check yet again with the court official. "Has the ruling been written up yet?"

"I think it's being done right now, Sir. Let us check." We move into an adjacent grimy room where a bearded stenographer is tapping away at the keys of an ancient typewriter.

"If you wait here a few minutes, Sir, you can take it with you." I'm relieved. For a while I was wondering if something was inexplicably wrong. The official leaves me gazing over the key-thumper's shoulder. As he taps away I'm slowly scanning down the lines.

An involuntary surge of adrenaline overwhelms my body. I'm shocked by the implications of what I am reading. I can't believe my eyes. The magistrate's written ruling is exactly the opposite of his oral ruling in the court. Now it's Bahram Yusuf, not we, who has occupation of Moonrise Bungalow.

Adrenaline is for flight or fight. I want to do both. I want to run away from this warped system. I want to cast aside the cold stone in my stomach, weighing me down with the realisation I've been deceived again. On the other hand, I want to fight. It's not right. It's a disgrace. Something has to be done.

"Hey! This isn't correct," I explode as the stenographer spins the document out and hands me a copy. "We're the ones who are supposed to resume possession, not Bahram Yusuf. That's what the magistrate said in the court."

He looks at me blankly and strokes his beard. "I only write what I am told to write, Sir. If you want to complain, go and see the Commissioner. His office is at his house."

I'm in luck. As I arrive at the impressive old British house, the sweating Commissioner is just returning from a game of polo. He is young and agile, and as he steps down from his big Land Cruiser I'm thrusting the report into his hands. In exasperation, I explain the miscarriage of justice which has been perpetrated right before my eyes.

He listens patiently and then lays a consoling hand on my shoulder. "Don't worry, Mr Lock. If it is as you say, just remember: there's always the courts." He turns on his heel and leaves me standing dumbstruck on the driveway.

There's always the courts? Haven't we just been to the courts? The Commissioner Sahib must have a lot more faith in the justice system than I do. Unless ... unless he's been on the receiving end of Barham Yusuf's largesse. Ah, now I get it. "Justice system." How ignorant of me. First there's justice, and then there's the system. In this case the system won out. Will it win out again if we have to appeal to a higher court?

I'm left wondering how much was paid to swing the ruling. And was something swung in the direction of our part-time bookkeeper, who denies any suggestion that he has failed in his duty? "My job is just to look after the money, Mr Lock," Nazeem responds in blank ambiguity.

✻

We have a great week in the Chitral valley. Matt and I climb over the snowline to explore remote, snow leopard slopes. We fail to see any, but on our second day out, Matt pulls a block of dark chocolate from his backpack. It is a memorable way to spend my birthday.

✻

Mr Nazeem lifts his head from his books. "Did you have a good week away, Sir?"

"Yes, thank you. We had a great time in Chitral." Did I notice a flicker in those guarded eyes? "Have you ever been to Chitral, Mr Nazeem?"

"Oh no, Sir. It's much too far away."

"That's strange. I could have sworn I saw you walking across a bridge in Chitral last Saturday."

His blank eyes stare through me for a moment, then he gives a muffled laugh. "No Sir, I was with my family." It's knock-off time, and he systematically locks away his pens and account books and the office cash-box. "Good night, Sir. I'd really like to go to Chitral one day."

Now I'm confused. Perhaps my eyes were playing tricks on me. Maybe my ledger-keeper has a look-alike up there.

I stay on in the office. I have to complete a donor report, due in a week. The late afternoon sun slants through the window and picks out a coloured object slipped between two filing cabinets. I'm curious. I thought I'd been introduced to everything in this office, but I don't recall seeing that. I pull it out. It's a small, pale-blue suitcase. *That's an unusual colour for Pakistan. Dark colours are all I've ever seen.* A couple of neurons fire in my brain. Wait—I've seen something like that before, but I can't remember when. I trawl through the library shelves of my memory trying to pick up a lead. Then I get a hit. I see the suitcase. A man is carrying it: a funny coloured suitcase for a man. I guess that's why my brain filed the incongruent picture. I want more detail, and gradually it comes. The man is walking. He's on a bridge in Chitral. It's Mr Nazeem!

Why did he lie to me? What is in this little suitcase? Is it something to do with this office? If it's not, why does Nazeem leave it here? It's not locked. I lift the latches and I'm in for a surprise. Lingerie! The contents consist entirely of women's lingerie. It's not the kind that the average Pakistani wife would wear. Janna's sources of local information have told her that most women sleep in a *shalwar kamiz*. Some even wear their *dupatta* to bed.

Sadly, I've been told that Mr Nazeem's marriage is not going too well. Perhaps the suitcase and the long-distance northern trips have something to do with that. The one thing I do know is that he has lied to me about Chitral, and about the illegal resident of Moonrise Bungalow.

But Mr Nazeem is not going to be with us much longer. It's clear that we need a full-time bookkeeper and one who can use a computer. Mr Nazeem is not prepared to leave his other job, or to learn computerised bookkeeping.

We farewell the secretive eyes with chicken patties and sticky *goolaab jaaman* dessert. I make the mandatory, complimentary speech. It's very short. Without looking us in the eye he mumbles a response, reaches between the filing cabinets and leaves with his pale-blue suitcase.

*

Every time I drive out of Peshawar at 4.30 am to be at the Abbottabad appeal court by 8.00, my sleep-starved body wishes that my bookkeeper had not kept so many secrets.

TWENTY-FIVE

TENNIS ANYONE?

AUGUST 1990

As much as we appreciated the remote, open skies of the Thar Desert, we are rapidly adapting to this bustling frontier capital. The provincial city of Peshawar and the sandy town of Mithi are like chalk and cheese.

Mithi has male-only tea houses made from sticks and rusty corrugated iron. Peshawar has some family restaurants. Mithi has fresh air and blazing stars at night. Peshawar has a blanket of vehicle fumes and pollution. Mithi has its small bazaar presided over by the benevolent Ganesh, the elephant god of good-fortune. Peshawar has countless bazaars, old and new, punctuated by mosques and minarets. Mithi has a sandy soccer field. Peshawar has all sorts of sports, including, yes, tennis.

I love tennis. My dad was crazy about it too. As kids we helped him pour the tar to make a court in front of the Kimba homestead. We spent countless cat-gut swinging hours on that farm court. I became the top player in our country district, and my twin brother was number two.

As I drive to my Peshawar office, my eyes are always drawn to the tennis courts in the adjacent army officer's club. Indeed, my whole tennis-starved psyche is craving for a hit. "I have to get onto a court again," I confide to Mike Cawthorne as he hands over his development responsibilities to me.

"Why don't you apply to the Club, Grant? I've been a member for years. They have squash and a swimming pool as well. I'll recommend you and Janna."

*

I think I inherited a goodly proportion of tennis genes from my dad's father, Steve Lock. He was the best tennis player in the northern Flinders Ranges. Known as the "Curly Comeback", he made the racquet look like a toy. On Saturday nights he would trade the racquet for a violin bow and provide the musical motivation for ever-popular country dances. He was a ruggedly handsome figure, with a shock of curly hair. Well, that's what his photos portray. I never met Grandpa Steve, so I never received any tennis tips from him. The tall northern champ died prematurely when a team of horses bolted.

*

I open an important-looking envelope, befitting the 150-year-old Peshawar Club. Originally established for officers of the British army, it is now the precincts of Pakistani army officers and their families. It's okay for Mike Cawthorne; he is a retired officer of the Royal Navy, with a head start over mere civilians. Perhaps we are naive in trying to gain membership, but the courts are calling and Mike has assured us he will do his best to get us accepted.

I open the letter and read it out to Janna.

> To the Most Honourable,
> Grand H. Lock Sahib
>
> Respected Sir,
>
> I have to advise your honour that the application to become a member of the Officer's Club has not been approved. The Committee is mindful that if you avail yourselves of the services of the swimming pool, AIDS could spread among our upright members and their families.
>
> I remain,
> Yours faithfully,
>
> The Secretary

Janna and I smile at the quaint Victorian English, though we smart at the insinuations, and we roll our eyes at the lack of information about AIDS. However, the answer is crystal clear.

But I'm not going to give up. I'm still hungry for a game of tennis, and I'm determined to get it.

*

My answer comes in the form of an invitation to play on the lawn court at Edwardes College, the oldest university college in Peshawar. "Why not come over and have a hit with our college team?" the principal suggests. "They are preparing for the inter-college competitions."

Dr Ronald Pont has become something of an advisor in my new project management role in the North-West Frontier. The long-serving Englishman and his wife, Molly, are both legendary surgeons and carry a wealth of information and inspiration. Versatile Ron has taken a break from surgery to head up the influential college.

After playing three enjoyable sets, I'm sipping iced lemonade while the principal and I watch the team further their preparation.

I turn to my host. "The bishop wants the Pennell School down at Bannu reopened, Ron. What do you know about it?"

"It was started over a century ago," the surgeon educator explains in his clipped English accent. "It was the second educational institute in the province, after this one. Rather amazing for such a remote place, but then, Dr Pennell was a remarkable man. Throughout British India it was famous for its academic and sporting standards."

I pour another glass of lemonade. "So what happened?"

"Unfortunately, mismanagement over the last couple of decades has brought about its closure. Now both the boys' and girls' sides are empty, waiting." He leans back in his chair. "You'll be starting from scratch: buildings to repair and replace, staff to find, curriculum to put in place. So there's a real challenge for you, boy."

I don't mind being called "boy" by the likes of Dr Pont, and although it doesn't all depend on one person, I know that the diocese is looking to me to get things moving.

"Well, I have a plan, Ron. I want to set up a steering committee and I hope you'll be on it." He nods. "I'm going down next week to check it out, and to talk to the Bannu locals."

"Just remember not to drive back after dark."

"Why is that?"

"The road passes through Dara, and that's a part of FATA, the tribal area. You wouldn't want to be driving through there at night."

"I'll have Samson, my assistant, with me."

The grey-haired sage looks me in the eye. "If you're in a convoy with police protection, all right. Otherwise, don't do it." He takes another sip of lemonade. "Unless you want to get kidnapped."

TWENTY-SIX

FATA

SEPTEMBER 1990

No seers or astrologers are involved, but by some kind of coincidence, the induction of the new Bishop of Peshawar is scheduled for the ninth hour of the ninth day of the ninth month, 1990. If you were superstitious you might say that all the numbers lining up makes for a propitious day. And so it would prove to be—for the kidnappers.

*

People are getting fidgety. We see them looking at their watches more frequently. It's not unusual for an official function to start an hour late in Pakistan, but this is getting past a joke. Whispers are circulating around the crowded cathedral. All eyes are on an empty chair on the podium. The bishops are all seated. The archbishop was half an hour late, but that was long ago. The time-driven Westerners assembled punctually, all except one: my friend and colleague Paul Murdoch.

The diocesan secretary moves through the rows and again questions the absentee's anxious wife, seated with her small children. "Mrs Murdoch, are you sure Paul Sahib is on his way? We can't start the ceremony without him. He has the gift to present to the bishop."

She nods her head, but what can she say? She is more worried than they are.

The secretary lowers his voice. "People are saying he is not coming because he has sour grapes that he wasn't chosen to be the new bishop."

"That's silly," she scoffs. "Everyone knows the Church of Pakistan doesn't select foreigners any more. Besides, he's never wanted to be a bishop. He has his hands full serving as diocesan treasurer. Please, Secretary Sahib, send someone to look for him. Perhaps he's had car trouble."

Indeed, the absent treasurer *has* had car trouble, but not of the kind his wife is imagining. The Secretary Sahib's search party finds the unlocked station wagon by the side of a little-used road. The gift and a briefcase full of cash are in the back. But there is no sign of Paul.

*

Two hours earlier. There isn't a big rush at the bank, so Paul has plenty of time. In his briefcase he has 20,000 Pakistani rupees. All the padres and church workers will be at Reverend Alexander's induction, and they will all be expecting their salaries before they return home. Then there is cash for the catering expenses for about a thousand guests. Things are going well, so he decides to look in on the new family that arrived just yesterday. From there, the shortest way to the cathedral is along the big irrigation canal.

Paul is enjoying the graceful flight of white herons when an inconspicuous, faded-green Datsun sedan draws alongside him. Instead of passing, it hangs back a little, in his blind zone. Three kidnappers are evaluating a potential victim.

The sedan moves level with the treasurer's small station wagon. Armed men hang out of the windows gesticulating with their firearms and signalling him to stop. Paul is unconcerned; guns are common this close to the Tribal Area. "Perhaps there has been some kind of accident in the village we have just passed," Paul generously assumes. "Maybe they need help." His compassion is about to be replaced by terror.

He slows. The Datsun aggressively moves forward and cuts him off. Three gun-wielding, scarf-covered faces surround his car, testing the locked doors. The butt of a rifle smashes a window and a swarthy hand reaches in. Paul's loud protests are silenced with a belt in the ribs from the glass-breaking Kalashnikov.

"Shut up and get out, *engrez*!"

They wrench him out and shove him into the rear seat. He's now totally immobilised, pinned between two burly Pashtuns. He hopes they won't see his cashed-up briefcase or the Persian carpet for the bishop in the rear of the vehicle.

The gang has been waiting to nab the child of a prominent Pakistani politician. But today the rich boy's driver must have used a different route. Never mind—this foreigner will do to trade for the release of jailed colleagues. In fact, a foreigner will work much better. "We'll keep him hidden in the mountains for a while and they'll soon meet our demands."

"*Raghlay! Raghlay!* Move! Move! Let's get out of here," the leader shouts through his scarf to the newly-installed driver. "This foreigner's vehicle will be a nice little bonus."

But the nice little bonus won't start. The frantic driver swings the key like a pinball control, but to no avail. He doesn't think to switch off the air conditioner. Paul is glad he has put off replacing that tired old battery. If only a vehicle would come by and see what is happening.

But that's what Ahmed Shaher, the leader of the pack, is worried about. "Out! Out!" he screams, and they drag the Canadian into the back seat of their little Datsun. Spewing gravel, they spin around and head west for the all-protecting mountains of FATA, the Federally Administrated Tribal Area.

The name may indicate federal administration, but it's an oxymoron. No outside government has ever effectively administered the strip of mountains between Pakistan and the peaked plateaus of Afghanistan. This is the future safety zone for Afghanistan's Taliban, the elusive al-Qaeda, and their joint affiliates, the resilient Haqqanis. It will also be the bastion of Pakistan's own emerging Taliban.

*

For millennia the wild, independent Pashtun tribes have shunned outside control as they have gone about their business of milking the traders passing through their barren, unproductive passes. Those who comply pay a price; the others are looted. Once it was Silk Road camel caravans moving the wares of the Middle East, Europe and Asia. Now it is Pakistani trucks hauling military supplies through the Khyber Pass to the anti-communist mujahidin. A decade later it will be supplies for the coalition troops fighting the Taliban. Whoever the victim, it's all remunerative.

Along with providing a conduit for drugs and weapons, the tribes enjoy another well established source of income: kidnapping. They kidnap boys to become Dubai camel jockeys, or for the sex trade. They kidnap girls for retailing as child brides, and they kidnap businessmen for ransom. Then there are the cars. They get kidnapped too.

Free-spirited and fiercely aggressive, the Pashtun tribes of FATA are not to be messed with, unless you can outgun them with lead or gold.

*

Even with his body jammed low in the Datsun's back seat, and wearing a blindfold to boot, Paul knows where he is going. It will be somewhere in those FATA mountains. During the first hour there are several stops. It seems there are negotiations going on for a third tribal party to take on the job of hiding him.

Back in Peshawar, the deserted vehicle has been found and the wages and gift are safe. The vexing question "Where is Paul Murdoch?" is taking on an intercessory tone. The first act of the newly appointed bishop is to call his people to prayer.

*

Finally the blindfold comes off. They lead the missing treasurer to a cave with a large open mouth. Three men are approaching from a nearby flat-roofed house. Ahmed Shaher is going through his captive's pockets. "You won't be needing this," he laughs as he removes the Canadian's wallet. "Nor these," and he pulls Paul's glasses from his face. "Nor this," and he savagely twists the gold wedding ring from the offended foreigner's finger.

He turns to the three newcomers. "Okay, you are getting good money. Be sure you earn it. Keep those chains on his feet and keep your mouths shut. We'll be back tomorrow." The Datsun roars off into the afternoon glare and disappears down the mountain track.

Paul's custodians are not the kind that drive vehicles. They are rather gaunt and their threadbare *shalwar kamiz* clothing needs replacing. They don't say much but they are not nasty. Abdul, the oldest of the group gives a toothy grin as he pockets Ahmed Shah's 400 rupees. "Make yourself at home, *engrez*. And don't worry, the police will never find you here."

Paul is sore and disorientated, but he feels he can communicate with these men. "*Soono, Janaab*—Listen, Sir. I have been sent by God to serve the people of Pakistan. It's not the police you should worry about. It is the Living God." The three look at each other but say nothing.

The Peshawar police commissioner has established rigorous checkpoints on all roads leading into the mountains. He's also testing all his FATA connections for information. There is nothing, absolutely nothing … until the photo shows up.

*

Two days have passed and Ahmed Shaher is restless. He hasn't been back to the cave. His plan is to delay for three days before opening negotiations.

"I can't stand this waiting around," he complains to his gang. "Anyone interested in a little car shopping?"

Shaheen Kokikhel rises. "Good idea! We need something to fill in the time."

"Okay," smiles the leader, "we'll catch the bus into Peshawar and ride home in style."

Style is a white Datsun sedan. There are so many around they are easy to resell as long as you have the right paperwork, and that's not hard to arrange. As usual the thieves will bluff their way through the checkpoint, or if necessary enhance the miserable salary of the checkpoint officers. But as Ahmed Shaher slows to join the queue of vehicles, he starts to panic. They are not only checking the occupants of each vehicle; they are meticulously checking every number plate.

He breaks into a cold sweat. "They're onto us, Shaheen. They're onto us." One hundred yards ahead is his stony FATA homeland. He guns the vehicle forward. The lawmen look up, leap aside and start firing at point blank range.

Two hours later a blue Toyota Hilux, bristling with armed policemen, roars into Malikdin Khel. "Commiserations, brothers. A son of your village is dead. He stole one car too many, and one person too many." The officer takes Paul Murdoch's passport photo from his pocket and slowly waves it in the faces of the gathering crowd. "We found this photo in Ahmed Shaher's wallet. Kidnapping foreigners is a serious business. Someone here knows where this Canadian is."

The police spokesman pauses and scans the hostile eyes of the men before him. He doesn't expect results this quick but he will get them one way or another. He is under big pressure from his boss, and his boss is under big pressure from the government and the embassies. The officer knows he will have to play hard ball. He lays down his ultimatum. "Ahmed Shaher is from this village. If you don't come forward with the information, we will come and burn down the houses of his relatives."

The load of police berets disappears in a plume of dust, leaving a crowd of villagers questioning each other. But no one here can help the police because Ahmed Shaher made sure he didn't tell anyone in his hometown.

❋

Back at the cave the Pashtuns are getting worried. "Where is Ahmed Shaher? He should have been back days ago."

It's the fourth night and the mosquitoes have gathered, looking for a fix. Abdul hates the buzzing blood-suckers. "You can feed the mosquitoes, *engrez*, not me. Tonight I'm going to rest in the house." He laughs as he rises. "Just don't run away overnight, okay?"

Paul joins in the banter and gestures toward his chains, which are now securely attached to the frame of a string bed. "How far do you think I could get, Abdul, dragging this thing?"

But Paul knows there is no need to drag that rough-hewn bed anywhere. By prolonged wiggling he slips the chains off his ankles and heads off into the moonlight. There are two mountain tracks, but both of them disappear into stones and rocks. Without his glasses it's bad enough, but banks of cloud are beginning to obscure the moon. He frantically scours the shadows to find the way of escape.

❋

"Did you sleep well last night, *engrez*?" Abdul calls as he climbs the slope to the cave. "I was truly concerned the mosquitoes may have carried you away."

There is no response. Why is the foreigner not answering? The Pashtun puffs into the mouth of the cave.

Paul raises his weary head from between his hands and forces a laugh. "It nearly happened, Abdul Jhi. They nearly carried me away, but I was saved by the *charpoy*." He waves his hand at the bed and the chains around his feet. "It was too heavy for them."

But inside he is struggling with God. Returning to voluntary incarceration was a deeply bitter blow. If tonight is clear, though, he will surely find his way out, before Ahmed Shaher and his henchmen come back.

But Ahmed Shaher won't be coming back, nor will the Canadian be testing the track again.

⁕

The worried senior jailor rides his donkey down to the local village. He can't get back to his colleagues fast enough.

"Ahmed Shaher and Shaheen are dead!"

"I told you that you're fighting against God," Paul reminds them, but despite his personal bondage, he's concerned for the families of the gunned-down gangsters. "I'd like to pray for the widows and their children," he says.

United by the terminal realities of death, the incongruent group raise their hands together, and the Canadian prays.

"*Mehribani, engrez*—Thank you for your kindness," Abdul responds. "But you won't be sleeping up here again." Paul's heart sinks; maybe someone has seen his foreign footprints on the dusty track.

The prisoner endures his fifth lonely night, chained in a windowless mud room while his guard sleeps just outside the locked doorway.

⁕

At dusk on the sixth day, anxious Abdul makes an abrupt announcement. "Get up, *engrez*, and follow!"

They lead the surprised prisoner two stumbling miles down Paul's previously unlocated ravine path. A spark of light appears from a high-walled *kor*, the fortress compound of the *malik*, the local clan leader. It's time to consult the turbaned chieftain because nothing happens on this mountain without his approval.

The Pashtuns go into a cross-legged, carpet-level huddle. "The foreigner is right. Allah is not pleased."

"This *engrez* is too much trouble."

"We could be next to go."

"But he is worth money. We could sell him off to another ransom broker."

An hour later the Malik rises and confronts the anxious captive.

They say that those who survive the first few days of a kidnapping often build significant relationships with their captors. This is true. The white-bearded tribal leader now speaks up. "This is not a good business, *engrez*. We are going to release you, right now. You will walk into Jamrud. It takes two hours. The first bus leaves at 4.00 am." He pulls a well-used note from his pocket. "Here's ten rupees, four for the bus to Peshawar and the rest for chai in Jamrud."

The Pashtuns lead the thankful Canadian out into the night, back to the head of the track. Paul's restored spirits are running on high. He can't wait to head downhill to freedom, but he pauses and looks into the eyes of his repentant warders.

Abdul speaks first. "*Engrez*, you are a good man. Will you pray for us?"

In the silver moonlight, Paul raises his open palms in the local fashion and prays a blessing on the poor mountain men, their struggling families and their stone-scouring livestock. Then the Pashtuns release their charge. "Go, Man of Prayer, go."

A wave of emotion flows through Paul. Release. Freedom. Family. Thankfulness.

But he is not home yet; he is still in the Tribal Area. Two hours later, a few of Jamrud's lights come into view as the FATA town closes down for the night.

A serious discussion breaks out between Paul's body and brain. His body speaks up first. "I'm aching. I'm so tired. Just find a corner to rest in till that bus leaves at first light. By 5.00 am we'll be safe in Peshawar, with family and a soaking bath."

But his brain disagrees. "There could be another ransom-minded entrepreneur showing up for that bus. Every radio listener in FATA knows you are out here somewhere. Don't risk this drug- and people-peddling town. If their dogs start barking, some watchman is sure to spot the foreigner. Look for a side road and bypass the place altogether. Just keep walking. Stick to the shadows lining the dried-up watercourse to the left. Keep going downhill. That will surely get you out of this wretched place."

His body argues back. “You must be crazy. You’ve bumbled along without glasses this far, but you could lose your way out there following sidetracks and all. Get real. I’m aching all over. I need rest. Right now.”

Paul’s imagination enters the debate. “I can see my wife and kids running to hug me. But then, I can also see myself chained up again, in some dark backroom of a house in Jamrud.”

Finally, brain and imagination overrule body. Body submits, draws on more adrenaline and concentrates on the prospect of good food and that soaking bath. An hour later, the weary man is drawn to the sound of falling water. An irrigation aqueduct spans the dry watercourse and it has a major leak. Paul lingers under the cooling shower. It’s not a bath, but his unwashed body luxuriates in its freshness.

Kilometres later, in the unfocusable gloom, the Canadian reaches the end of a fading road. It goes nowhere. His body speaks up. "See! I told you so. Now we’ll have to turn back to Jamrud and wait for the bus.”

“No way!” says his brain. “Look! That glow in the distance has to be Peshawar City. Just follow the plan. Forget about tracks and roads. Forget about fields and stones and trees. Just walk towards the light.”

At dawn of the seventh day, a sleepy police guard peers through the gloom and hails a haggard figure. It has taken eight exhausting hours of cross-country resolve, but Paul has walked out of FATA to freedom. Midmorning, after debriefing at the precinct and ministry, there is a family reunion. God is good.

*

About twelve months prior to Paul’s deliverance, another Canadian aid worker, John Tarswell, disappeared without trace. Friends went looking for him at his Peshawar home. There were lights on and the doors were unlocked, but no John. His heavily pregnant wife had left a month earlier and John was about to fly out to join her for the birth. He was never seen again.

It’s not easy to say “God is good” in the face of such suffering and injustice. What kind of God would do that? We conveniently forget that he himself is no stranger to suffering, no stranger to injustice.

TWENTY-SEVEN

GUN TOWN

1990

"For my birthday, I want to visit a gun shop in Dara," announces Matthew.

"Me too," says Angela, his older sister, who is always looking for an adventure.

So during the winter holidays I drive the family to "Gun Town". The main bazaar of Dara is lined with gun shops. For more than a century, they've been manufacturing working copies of every notable firearm in the world. In amazingly simple workshops, they turn out fake German Lugers, Winchester shotguns and AK47s. They supply a brisk and affordable demand from the gun-loving Pashtuns.

"And don't forget I want to fire a Kalashnikov, Dad," fourteen-year-old Matthew reminds me as we pull into town.

"Me too," says Angela.

"What about you, Maria?"

Maria shakes her head. Bragging to her class-fellows about discharging the world's most popular offensive weapon holds absolutely no appeal for our second daughter.

We park in front of a row of eight-foot-wide gun shops. Janna opens her door, then rapidly slams it shut again. "Someone is shooting out there, just behind those shops. This is a bad idea, Grant. It's not safe."

I give her hand a squeeze. "Don't worry. The buyers always try before they buy. Samson and I often hear them when we're passing through."

Stepping out of our vehicle, I feel a firm grip on my right arm. I turn to face a clean-shaven local young man wrapped in a winter *chaadar* (blanket). He steers me aside for a couple of steps and begins speaking in confidential tones.

"What will it be, Sir? White opium, black opium, marijuana or whisky?"

"I don't use any of those." I shrug my arm free.

The smooth salesman reattaches his tentacles. "No, Sir! No, Sir! That doesn't matter at all. This is business, strictly business. It's all very cheap. You'll turn a handsome profit, Sir."

"Not today, thank you." I detach myself again and lead my waiting family into a narrow gun shop. The old proprietor welcomes us. "If you want opium at any time, Sir, I have plenty, and it's much better quality than that rogue sells."

I disregard the offer. "Sir, it's my son's birthday and he's always wanted to visit a gun shop."

"*Moobarak ho*, young man! Congratulations! You are all most welcome in my humble shop. I am indeed honoured." The affable old man has already sent his young helper to bring us drinks. Five bottles of Sprite and a plateful of tasteless local biscuits are set down before us. The shopkeeper readjusts his pure white turban and watches us as we enjoy his hospitality.

"And what else can I do for you, young man?"

"Sir, can you show me your guns?"

In no time the birthday boy has inspected all manner of firearms, from ancient flintlocks to modern automatics. Our friendly proprietor assures us that the local product is every bit as good as the original, but we all know that is not true. Of course he has some originals on hand, at four times the price.

"And if there is something you want," explains the weapons exhibitor proudly, "if it's not in my shop, I can soon get it for you."

Keeping a straight face I respond, "Do you have any rocket launchers?" It's just a joke. I'm not expecting this dusty mountain town to supply such sophisticated devices.

The old man's countenance falls. "I am truly sorry, Sir, there is not one available anywhere in Dara. But we do have a shipment coming in next week. There is a big demand in Afghanistan. I could save one for you."

I gulp, decline the offer and turn my attention back to Matthew.

The old man takes up my lead. "Now, young man, is there anything else I can show you?"

By this time Janna and Maria have both drifted back to our sun-warmed vehicle and have their noses in books.

"Sir," Matthew says, "I would like to fire a Kalashnikov."

"Me too," Angela chimes in.

The old man cheerfully reaches for the weapon and a couple of clips, loaded full of bullets. "Absolutely," he says, then casts a half look at me. "Of course, your father will have to pay for the ammunition."

"Of course. Just don't set it on automatic, that's all."

We follow him out of the back of the shop and he directs Matt to fire at a large boulder on the barren mountain that rises abruptly before us. Then it's his older sister's turn. "Hey! This thing really kicks!"

"Try again, Miss, *Sahiba*," the gun-seller encourages her, "but hold it hard against your shoulder."

I can already see Angela crowing to her suitably impressed Year 12 classmates. After I fire a couple of rounds we return to the shop. All in all, Matt thought it was a pretty neat birthday.

❋

Meanwhile, further south, Pennell's derelict girls' school remains a dust-collecting reminder of the empowering benefits of female education. As long as the dust continues to collect, there's an ongoing unfairness toward the girls of Bannu.

It's my job to remedy that.

❋

The summer of 1992, two years later, is particularly hot. For more than a year I've been making regular visits to the defunct school at Bannu. Things are moving on the boys' side, but right now we are stuck. Before we can start rebuilding the girls' side, we have to force an eviction.

Limping, white-bearded Anwar was the school's watchman and he always lived on site. Years ago, when the school was closed and the girls moved out, Anwar and his family stayed. He claims he is still owed wages. I've checked the ledgers and it's not true, but he and his children, and now grandchildren, have little incentive to move. In Pakistan possession is ninety-nine hundredths of the law. Until the old *chaokidaar* is out, rebuilding cannot begin.

Crafty Anwar makes sure that some of his womenfolk are always in the rent-free building. With the cooperation of the police we could physically remove the males, but it would be suicidal to lay hands on their women.

We don't want to use the courts; they are corrupt, unpredictable and slow. Fortunately, the community tide is running strongly against old Anwar. He's had a lot of visits from Bannuchis who want the school reopened. Samson, my young Pakistani assistant, has been preparing the ground with a juicy carrot: big concessions for a couple of Anwar's granddaughters when the school is operating again.

*

An hour south of Peshawar, on our way to Bannu, Samson and I are driving across the mountainous tongue of the Tribal Area that juts eastward into the North-West Frontier Province. We left late and as we approach "Gun Town" we are both getting hungry.

"Let's stop in Dara for some *pakoras* and a Coke, Mr Lock," suggests Samson through his big moustache. Those tasty, deep-fried pastries are Pakistan's version of a fast-food burger and I readily agree. At night we wouldn't be stopping in this notorious FATA town, but it's fine during the day.

In front of the gun shops is a row of *pakora*-sizzling roadside carts. We pull in and I salute Matthew's old Kalashnikov mentor as he rises from his stool in front of his shop. He lays his hand across his chest, indicating he is at our service. But today we are in a hurry. Samson grabs the hot *pakoras* in their newspaper packets and we resume our journey south.

We should have relaxed in a tea house and consumed them at leisure. Ten minutes out of Gun Town we join a long line of stationary vehicles on the steeply descending Kohat Pass. Slewed across the narrow, twisting road is an empty truck. Wheels in the air, it's a helpless inverted tortoise paddling its black, futile feet. It's not going anywhere, and neither are the ever-growing lines of traffic on either side of the wreck. With a rocky mountain face on the left and a seven-hundred-foot drop on the right, it was a stupid place for a truck to try and pass its competitor. Munching our *pakoras*, we look over the steep precipice. There are no recent additions to the twisted matchbox-sized wrecks below. The successful competitor must be well on his way to Kohat to claim his prize: the next job. It's not a good place for diesel-driven Ben Hur tricks.

"Why don't they show a bit of patience on these narrow passes, Samson? They take so many risks."

"Most believe that Allah has appointed a day for them to die," he says. "If it's today, it will happen. If it's not, they will be okay."

"Bang goes personal responsibility," I comment, "and sensible driving."

Down at the head of the line of waiting vehicles, an ant's nest of frustrated drivers swarms about. They shout and gesticulate conflicting orders to another lorry that has just pulled the helpless metallic tortoise to its feet. There is a loud cheer as the traffic starts moving again.

We reach Bannu in time to visit our long-term squatter. A bit of Samson's carrot and a lot of the locals' stick appear to be working. The old man can smugly resist the intermittent pressure of the visitors from Peshawar, but not the continuous scorn of his Bannu community. He is blocking progress. Samson is quick to sense the mood swing.

"Look, Anwar Jhi, we thank you for staying to protect the property while it has been empty," he says. Old Anwar gives an approving grunt to the face-saving comment and Samson continues to pour it on. "You are a good man, Anwar Jhi, and to show our appreciation we will call in some donkey carts right now and move your belongings to your brother's house—at no cost to you, of course."

Anwar eyes the four steely-faced community leaders standing behind us and gives a reluctant nod. As we close the gate behind the Anwar family, women and all, I am elated. This sort of thing can drag on for years.

My joy, however, is short lived. I hear a shout from Samson. "Come quickly, Sir! We have another problem."

Samson leads me to the rear of the derelict classrooms. A flat-roofed, mud-brick storeroom has recently been constructed inside the schoolyard, with a doorway cut through the wall to connect it to the adjacent bicycle repair shop. I screw up my nose. Old Anwar's family has been using one side as a urinal.

My euphoria at evicting wily Anwar is dissolving like the great blocks of ice being hawked from barrows throughout the roasting town. I'm starting to feel cranky about the frustrating one-step-forward, one-step-back Pakistani property polonaise.

"This has to go, Samson! It's illegal, and it's right where we're going to build a decent toilet block for the girls."

We find the offending shopkeeper in the midst of an array of disassembled bicycles. They are all machines for males; no female would dare ride a bike in this deeply conservative town. With no apparent logic or order, countless parts liberally decorate the grimy concrete floor.

Mohammad Afzal knows he is in the wrong. No doubt he was counting on the school remaining empty and, if space is there, why not use it? I deliver an ultimatum: "Sir, if you don't start to remove this storeroom today, we will bring our workmen and do it for you first thing tomorrow morning."

Like a cornered animal, the proprietor leans from one foot to the other. Inquisitive men are gathering in the doorway and it's getting a bit embarrassing. Samson presents a hand-written agreement of compliance. Mohammad Afzal wipes his oily hands on an even oilier rag, takes the pen and meekly signs the document. His hand shows compliance, but his eyes do not.

TWENTY-EIGHT

SHOOT ME FIRST

BANNU, 1992

Mohammad Afzal does nothing, so next morning the demolition begins. The sun blazes down on the backs of my sweating Pakistani workers as they swing picks into the mud-brick walls and shovel rubble away. I want to get the work done before the honour-intoxicated local Pashtuns start causing problems.

Unfortunately, problems come all too quickly. Samson's urgent voice breaks my concentration.

"Sir! Sir! You must come outside! They have guns!"

I march resolutely to the gate. This is what I feared. The crowd outside the walls is in uproar, a sea of shouting beards. Some are waving guns over their heads. I too am getting angry. They all know that Mohammad Afzal had no right to build inside the school grounds and that he agreed that we remove the building. What's all the fuss about? The fuss, of course, is that one of their fellow-Pashtuns has been humiliated by an *engrez* unbeliever. They have closed ranks to defend his honour.

The noisy mob surrounds diminutive Samson and me. Eyes dilated, their burly leader shouts his demand: "If you don't stop your workmen, we are going to shoot them!" I stare back. He repeats his threat and my angry resolve boils over.

"If you're going to shoot my workmen, Sir, you'll have to shoot me first!"

The crowd falls silent, and hundreds of angry eyes strive to stare me into submission. Inside I'm fuming. Can't anyone do anything in this country without someone's precious honour being challenged? Honour is such a convenient word. Selfishness would be a better one most of the time.

I've been confronted with eyes like this before: the wild eyes of a mob of half-ton bulls that all turn as they realise they are about to be driven into a set of confining cattle yards. All that lies between them and the freedom of their paddock is a guy with a wide-brimmed Akubra and a lashing stockwhip. They know that if they charge together he'll have to give way, but which bull will take up the challenge to activate the mob? It all comes down to resolve.

The time-warp of staring silence is again broken by my loud voice. I have the good sense to launch my question with a dose of overblown, cultural respect. "Honourable Pashtuns of Bannu, *baat soono*—listen. This is not for me. This is for you, the respected citizens of Bannu." A touch of flattery holds their bulging eyeballs in check. "Tell me," I shout, "how can you proud Pashtuns compete in Pakistan if you don't educate your girls like the Punjabis do?"

Ah, that's stalled them a bit. There is one thing Pashtuns can't stand and that is to be overshadowed by Punjabis, the most progressive and influential ethnic group in the country.

The iron-hard face of the leading beard doesn't change, but I sense his brain is working like that of a football coach at the strategic half-time break of a closely fought match. His dark eyes hold mine and I'm expecting another vitriolic outburst. Suddenly his countenance softens and he reaches for my arm.

"*Engrez,* why don't you come and have a cup of tea?"

A cup of tea? I'm confused, Mr Beard. One moment you have this wild mob psyched up to pull the trigger and the next you want to drink chai. Has the logic of my question changed your heart? Or is it that you Pashtuns respect a show of bravado? Perhaps it's just a clever manoeuvre to derail my resolve. Well, if you're a serious chameleon I'll have a cup of tea with you—but the girls' school locomotive is not going to be derailed if I can help it.

The Beard takes my arm with both hands. "Come, *engrez*. I think we can work this out."

The guns are lowered, and, like the Red Sea, the crowd parts and Samson and I are escorted to a nearby tea house. We are directed to sit at a table at the rear of the smoky room. Four tall, turbaned Pashtuns pull up chairs, making my trusty assistant look like a hand puppet. Now the Beard is all congeniality. He's ordered the best cardamom chai, along with mutton and chicken kebabs.

He thrusts his hefty hand into mine. "My name is Ibraheem. I am the Chairman of the Shopkeepers' Association of Bannu."

I can tell by the quality of the cloth in his *shalwar kamiz* that the position is a rewarding one. I introduce myself and he responds as if we grew up together. I try to raise the subject of the illegal building, but the Pashtun silences me with a wave of his hand. "After, Lock Sahib. After the food."

I am all the more wary as a Pashtun proverb comes to mind: "When you can kill with sweetness, what is the need for poison?"

Sweetness arrives in the form of mouth-watering kebabs with fresh *naan*. I'm not sure where all this is going, but the kebabs are delicious.

Ibraheem wipes his mouth and beard with the back of his hand and leans back in his chair. An approving belch emanates from his ample abdomen. "Now, Lock Sahib, we can talk." I'm more than ready. I was hoping to be halfway back to Peshawar by now, but this has to be settled, even if it takes the rest of the day.

"What you say about Punjabis getting ahead is absolutely right, Lock Jhi, and I agree with the need to educate our girls."

I'm pleasantly surprised, but as he continues I find that he approaches female education with a different mindset to mine. "These days, an educated girl brings a much bigger bride price. My neighbour just arranged a marriage for his daughter who graduated from medical college. He married her off to a wealthy cousin for a very handsome sum."

Yes, Ibraheem, I've seen it before. Put the girl through medical college so she can put on the all-important white coat and stethoscope—but there is no intention of her ever practising. No intention of exposing her to filth or having men working around her. Hooray for those who do go on, but for some it's just like fattening a heifer for the cattle market.

Even then, though, a girl's education will benefit her family, and her society. "Ibraheem Sahib," I say, "it's a well-known fact that the country that educates its women is the country that develops the fastest."

The chairman treats my comment as irrelevant. He has his own agenda and it's all about one of his Association members. "By all means, let us proceed with the girls' school, Lock Sahib. We give you our blessing. But please consider the position of our colleague, Mohammad Afzal."

I've been waiting for the barb and here it is. "Ibraheem Jhi, his extension into the schoolyard has to go."

"But he is such a poor man ..."

"Then I am sure that his fellow shopkeepers will assist him."

"But think of his honour."

"To build on someone else's land is very bad. His honour will surely be restored when it is removed."

Ibraheem is getting frustrated with me. He turns and launches into an animated conversation in Pashtu with Samson. His colleagues join in and make supportive noises when required. It hasn't been verbalised, but in this bribe-driven society I know exactly what they are thinking: *You are going to rebuild the school. That means a big contract. A fat contractor is going to slip you a lot of money to guarantee he gets the job. Why shouldn't we get some of that? Therefore, we won't move Mohammad Afzal's storeroom until we get paid for cooperating.*

I grimace inwardly as I recall the year Transparency International ranked Pakistan as the world's second most corrupt country. One Pakistani wag complained, "If only we had slipped some money to the organisers, we would have come in as number one!"

Ibraheem is getting nowhere. Samson has assured them that I will not get any kickbacks, bribes or under-the-table compensation from contractors in the school rebuilding project. It's all for the benefit of the Bannuchis. Over the next five hours, the chairman calls in other town dignitaries and a senior lawyer to argue the case for preserving Mohammad Afzal's honour.

I keep repeating my mantra: "This is not for me. This is for you. This is for your daughters." Then in an inspired moment I add, "... just as Dr Pennell Sahib would have wished."

Pennell is a legend. A brilliant student, he was a triple gold medallist at medical school in London. Perhaps his mother should also have received a medal: to avoid separation from her only child, Elizabeth, the godly widow, sailed with him to India. In 1893 both arrived here in Bannu, in the remote north-west corner of the British Raj. Pennell never saw his forty-fifth birthday. While operating on a septic patient, the surgeon contracted fatal blood poisoning. He died in the hospital he pioneered. Thousands of Muslims, Sikhs, Hindus and Christians gathered to mourn his death.

In Bannu the selfless doctor is still considered to be something of a saint, and mentioning his name strengthens my case. I can feel that the weight of honour is starting to move in my direction.

Chairman Ibraheem has exhausted all of his options. With the Pennell card on the table he now has an acceptably honourable escape route. He sits tall in his chair, places his hand across his chest and magnanimously announces, "Lock Jhi, for the sake of Dr Pennell Sahib, go ahead, remove the building." Then he adds in an accommodating tone, "And if there is anything we can do for you, anything at all, I am at your service." I wish he had said that, and meant it, five hours ago.

I heave a sigh of relief and dispatch Samson to get our workers moving again. "Tell them to flatten it fast, Samson." I look at my watch. "I'll leave you down here to finish the job. I have to get back to Peshawar. Janna and I are driving to Murree tomorrow. I'm chairing a school board meeting, and of course we want to see our kids."

There are landmark days in everyone's working life. This has been one of them. We've seen the disgruntled old *chaokidaar* leave without litigation, and we have survived a confrontation with the local businessmen. And, in a back-handed way best understood by Pashtuns, we have strengthened the respect and support for us in the community.

"You've done it, Sir," Samson congratulates me.

"No, Samson, *we* have done it," I respond, recognising the powerful input of my micro-sized assistant. He has a name like Goliath's but performs like a David, loading his sling with cultural stones and a few well-directed carrots, all for the girls of Bannu.

*

I'm five twilight miles north of Bannu. Later on I'll have to join a police-escorted night convoy to drive back through Dara, but that's okay. I can be patient; it's been a tension-loaded day, but the girls' school is another step closer. I'm emotionally exhausted yet still charged with adrenaline. I slow a little, roll down the window, thrust my head into the evening air-stream and bellow a stress-releasing shout of God-directed thankfulness. "Hallelujah! Hallelujah!"

At this time of evening there is a lot of rural roadside activity. Farmers carry their hoes back from the fields. Boys shepherd their goats back to the villages. Countless children run and play on the edge of the road. Careful driving is the order of the evening.

The thing that I fear most in this country is the agonising thump of flesh on the bull bar of our Toyota. Tomorrow, on our way to Murree, it's going to happen.

TWENTY-NINE

THE SICKENING THUD

GRAND TRUCK ROAD, 1992

She is running fast across the divided road. Trees in the median strip obscure my view. I do not see her until it's too late. I brake and swerve hard, but there's a sickening thud as flesh meets steel. This is the noise I've feared most on Pakistani roads, and now it's happened. Running back, I can see there is nothing I can do. She's dying in a pool of blood.

In forty seconds forty men gather around.

It's all happening on the Grand Trunk Road, between Wah and Taxila. The Mughal emperors travelled this same route, enjoying cool Kabul in summer and returning to warm Delhi in winter.

The crowd is in a nasty mood. "Look what you've done! She's badly injured."

I'm a cattleman and I know this cow is more than injured. There are only a few more twitches left in her dying body. Thank you, Lord, that it's not one of their daughters. The animal's only value now is her meat and hide.

Another upset voice asks, "What should we do?"

"Point her toward Mecca," I quickly recommend, "and cut her jugular, then you can use the meat, if you do it right now."

They all stare at the beast. No one moves. Her twitching stops. An accusing voice pipes up, "Look! Now she's dead! You'll have to pay for this, *engrez*."

Janna is about to get out of the Hilux. "Stay in the car, Janna!" I shout. "This could get nasty!"

She slams the door, locks it and calls me over. "Any hope for the cow, Grant?" she asks through the open window.

"None! She's dead. They shouldn't let stock gallop around like that. This is the Grand Trunk Highway, not some village lane."

"They look pretty angry. What are we going to do?"

The crowd is tightening around us, eyes burning with antagonism.

I'm frightened. My adrenaline says, "Get in that vehicle and get out of here, pronto." But if it won't start they'll be livid, and who knows what they will do?

"Eh, Amreecan!" shouts the accusing voice. "The cow is dead, now you will have to pay, or do we call the police?"

I'm about to rebut his assumptions about my nationality when suddenly I recall advice given to me only last month. "Grant, if you ever hit someone's animal and it's not your fault, you should go on the offensive. They only see your foreign dollars and they'll squeeze you for all they can get. And don't get the police involved otherwise you'll end up paying much more."

In that moment I decide that I am not responsible, and that I'm going to take that advice seriously. I walk to the front of my Hilux and survey the damage. Eighty eyes follow me. I make angry noises as I check the crumpled bodywork. I turn on the agitated pack.

"Look at this!" I point with both palms. "Look at all this damage!"

My adversaries are all wrapped in *chaadars* for protection against the early morning breeze. I look them in the eye and raise my voice. "Where's the owner of this cow? I want to see him." No response. I look under the vehicle and let out a furious growl. "Oh no! Look at that! Probably wrecked my front suspension as well." I open the bonnet. Acid is leaking from a big crack in the battery. I give an angry groan. "That means a brand new battery."

I eyeball the team of blankets, upping my offensive. "This is going to cost a lot of money to fix. More than 20,000 rupees! Where's the owner of that cow? I have to see him. He has to pay to fix my vehicle."

No owner appears. The tallest blanket steps forward and takes up the case for the prosecution. "Okay, your car is damaged a bit, but what about the cow? The cow is dead!"

A steady stream of vehicles whizzes past us as I aggressively take up the case for the defence. "Look, you men! You know that cows shouldn't be galloping across the highway. I've driven all over your country for ten years and I've seen plenty of goats, buffaloes, cattle and camels, but none of them running around like that cow. How am I to see an animal if it rushes straight out of the trees?"

Their eyes indicate that the defence's case is gaining ground. I continue, "If anyone has a wild cow they should keep it tethered till it settles down." I see a couple of faint nods from the back of the jury. I press my original demand with renewed vigour. "Where is the owner of that cow? He is responsible. He has to pay for the damage to my vehicle." I'm desperately hoping he won't appear. "My repairs are going to cost him a lot of money. Where is that man?"

The jury of blankets look at each other and they mumble among themselves. A tall spokesman steps forward. "Look, *engrez*, why don't you just get going?"

His words are like good news from a far country, but I don't want to appear too eager. "What!" I protest, "I can't leave till I've seen the owner of that cow. He owes me money."

There's a pause while the spokesman deliberates. Then, with a strong hint of malice in his voice, he repeats, "Why don't you just get going?"

"Well … all right. But I'm not happy. I'll go, providing my Toyota will start. The battery's been wrecked, you know."

I move slowly, but I can't get behind the wheel quickly enough. I turn the key and the weakened battery struggles to power engagement with the flywheel. Click. Click. Click. There's fear in Janna's eyes. I try again. Hallelujah, the starter motor engages and the diesel roars to life.

As the crowd disappears in my rear view mirror we both heave a sigh of relief. "Phew," Janna says, "that was close. I've heard of angry crowds burning vehicles in situations like that!"

THIRTY

ROYALTY

PESHAWAR, 1995

After six years we have moved from "Ararat". The bored murderer continued to throw flowers from his side of the lane, and Janna continued to ignore him. Following one particularly violent rain-storm (fortunately not of the forty days and forty nights kind), our Afghan neighbours came to help clean out the mud left by a foot of filthy water. We became good friends, and Janna and I learnt a lot about the civil war that rages in their homeland. Ironically, the mujahidin groups who squeezed the Russian invaders out are now fighting each other for control of their country. It is just as the third Trucketeer predicted six years ago.

*

We've moved to a nearby three-story block of six flats. We are in Flat 3. In the flats below us there are two different kinds of royalty. In Flat 2, Ayisha has genuine royal blood from the old Kingdom of Swat. Then there is "Mrs Major" in Flat 1, directly below us. No one uses her real name. It's just "Mrs Major", spoken in hushed tones. It seems that when her unassuming husband retired, his wife inherited his title and rank. Unlike petite Ayisha, portly Mrs Major hasn't a drop of royal blood in her veins. But she rules the flats like a military queen, or at least tries to. Being directly above regimental headquarters, poor Janna is right in the firing line. There are days she is glad she is in the bishop's office doing his secretarial work.

Mrs Major marches up the stairs, bangs on our door and goosesteps across the threshold. "Mrs Lock, you have cut down my precious bougainvillea! You have destroyed it!"

"No, I haven't. I've just trimmed a few of the laterals growing across our window." Janna is regretting that some telltale clippings fell as she leaned out to expedite the pruning. "We couldn't even see out of it."

"Next time you must speak to me first!" Then her military tone moderates. "And, Mrs Lock, I note you have a new pair of high-heeled shoes."

Janna is confused by the more civil comment. However, our visitor is about to leap out of the trenches and resume the charge. "Yes, I know you have new shoes because they tap, tap, tap around on the floor and keep my poor husband awake. He goes to bed early and he must get his sleep. You know he has high blood pressure."

No one is game to suggest that the biggest cause of his blood pressure sleeps next to him every night.

"But Mrs Major, I'm wearing the same plastic slip-ons that I've worn inside all year," Janna says bravely, wondering if she's about to be court-marshalled.

"You need to remember," blurts out the military machine, "that the Major has honourably served his country in three wars against India, and he deserves his rest."

Receiving clear distress signals on my auditory radar, I leave my work and reinforce Janna in the living room. I'm glad I happen to be on reserve duty at my home desk, because for some time I've been preparing a counterattack with a not-so-secret weapon.

"Mrs Major," I interrupt from Janna's side, "since we are talking about sleeping, do you realise the Major Sahib actually keeps us awake at night?"

There is a startled look of incredulity on her face, as though I have stooped so low as to use germ warfare in combat. "What are you talking about, Mr Lock? Your wife is the one clip-clopping on the floor all night."

It's time for me to detonate the fuse of my war-ending missile. "I know Major Sahib can't help it, but he snores so loudly below us that it often keeps us awake, even when our window is shut. The Farzeens in the flat above us can hear it too. They thought it was me."

Janna is no longer stranded on the battlefield. "Perhaps," she bravely suggests, "the Major Sahib has sleep apnoea?"

Mrs Major huffs and puffs, but she knows that the intelligence report from across the lines is absolutely true.

"But, Mrs Major," I genuinely add, "it's all part of living together in flats. We all have to learn to give and take a bit, don't we?"

Face aghast, she turns on her heel and beats a retreat down to the Flat 1 bunkers. "No respect for returned soldiers," we hear her expounding as she departs. "No respect at all!"

*

It's no wonder that the other five women in the block decline to invite the military queen to their eleven o'clock morning tea chitchats.

"Five of us," explains Janna, "and five different mother tongues, but we all know some Urdu, so it works."

They all love Ayisha from Flat 2, the one with real royal blood in her veins. She is refined, educated and quietly elegant. She buys her expensive perfume on visits to Dubai, but she never flaunts her genes or wealth. Ayisha is a member of the old royal family of the small northern kingdom of Swat, which long ago became a district of Pakistan.

"Her unaffected nature reminds me of Princess Diana," Janna shares with me.

"Except," I quip, "that Ayisha is a royal who has become a commoner, and Diana is a near-commoner who has become a royal."

"Well, I'm going to take her with me next week when I line up to see Princess Di."

Although the royal family of Swat doesn't rule any more, they are still highly respected. In fact, Ayisha's father is currently Governor of Peshawar. Ayisha insisted we drink tea with her parents in Government House. After her father showed us his beautiful aviary, we all sat down to sip tea from translucent Royal Doulton china. I talked current affairs with him while former governors made non-verbal contributions from manifold portraits staring down from the reception room walls.

*

Right now Ayisha's biggest concern is losing young Shahbaz to boarding school. Janna can empathise.

"Little Shahbaz is so small , and I will miss him so much," Ayisha confides, "but his father insists that he goes to the same school that he attended in Lahore. That's hundreds of miles away!"

Ayisha is married to Gul Mohammad, a landlord, whose fertile, irrigated fields are an hour from Peshawar in the direction of Swat. I quite enjoy Gul Mohammad's blustery sort of rugged company. While his wife is truly a royal, Gul Mohammad is more like the frog the princess kissed. A tall, vigorous hunk of a frog, he dotes on his two little froglets. He has firm plans for his small son to start Grade 1 in his Alma Mater in the Punjab. Shahbaz's name was put on the waiting list the week after his birth.

Gul Mohammad sometimes invites me to watch cricket on his big screen TV, and we compare notes on agriculture and life in general. "Mr Grant, "he says, "when you are away for days on your project trips, I note Mrs Janna is left all alone."

I nod, realising that most Pakistanis grow up in an extended household and have problems with being in a house by themselves.

"Isn't she afraid?"

"Not really. She's used to it."

"Well, if she ever has any trouble, tell her to ring down here and I will be right up there with my new Winchester shotgun."

I thank him profusely for his genuine concern. I also know he would love to have an excuse to test the trigger of the fancy weapon he has just added to his imported collection.

*

A day's drive north-east from Peshawar, Ayisha's emerald Swat Valley is a special place. We have spent some memorable family holidays among its many orchards and mosques.

Kalam, at the head of the valley, is our favourite destination. It is wedged into a magnificent arena of snow-covered mountains. We hike among waterfalls, glaciers, mistletoe forests and alpine pastures. From the flock of river-hugging hotels, it is clear that Kalam is a favourite summer holiday place for Pakistanis as well.

But the area is not all sweetness and light. There are nation-dividing tensions in the valley. The idyllic Swat has always been a nesting ground for Islamic fundamentalists. They punctuate their anti-government demands by burning tyres across the main roads. It's not funny when your family is eye-balled by a clutch of armed, black-turbaned men who are blatantly recruiting for the jihad. Their piercing eyes have a message:

Now is not our time, but it will come. Then you hated Americans will not be tolerated.

Those eyes are right. In time fundamentalism will morph into Pakistan's Taliban and the hotels will be mostly empty. In fact, by 2009 almost all of Swat will be deserted. Two million locals will flee from their valley while Pakistan's army attempts to eliminate the Taliban malignancy before it threatens the entire nation.

In Swat, as in any place on the globe, tourism and lack of security do not mix. Few people know that Pakistan is a tourists' paradise. Apart from the north and south poles, Pakistan has more glaciers than any other country. Nine of the world's twenty highest peaks raise their snowy buttresses in the "Land of the Pure". But different Islamic groups have varying ideas about what is "pure". The Taliban want to take Muslims back to the Arabic Middle East of the seventh century. Although liberal-thinking Muslims declare that this is not the way to go, it seems that the Holy Quran is on the side of the fundamentalists and the Taliban.

*

The women are gathering for their morning *gup-chup*, chitchat, over tea. Janna discovers all sorts of things at these female gatherings. She finds out why there are fresh bloodstains on the stairs: Flat 4 has slaughtered a goat as a sacrifice for the health of a sick son. She learns that Muslim women are not allowed to pray during menstruation. And Mrs Major's latest edicts are always discussed in appropriately hushed tones.

*

"Where is Ayisha today?" Janna asks as she arrives late for today's tea and biscuits.

"She has taken the two children shopping," Salma from Flat 6 smiles. "She has to get clothes for Shahbaz to go into boarding school in Lahore." Salma is on a high; she is going to have her first baby. "Thank you, Sister Janna," she says, "thank you. We have wanted a baby for years. I've been to many holy men to pray and make offerings, but it's only since you prayed for me that I have become pregnant."

The mother-to-be cocks her head. "What's all that noise? Do you think Ayisha is back early?"

Everyone can hear it now. Below, car doors are slamming and people are rushing into Flat 2. Voices are raised, and then there's a loud, agonising, masculine wail.

Salma springs to her feet. "That sounds like Gul Mohammad," and she rushes out.

Two minutes later she reappears, her face ashen and a hand covering her mouth. "It's Ayisha," she whispers.

"What has happened, Salma?"

"A bomb was thrown into one of the clothing shops downtown. There was a terrible fire. People were trapped inside. There was only one way out, and it was cut off by the blaze." Salma throws her hands over her face. "Ayisha couldn't get out. She was burned to death!"

The women gasp. "And the children? Shahbaz and his little sister?"

"They … they are gone too."

The four stare at each other, their thoughts full of pictures of their dear friend and her two small children, and their ears full of the screams of Gul Mohammad, sobbing and wailing below.

*

A few weeks later, Janna is all excited. "I've seen her, Grant! I've seen Princess Diana!" She dances about like a little girl.

It's been a heavy day of meetings for me, including a low-cost housing feasibility study. My dancing girl meets me at the door. "She was wearing a red dress with white spots. I couldn't have found a better location if I'd tried."

"How did you do that? Weren't you a bit late in leaving?"

"There were masses of people and police all along Saddar Road. I was heading for some spaces around the white mosque, and then the morning prayers finished and all the men came streaming out. I was surrounded by a great crowd of men all jostling to be up the front. I was the only female, and you know what they are like with foreign women: a mixture of embarrassment and chivalry. The crowd parted for me, and next thing I know I'm in the front row. And there she was," Janna claps her hands, "standing in the back of an open vehicle, coming down Arbab Road, straight toward us at the T-junction."

I lower my computer bag. "Wow! That was a good place to be."

"As the vehicle slowed for the turn, she scanned the mass of turbans and white prayer caps and then spotted me, the only woman in an ocean of bearded men. She looked straight at me and gave me a knowing smile, and waved back to me. I couldn't believe it. Here I was, a woman from the sticks of Australia, surrounded by Pashtun men in a far corner of Pakistan, and Her Royal Highness, the Princess of Wales, the most popular woman in the world, saw me and smiled and waved at me! It was as though she had come all the way to Peshawar just to see me." Janna dances around the floor in another paroxysm of youthful exuberance. "I still can't believe it!"

"I wish Ayisha could have been there with you," I comment.

Janna stalls in her girlish spin as I mention our downstairs neighbour. We look at each other and share the same sadness.

A faint whiff of French perfume no longer drifts up the stairs from Flat 2. The curtains are drawn, and it is empty. Gul Mohammad moved out the day his royal wife from Swat, and his two little children, didn't come home.

THIRTY-ONE

SPECIAL MEAT

1997

There is a pair of well-worn, very muddy shoes outside our door. On the inside, a faded shuttlecock burka hangs on a hook, and the sound of scrubbing comes from the kitchen. I'm getting organised to leave for my office. Today I meet with European donor partners who support our apprenticeship scheme and education for slum kids.

Janna looks up from the rattling keys of her word processor. "You know, the thing I admire about Zu Bibi is her faithfulness. She comes across those muddy fields and catches a horse-drawn *taanga*, rain, hail or shine. She might arrive late but she always comes. I'd never get all these letters done for the bishop if I didn't have her coming part-time to help around the house. She's fantastic."

I nod in agreement and kiss Janna goodbye for the day. She is usually snowed under with high priority letters and reports for the leader of the diocese. She is a real asset to Bishop Sahib: a great typist, reliable and, above all, discreet.

There is a quiet call. "Sister, I am going."

Janna goes to see her helper to the door and give the customary hug and three kisses, on alternate cheeks. Zu Bibi's hug is a little longer than usual. "Sister Janna," she says, "you are my friend and I need your help. Could you give me a small advance on my wages?"

Janna is not fazed. Zu Bibi always has a good reason, and she always pays it back. "What is it, Zu Bibi?"

Tears come to the Pashtun woman's eyes. She has had a hard life—looks fifty but is only thirty-five. Her first husband died from TB and she has recently remarried a much older man. Her only son is the reason for the request.

"Abid is in jail."

"What has he done this time?"

"Nothing, Sister Janna. He was just delivering some parcels."

"Ah, but what was in the parcels?"

"It was medicine."

"Medicine?"

She looks a bit sheepish. "It was heroin. But it wasn't his fault. Who can resist the will of Allah? It was destined that the police should find out."

Janna is mentally grappling with the theology of everyday Islam. Allah requires that each person submits to his laws. They must do more good deeds than bad deeds to weigh down the heavenly scales. But what kind of God is it that expects good to be done yet overrides a person's will and compels him to do evil? It's a cop out, an escape from personal responsibility. It's not a good basis for society to operate on.

Janna returns to her desk and brings the money and her wages notebook. "Put your mark here, Zu Bibi. I hope you are successful with the police. Why doesn't Abid get a regular job?"

Zu Bibi hugs her again. "Jobs are hard to find, but he is trying." She drops the cloth over her face and disappears down the stairs.

A month later the books are balanced on pay-day. The faithful worker has another request. "Sister Janna, I need some special meat."

"Special meat? What do you mean special meat?"

The Pashtun woman can't bring herself to utter the word *soor* (pig). "Special meat, Sister Janna. You know—special meat."

Janna realises what she means. "What do you want pig meat for, Zu Bibi? That is *haram*, unclean, for Muslims."

"But my doctor says that special meat is the only thing which will cure my joint pains. You are a Christian, and a foreigner. You must be able to get it for me."

Janna figures the doctor is a *pir*, a holy man who mixes Islam with all sorts of black arts and bizarre medication. "Zu Bibi, we don't eat it in Pakistan. It would not be right that we upset our Muslim friends. I know it is available in Islamabad, but we have no plans to visit there for a good while. Anyway, I don't think it would do anything for your rheumatism. I recommend that you save your money."

Zu Bibi is not listening. She has the information she needs. "I really must have some," she declares, and shuffles off in her anonymous garb.

A week later Zu Bibi confides to Janna in a quiet whisper, as though she is going to be struck down if she says it too loudly, "I have the special meat, Sister Janna." She reaches into her bosom and pulls out a small calico bag that is tied around her neck. Then she carefully withdraws a hard, brown piece of salted meat. It looks a lot like dried corned beef. Janna is not impressed.

"I went to Islamabad," Zu Bibi says, "and asked a lot of questions, and I found the man who sells it. He said he gets it from the jungle hunters who shoot the wild animals for sport. You are the one who knows what special meat tastes like, Sister Janna. Now you must test it for me."

Janna curls her nose and makes unacceptable excuses. Undeterred, her helper separates a sliver of meat from the uninviting blob and thrusts it at her employer.

"I must be sure it's special meat, otherwise I have spent all my money for nothing." Whatever it is, Zu Bibi has wasted her money, unless her condition is psychosomatic.

Janna recoils. Who knows where that blob has come from, who has handled it and where it's been? It's better not to think about it.

"I know it will work," asserts the village woman, "as long as it is special meat. Try it, Sister Janna."

Janna stares at the uninviting morsel, then back into the round face of her expectant helper. But she is more than a helper. She has become a friend. That swings the deal; friends do things for each other. The tester closes her eyes and nibbles the grimy morsel. It has a smoky, salty taste, with a faint pork flavour.

Maybe it is salted pork after all, Janna thinks. *I'll give it the benefit of the doubt—otherwise she'll be devastated.* "Yes, Zu Bibi, it is special meat."

Some of the work-worn lines on the helper's face immediately dissolve. She beams. "Thank you, Sister Janna. Thank you. Now I will have some."

She goes to the kitchen, takes a fragment from the blob in the bag and grinds it with a small mortar and pestle. Then she stirs it into a glass of water and religiously drinks it all. "I will do that every day till it's all gone," explains the Pashtun, "then my pain will also be gone." She smiles and reaches behind the door for the mop and makes preparation to clean the daily layer of dust and uncombusted traffic pollutants from the floor.

That evening Janna tells me what happened. "Grant, I still can't understand why that Muslim *pir* would recommend something which is prohibited in Islam," she muses. "How can something which is supposed to make them unclean cure them?"

"Remember when we were kids? The nastier the medicine, the more effective it was supposed to be." The memory brings the taste of cod liver oil to my mouth. "Perhaps it's a bit like that. Or maybe 'stolen fruit tastes the sweetest'. Or the *pir* has come up with a good money spinner. We'll see."

*

After a month of hope and anticipation, the special meat turns out not to be so special after all. "Sister Janna," Zu Bibi says, "I need one of your Australian Dispreen tablets. My joints are giving me big trouble today. Your tablets work so much better than the Pakistani ones."

"I know," Janna agrees. "Half the drugs in this country are *nuqli* (counterfeit) and mostly clay." She hands Zu Bibi two tablets. "Take these and make some tea for us before I go to the bishop's office."

The two women sip their tea while the Aussie Disprin goes to work. Zu Bibi reaches into her cloth bag and pulls out a large, legal-looking manila envelope. "You must keep this safe for me, Sister Janna. It cannot stay in my house any more."

"What is it, Zu Bibi?"

"I cannot read, but it is the ownership documents for a one-roomed mud-brick house in Charsadda. When my mother died, there was no one else, so it was left to me. I get a little bit of rent from a distant cousin."

"But why give it to me?"

As though she fears someone is listening at the door, Zu Bibi drops her voice. "When I married Gul Khan, I thought he had feelings for me. I thought he wanted to care for me. But I was wrong. He only wants my tiny property. Now he thinks he has the right to take it."

Janna listens. In this culture, a woman without the covering of a man is like a dismasted yacht drifting in the path of an approaching tsunami.

Abid, the son, seems slothfully incapable of protecting his hardworking mother. No wonder she agreed to marry the "supportive" Gul Khan.

"He has threatened to beat me if I don't give him the papers. He's getting very angry and abusive. I didn't think he was a violent man, but he has seven guns in the house."

Janna nods as she recalls her visit. She personally counted the guns while Zu Bibi boiled the chai out in the courtyard.

"If I do not have the papers, how can I give them to him?" She smiles as though this will solve all her troubles and then changes the subject. "You look tired, Sister Janna. You sit too long at that letter writing machine." Forgetting her own pains and problems, the village woman compels Janna to lie face down on the nearest *toshak* (floor mattress) and proceeds to pummel and kneed her muscles.

Janna is thinking through the gravity of her helper's position. No one asks too many questions about domestic accidents. "You must be very careful, Zu Bibi," she mumbles through the painful bliss of the massage.

A British friend of Janna's, red-haired Susan, is also worried about Zu Bibi's predicament. "Zu Bibi is an amazing woman, Janna. When she comes to clean my house, she insists that I teach her to read. I give her half an hour a day, and she is going really well. She says it will give her more control of her life, and of course she is right."

"You don't suppose he would put petrol in her kerosene cooker so it blows up when she lights it, do you?"

"It happens often enough, Janna. It's a neat way to get rid of an unwanted wife. 'Accidents will happen.' Sometimes they don't even risk losing the stove. Just pour fuel over her and strike a match. If the burns don't kill her, the infections will."

It sure is a lottery when a girl moves in to live with her husband, his mother and all his family. "I hope Zu Bibi is okay when we are both on home assignment," Janna says.

*

Several months later, when we are back in Adelaide, a letter arrives from England.

> Dear Janna,
>
> We hope things have been going well for you in Australia. It's always such a huge adjustment, isn't it? We've only been back in England a week and today I got bad news about our faithful helper.
>
> Zu Bibi is gone.
>
> It's so sad. Apparently there were no suspicious circumstances—except when we left last week she was fit and well. I wouldn't be surprised if it was poison. I had to give the documents back to her when we left. I don't know what she did with them or who has them now, but I suspect Gul Khan is a very happy widower. And who knows, that lazy son of hers might have been in on it as well.
>
> Love,
>
> Susan

THIRTY-TWO

NOT A BAD INNINGS

1998

The early morning phone connection from Australia is not good, but I can tell from Janna's drawn face that the news is even worse. "There's nothing more they can do for Jeff's brain tumour," she told me after hanging up. "We need to go home very soon, not in three months' time."

I scratch my head. "We'll have to tell Bishop Mano. I'll organise a meeting."

"That won't be easy."

Bishop Mano was appointed as Bishop of Peshawar three years ago. If his predecessor, frail Bishop Alexander, had not survived a coronary and then a kidnapping, Mano RumalShah may have been required to step into the position much earlier. Now, in some form of organisational osmosis, all problems, big or small, filter their way through to his office. Although he has cut the flow by delegating work to others, both the cream and the flotsam seem to rise to the surface of his paper-laden desk. It's the way the culture works, and things are slow to change.

Bishop Mano squeezes us in at the end of the day. We arrive just as Jarmu John, the old school cleaner from out at Mardan, hobbles out. Despite his age, he won't accept retirement from either the school's principal or the diocesan education director; he has to hear it from the bishop himself. Mano RumalShah has bigger things to deal with, like the ransacking of the Christian township of Shanti Nagar by militant Muslim mobs, but he graciously hears old Jarmu John out.

When it's our turn for an audience, I explain the situation. "Janna's brother's brain tumour is out of control, Bishop Sahib. They can't do anything more for him."

Janna's eyes are moist. "He's my only brother. It was probably the years of paint solvents that did it, in the crash repair workshop."

The bishop is tired but he makes empathetic noises. His parents have had their share of serious health issues lately.

"Bishop Sahib," I say, "we'd like to leave for our triennial home assignment within three weeks and not three months as we all expected."

Bishop Mano does some quick mental calculations. "That means you'll be back in September. I think we can manage without you for six months. Your contractor should have completed the nurses' quarters at Bannu hospital by about then."

I'm feeling uncomfortable. Janna and I look at each other, and then I drop the bomb-shell. "Bishop Sahib, we have thought and prayed about this a lot, and … we won't be coming back." There is a lengthy silence as he absorbs the news.

"We don't know how long Jeff will hang on, so we plan to take some study leave as well." The Bishop's silence continues. "And I think it's time to hand over the project work to locals. Samson and Sohail are well trained now. They can continue to support whoever takes over my role."

The ecclesiastical leader finally responds, but he's still looking shell shocked. "Not coming back. How long have you been here now?"

"Ten years, Bishop Sahib."

"Well," he says slowly, "that's not a bad innings."

*

Like most Pakistanis, Bishop Mano loves cricket, so it's not surprising to hear him couch his response to our announcement in cricket parlance. Pakistan recently won the Cricket World Cup. The nation was euphoric not just because they cleaned up arch-rival India but because they conquered the whole world.

In Peshawar big events like weddings and World Cup wins are enthusiastically celebrated by discharging rifles into the air. It wasn't so bad with the old single-shot *jezeels*, but with automatic weapons there is a lot of hot lead up there. When the celebrations begin, it's smart to move indoors. Our neighbour Atiq was a bit slow. When he lingered on the balcony, he took a slug in his right arm.

"Cricket?" some mystified American friends laughed one day. "It's all a mystery to us. What other game in the world do you play for five days without producing a winner?"

"Come on, guys," I challenged them. "You do language and culture study for years. Cricket isn't just an arbitrary game here—it's culture. Learn a bit about it. They'll love you for it." I could still see the scepticism in their eyes. "Look, a few words of cricket language might help you out of trouble one day."

The unbelieving cricket *kafirs* scoffed.

"Let me give you an example. Janna and I were on the road once just after the United States had fired a missile at another Islamic country. We were stopped at a checkpoint by a very serious member of the Pakistan army. He held his rifle at the ready and ordered us out of our vehicle.

"'Are you Amreecans?' he demanded.

"'No, no!' I said. 'We play cricket! We're Australian.'

"He lowered his gun and visibly relaxed. 'Ah yes! Dennis Lillee and Steve Waugh.'

"'And Shane Warne,' I added.

"He grinned. 'Sir, why don't you come and have a cup of tea with us?'"

My Stars and Stripes friends were not convinced. "That's all right for you—you're Australian."

"Well, just congratulate them on the World Cup and the great job Imran Khan did as their captain. Remember, Pakistanis love cricket."

I didn't tell them that I got an extra ten rupees off every tin of motor oil when I asked for my Allan Border discount.

Cricket must be one of the most enduring legacies of British rule. It's played in dusty village fields, on the streets and in the stadiums. And I sometimes think it's the common denominator that has kept Pakistan and India from more border scraps.

I mentally agree with my boss. A decade has been a pretty good innings. But it's only been by the grace of God we have kept up the run rate. It's partly the length of the innings that is forcing us to declare. For the last couple of years, running between the wickets seems to have been much more demanding. Maybe there have been too many away games and not enough on the home ground.

For some time now Janna has been chiding me, "You have to slow down, Grant. You have too much on your plate. Driving all over the province to keep the projects going, and working till late at night on your computer—you'll just burn yourself out. Then you won't be any use to anyone." I'm starting to agree with her logic.

"Remember what you read in Stephen Covey's book? That basing your happiness on your ability to control everything is futile." I nod. I know she's right.

Maria's visit was a turning point. Last year we had the delight of having our second daughter with us for ten months. She came as a volunteer to teach English as a Second Language, and she was a real hit with the young Pakistani and Afghan women.

"I can see that teaching English is a great way to get to know the locals," I told her.

"Dad," she said, "it's so important for them, and for their countries, to get English."

"I reckon I'd enjoy doing that for a while."

"Why don't you? You could do a course in Australia during your home assignment, then come back and teach English. The change would do you good."

The seed was sown and it grew. I visited the men's English classes and I was enthused. I felt I'd like to empower people like that, even though I'd been doing lots of empowerment with my guys in the project office for years.

*

With Bishop Mano's cricketing metaphor still ringing in my ears, my mind flashes through some of the events of the last ten years.

"Limited overs": The little Suzuki didn't stand a chance as it pulled out onto the highway in front of the speeding bus. All its passengers were crushed. We were among the two thousand mourners. Inside one of the five coffins was the mangled body of a lively, intellectual Pakistani mother. Talat Peters had just started managing five schools that changed the lives of "Sweepers' kids", the children of poor Christians. Janna supported Talat professionally and they were close friends. Sadly, that was a limited overs event.

A "six": Janna worked hard by extension and completed her Masters studies on culture with straight As.

Another "six": "You'll never get permission to build a school in Risalpur, Grant. It's a military town, and we've been trying for thirty years." But after two years of visiting army headquarters in Rawalpindi, I came back with the necessary piece of paper.

A "run out": The Moonrise Bungalow case dragged on and on. After many years we finally won. We dropped a catch early on in the game, but Barham Yusuf was run out in the end.

"The members' stand": Since we reopened Bannu School, the classrooms have filled with both Pashtun boys and girls. There is vigorous teacher training and strong leadership from Paul and Belinda Cooper, educators from New Zealand. More buildings are going up and ultimately it will have nine hundred students. (It will later go on to be widely acclaimed for academic excellence, and the girl's side will gain college status.) The nearby hospital will open again soon. I can see Dr Pennell rising in the members' stand to applaud this double century.

Another "century": Except when she was clean-bowled with two attacks of hepatitis, Janna has been on call for Bishop Mano's correspondence at all hours of the day and night. She has also scored with the local women, even though several of them cunningly stole her purse while they chatted on a horse-drawn *taanga*. Those runs all add up to another century.

The "umpire": The bishop wanted to run clean elections for the diocese and asked if I thought it could be done. "The problem, Bishop Sahib," I explained, "is that delegates are unable to vote with their hearts when everyone is watching them raise their hands. I can do it if you let me organise a secret ballot." Despite the accusation that we mixed magic into the food so people would vote the way we wanted, it was the cleanest elections in the history of the diocese, and I was the umpire.

A long "test": "Sir! Sir! A semi-government department has just pulled down all the fences you put around our ten properties at Thandiani." I was stunned. Samson continued his phone report from Abbottabad. "And they say the land is theirs because the Christians can't prove ownership." All sorts of human rights issues surged up within me. I was positive they were wrong and I set out to prove it. There were some vital documents we didn't have. They wouldn't be easy to get but I knew where they were: hidden away in the said department's locked document room.

Finally I got the Commissioner's permission to search the files: "Go ahead, Mr Lock, they are public documents." They may have been public documents, but there were some worried officials who definitely didn't want me to see them. For two days I sifted through thousands of pages, some one hundred years old, all the time carefully watched by the department's hawk-eyed staff. Bingo, bingo, lots of bingos, but it took seven frustrating months to get permission to photocopy them. After another three years of careful compiling, legal presentations and regular meetings, the Chief Secretary agreed that it was Christian land.

"No Pakistani could have done that, Mr Lock," the Archbishop told me. I was relieved that justice had finally been done, but it had been a long test.

In fact, overall it has been a gruelling "series". Watching for the cunning spin. Racing to the boundaries of a province bigger than Tasmania. Bowling flat out for the whole match. Yes, it has worn us down. But now Janna and I know that the Third Umpire has given the signal for us to toss the ball to others, and to change grounds.

During the 1980s millions of Afghan refugees found shelter in camps around Peshawar. Things rapidly changed for the frontier capital. The BBC called it "the dirtiest city in the world". *Newsweek* called Peshawar "a cradle of terror" and "the capital of militant Islam". Yet, despite the bad press, Janna and I will miss this ancient Silk Road city with its cosmopolitan population and Wild West atmosphere.

*

Samson and Sohail have long faces. "I don't think we will last long once you are gone," says my frail chief assistant. "There is a lot of politics in the diocese and we may be replaced." That pains me deeply, but I console myself that their training will stand them in good stead when I, the current captain of the Project Team, move to a different club. I just have to accept that the "selectors" may have different ideas about the team's future makeup.

Back in Australia we get the news by email. "Samson fell sick. He was put off, and then he got worse and couldn't leave his bed. He died last week."

I send our condolences, but in my mind a question lingers. Was it his sickness that caused him to leave the job, or was it leaving the job that caused his sickness? He'd given his all for me and for the projects, but with a frail constitution and smashed self-esteem, I reckon he just curled his small body up and died of a broken heart.

THE CAPITAL

NORTH-EAST PAKISTAN

1999–2003

SEPTEMBER 11. COALITION ENTERS AFGHANISTAN

1999 | 2000 | 2001 | 2002 | 2003 | 2004 | 2005 | 2006 | 2007 | 2008 | 2009 | 2010

LED BY THE TALIBAN | HAMID KARZAI PRESIDENT OF AFGHANISTAN

THIRTY-THREE

THE SNOW PRINCESS

ISLAMABAD, 1999

She's twenty-two and tall. Her skin is like alabaster. Looking into the mirror, she complains that two teeth are crooked, but no one else can see it. She is not aloof, but she moves in a regal way and never rushes. "Why would I want to hurry?" she says. "I've had four years of imprisonment with no need to rush at all." We call her the Snow Princess. Her real name is Mariam, but we seldom use it because she is on the run. If the Taliban find her she'll be dragged back to Afghanistan to be flogged and shot for adultery.

*

We are in Islamabad. Janna and I have enjoyed an evening meal with Heather, an experienced English as a Foreign Language teacher. After a year back in Australia, we've recently arrived in Pakistan's capital and are keen to learn about our new vocation: teaching English to adult Afghan refugees.

"Our teachers are all foreign professionals, and all volunteers." Heather is removing our empty plates. "We have separate classes for men and women."

"How many students?"

"Currently about five hundred a day, all adults, and there's a long waiting list." She gives a proud smile, "We *are* the best English teaching outfit in town."

"And what's their background?"

"Lots of terrible war stories. Most are reasonably well educated in their own language and have some resources; otherwise, they'd be in a refugee camp."

She passes around the after-dinner mints she's been hoarding. "They're either dead keen to get English to go back and rebuild their country, or they're too afraid to go back and want to try for a Western visa."

Heather Bellamy is a feisty blonde from a small country town in British Columbia, Canada. Versatile and resourceful, she has a huge heart for needy women. Her students love her and appreciate the fact she's learning their Dari language.

There's a banging on the high metal gate. Janna and I look up.

"Don't worry," says Heather. "Afzal the watchman will get that." She looks at her watch. "I don't know who'd come this late at night."

Bang-bang. Bang-bang. BANG-BANG.

Heather's getting annoyed. "Where is the man?" Her blood pressure is rising in direct proportion to the amount of unanswered gate banging. "Surely he can't be sleeping through all that, though it wouldn't be the first time." She thrusts back her chair and stalks outside to confront the recalcitrant *chaokidaar*. He's nowhere to be seen.

The banging increases in urgency. It's not wise or fitting for a woman, particularly a single foreign woman, to open a gate to nocturnal strangers. That's the responsibility of the *chaokidaar*.

I rise. "Don't worry, Heather. We'll come with you."

"I get a lot of visits from my students," our hostess says as we walk down the path, "but not at this time of night. Just one little whisper about a girl in the streets after dark would doom her family's honour and her marriage prospects, and her sisters' marriage prospects as well."

Heather calls out from behind her high walls, "*Ki bood?*—Who is it?"

A female voice replies in a loud Afghan whisper, "Quickly, let me in!"

Heather is surprised by the gender of the gate-banger. "Who are you? What do you want?"

"Quickly, let me in. Please! Please!"

Knowing that Janna and I are right behind her, Heather relents and slides the bolt.

The young woman is carrying a bundle under her all-enveloping *chador*. She steps inside. Unexpectedly, a shrouded man carrying a small suitcase swiftly steps in and stands behind her.

"Are you Sister Heather?" the female asks urgently.

We get a glimpse of her young face. Her skin is pale and translucent.

Heather looks apprehensively at the silent male, then back to the young woman. "Who are you? What do you want?"

The visitor holds up a slip of paper. "I have this address. I must find Sister Heather." There's both desperation and expectation in her voice. "You *are* Sister Heather, aren't you?"

Heather pauses defensively. *Oh no. Not again. Will I have to be the human lie detector, trying to winnow through the truth and lies of desperate Afghan visa seekers?*

The young woman looks intently at Heather, waiting.

"Yes, I am Sister Heather," the Canadian answers.

A wave of relief ripples through the young woman's frame. "Sister Heather, six months ago you met Feroza, a widow from Kabul. Do you remember? The UN was sending her to Sweden."

"Yes, I remember Feroza. She told me that several years ago a warlord had kidnapped her oldest daughter and she never saw her again. I promised to pray for her."

Tears well up in the girl's eyes. "I am the one who was kidnapped. I am Mariam, Feroza's daughter."

Heather's jaw drops. "And who is this?"

"This is Jawad; he has helped me to escape. He saved me." The bundle under her *chador* moves. "And this is my daughter, Salma."

The two women stare at each other, then the young mother falls into Heather's outstretched arms. Both sob with joy and relief as they break their long embrace.

The young mother stiffens and her tone changes. "Sister Heather, no one must know we are here or the Taliban will come for me." She glances at the shrouded man. "They will come for us."

Heather immediately comprehends. Only last week one of her students confided that she and her husband have moved several times to keep ahead of the searching eyes of local Taliban spies. Her husband is so afraid he only works at night as a taxi driver.

"Yes, you are right, Mariam." She bustles us all inside, repeating a Dari proverb: "'Walls have mice, and mice have ears.'"

Mariam drops exhausted onto the living room's blue *toshak*. Jawad chooses one on the opposite side of the room. He's about twenty-five and has a handsome, open face. At that moment we hear the bolt of the metal gate slide open, then shut. The missing watchman coughs to affirm he is on deck. Tomorrow he will undoubtedly vow he never left his post. Heather knows she will have to swear him to secrecy about her visitors. She will have to trust him; there is no choice. But he's new, and there's something about him. He spends all his free time chatting at the mosque up the street. There could be mice in the walls of that mosque—little mice with big Taliban ears.

Heather and Janna make the weary Afghans comfortable with green tea and leftover lasagne. They almost fight to cuddle sweet little Salma. Despite the fatigue, Mariam continues to exude the bearing of one who comes from an educated, self-assured family back in Kabul.

"I'm sorry, Jawad," Heather announces, "but it's not fitting that you sleep here. I've rung my friends, the Browns. They will come for you shortly."

There are a lot of unanswered questions in the air. How did Mariam get Heather's address? How did she escape from the warlord? Is he looking for her? Who is silent Jawad and how did he save her?

Mariam takes a deep breath. "Sister Heather, let me start from the beginning."

THIRTY-FOUR

KABIR TAKES A WIFE

"It all started four years ago. I was eighteen. We lived in a large house in central Kabul and I loved high school. My father had big plans for us all and encouraged us to study hard. He was very busy, but he always brought us back something special when he went to other countries for conferences.

"That all changed when Kabir, the young warlord, saw me walking to school with my friends. He watched us from his pickup. It had a pile of armed men on the back. I never even looked at him, but my girlfriend said that he couldn't take his eyes off me. 'If my father finds out he'll be in big trouble,' I told her.

"My father soon found out because Kabir sent his cousin to ask for me. Father was furious and sent him away. 'There's no way I will have some illiterate warlord marrying my daughter,' he told me. I agreed wholeheartedly. At that time in Kabul all the groups were fighting each other to fill the gap left by the communists. The gun ruled, and Kabir had a lot of men with a lot of guns."

Mariam pauses and gives a deep sigh. "If only it had been different. Kabir simply sent twenty of his mujahidin fighters to come and grab me. When those men broke into our home, they pointed their guns at us and warned me, 'If you scream we will shoot all your family.' I screamed and struggled anyway, all the way out the door and into their big vehicle.

"My dear father was so upset. I could hear him shouting, demanding my release. I looked back. Kabir's men were laughing and pushing their guns deeper into his ribs. Then his knees gave way and he crumpled onto the doorstep, gripping his chest. My mother was leaning over him. As they drove me away I tried to call out to him. Deep inside I knew he wouldn't survive. I knew I would never see him again."

Mariam wipes her eyes and then speaks through the tears. "Kabir took me to a secluded area and locked me in a house where no one could hear my screams. He left me there with an old woman, and guards outside. He was away fighting for many days. I just wanted to die. I found the old woman's medication and tried to kill myself. It didn't work. Then the rocketing started. The Taliban were taking the city and rockets were falling all around us. I prayed to Allah, 'Please send a rocket on me before Kabir gets back.' When he returned I tried to fight him off. Finally, after four days, he tied me to the bed and had his way with me.

"Later he took me to his extended family's house where he lived with his parents and brothers and all their families. It became my jail for four years. The women and children watched me all the time. I was never allowed out on my own. At night my mother-in-law would sleep with me. Then, any chance of escape disappeared altogether."

The young mother takes a sip of green tea. "Why was that?" I ask, amazed at what she has endured.

"The Taliban finally took Kabul, and any woman found on the street without a male relative was whipped or jailed. If I'd escaped and Kabir's family hadn't caught me, the Taliban would have."

We're wondering how she could be here in Pakistan, in Islamabad. We listen spellbound.

"I became pregnant and had a son. Everyone was celebrating, until the poor little boy died. Later I had Salma." Her eyes drift to the sleeping bundle at her feet. "But they considered me a failure because I didn't have another boy. They're so illiterate, but they keep all the religious observances.

"I refused to fast with them during Ramzan. 'You're nothing but a *kafir*, an unbelieving heathen,' they told me. 'Because you don't keep our holy fast, you bring Allah's shame and punishment on our household.'

"'Why should I fast every day for a month?' I asked them. 'Since you brought me here my whole life has been a fast. You are all hypocrites! You fast to gain spiritual merit so God will answer your prayers, but you are wasting your time. How can God hear your prayers when you are doing such a terrible thing to me?'"

As she continues we see some of the fire that must have kept her going. "One night bad news came. What I had wished for myself was the fate of Kabir. He had seen that the Taliban was taking over the country, so, as is the custom with all warlords, he conveniently changed sides. He was out with the Taliban fighting the Northern Alliance when a rocket fell. They couldn't even find a few pieces to send back for a proper burial. All the women wailed and wailed, but my eyes were dry. How could I weep for my violent husband, the man who had dishonourably kidnapped me and caused my father's death?

"My mother-in-law raised her arms and screamed at the ceiling, 'Oh my dear son, who is the person who prayed that you should be torn to pieces like that?' Then they all looked straight at me. Their eyes burned with hatred. 'Just let me go,' I pleaded with them. 'Now that Kabir is dead, why don't you just let me go?'

"My mother-in-law stopped her wailing. 'You think you can just get up and leave, girl? It's impossible to let you go.' Then she sneered at me. 'You and the baby are the property of Kabir. Now he has gone you will have to marry his younger brother, Rahematullah. The family's property always stays with the family!'

"'Just let me go!' I screamed. 'Haven't I been through enough? Just let me go!'

"They all stared at me. I felt like a mouse cornered by a brood of cobras. 'This is the custom of our clan,' pronounced my mother-in-law. 'If you do not marry Rahematullah, we will kill you. No one will know, and no one will care.' I felt utterly helpless and alone in the world. I could hardly eat."

Mariam's voice drops as she relives her abandonment. "I couldn't run away. They watched me like hawks. I thought again of suicide. I'd heard of desperate women at Herat dousing themselves with heating fuel and setting themselves alight. But there was little Salma. She was the only thing that made my life worth living. And then Kabir's creepy brother got me, just like he got Kabir's spare guns and his old clothes. I wasn't a person any more. I was just a hand-me-down. A thing. And Salma, she was just a thing, and they would marry her off before she was twelve."

Salma makes a noise, but resettles. Mariam's face lightens. "Then something happened that gave me a tiny ray of hope.

"I was with the women in the bazaar and they were arguing about prices with the cloth merchant. I thought I heard a voice I knew. The neighbouring shopkeeper was talking at the front of his shop. I recognised him immediately. It was Jawad, my older brother's friend and class-fellow."

At the mention of his name, handsome Jawad stirs in the corner. Mariam makes a slight gesture toward him. "He often visited our house before my brother moved for higher studies, and we all visited Jawad's family. I was so excited when I saw him. Of course, he couldn't recognise me as I was fully covered with my burka. But I noted the name of his shop, and from that moment things seemed brighter. Now I had a link with the outside world. Somehow I had to find a way to make contact."

"I used to talk to the neighbour's wife when we were hanging out washing on our balconies. She at least had a heart. I think she felt sorry for me. I secretly prepared a letter for my mother and another for Jawad. The neighbour's wife agreed to take them to Jawad's shop. My mother got a letter back to me via Jawad and my neighbour. She was just leaving for Islamabad. She said there was no hope for her in Kabul and she would try to get a visa for the West."

"That's when she met me," Heather chimes in, "and I promised her I'd pray for you and help you if you ever escaped." She shakes her head in disbelief.

"My mother somehow got a letter back to Jawad from here in Islamabad," Mariam continues. "She told me what a wonderful person you were and that if I ever escaped I must find you at this address"—she waves the slip of paper in the air—"because you are a good person."

"But Mariam," asks Janna, "how did you escape?"

"Kabul is extremely cold at this time of year. Two nights ago all the men of the house left to meet with other men somewhere. My mother-in-law said, 'Let's all go to the warmer rooms now that the men have gone.' They all trooped off. Salma was asleep and I was the last to leave. Suddenly, for the first time in four years, I was alone. This was my chance. We always kept a bag packed in case there were rockets. I grabbed Salma and my bag, hid them under my burka and ran."

"Weren't you afraid of the Taliban in the streets, Mariam?"

"*Beeshuk!* Of course! But there are no street lights in Kabul now, and the streets were empty. I stumbled my way to where I knew Jawad's family lived and banged on their door. I thought they would never come. I pleaded for help to get me out of Kabul. The family panicked. They said they could all be killed. 'You must go back. Don't be a foolish girl; you must face what Allah has ordained for you. Why should *we* suffer?"

"I threw myself on Jawad's feet and cried out, 'You are my brother's best friend. I will never go back. Take me to Pakistan or shoot me right now!'" She looks over at her travelling companion with admiration. "Jawad is my brother's brave and honourable class-fellow, and he agreed to try and get me out."

"At first light next morning we went to the Pakistan bus stand. Jawad posed as my husband. It was very risky. We could have been killed for adultery. Just being with another man is all the proof they need. He bought the tickets and we went to the back of the empty bus. It took an age to fill. It was about to leave when a young Taliban soldier with a Kalashnikov jumped on and slowly scanned up and down the aisle. I thought he would hear my heart racing. For once I was glad to be underneath a burka. The same thing happened when we changed buses at the border. Last night we stayed in a cheap hotel near the bus stand in Peshawar."

Janna gives me a knowing glance. One of my staff lived out that way when we worked in Peshawar.

"We caught a minibus to Islamabad and then a taxi driver helped us find your house." Mariam gives a weary smile and slowly looks around the room. "I can't believe I'm here!"

It's been good for her to unload and it's been good for us to listen. The Browns arrive for Jawad. Before they go, we all give thanks to God for his goodness.

"We'll get you to the United Nations refugee office tomorrow, Mariam," Heather announces, "and you can hide in your burka when we are out. I'll tell the *chaokidaar* to say absolutely nothing to anyone."

"Heather Jaan, I am so tired, but can you please try to ring my mother in Sweden?" The phone dials, and then Mariam says, "*Madar-e Jaan*—Dear Mother." There's a pause on the Swedish end followed by a scream of surprise. It's a wonderful phone call.

But the telephone can convey bad news as well as good.

THIRTY-FIVE

RETRIBUTION

Four days have passed and Jawad is preparing to return to Kabul. His job is done. He has upheld his honour as a friend and a class-fellow. Janna and I email our friends and family to solicit prayer for Mariam, the young Afghan widow. We cannot mention her real name. We need a pseudonym. I visualise the winter snow in Kabul and Mariam's regal bearing, and I write, "We'll call her the Snow Princess." Referring to unnamed Jawad I write, "... and for once the preservation of honour has not led to retribution".

But my assessment is premature.

The phone rings. It's Heather and she's in a flap. "Can you come around right now? Things have gone terribly pear-shaped. We can't discuss it on the phone."

Heather's *chaokidaar* lets us into her small high walled compound. I greet him. "*Salaam alekoom*, Afzal."

"*Vaalekoom Salaam*, Lock Jhi."

There's something strange about his expression. *What's that funny little smile about, Afzal? I hope you haven't spilled the beans, mate. Heather's warned you to say nothing, but with your family out there in the village you have to talk to someone, and there are mice in those mosque and tea house walls.*

The Snow Princess has been weeping. Her eyes are all red.

"What's going on?" asks Janna.

Heather gestures toward the *toshaks*. "Sit down and I'll bring you up to speed. Jawad was just around here with the Browns. He was terribly upset."

"I thought he was leaving to go back to his shop in Kabul."

"That's not going to happen now, Grant. He rang his family and he got dreadful news. Two of his brothers are in jail."

"In jail?" Janna's jaw drops. "What for?"

"Mariam's in-laws want their 'property' back. They've been to the Taliban, and the Vice and Virtue squads are out looking for the 'runaway adulterers'. They have alerted their Pakistani network as well. And worse still, they've grabbed Jawad's brothers along with two of Mariam's cousins and thrown them into jail. They'll stay there until the runaways are found and brought back. That's what Mariam is so upset about."

Heather opens a plastic container Janna brought. "Ah, Salma loves these Aussie Anzac biscuits. Thanks for all the cooking, Janna. It's a big help." Her frown returns and she continues, "Jawad was sweating when he told me. The families has been given twenty days to bring the runaways back or there will be worse consequences, and with the Taliban that could mean anything."

Mariam is moaning. "I am not a robber. I took nothing but my baby."

We look at Heather for an explanation.

"The in-laws have laid charges against her for stealing two of their carpets, plus their gold and money."

"As if I could carry two big carpets as well as Salma and my bag," bursts out Mariam. "I am not a thief! *They* are the thieves! They stole me from my family, and they stole four years of my life. Now my cousins and Jawad's brothers are in jail!" She buries her head in her hands and her exhausted tear ducts service her grief.

"But if they find her, that means cutting off her hand, doesn't it?" Janna asks.

"They probably wouldn't get to that," says Heather. "Adulterers are taken to the soccer ground and shot at half time." She passes the biscuits. "Jawad was in an appalling state. He said it wasn't fair. He shows honour to his class-fellow and then this is what he gets. He said he should have listened to his family. Now they are being punished because of his decision."

"Poor man," Janna commiserates. "It was such a brave thing to do.

"What now?" I ask.

"Of course, he can't go back." Heather shakes her head. "He'd be promptly shot by the Vice and Virtue squads."

"Could you take him to the UN Refugee Committee like you have Mariam?"

"Maybe, but it's different for him. The UN has registered Mariam as a woman at risk, and that means she goes to the top of the waiting list. But Jawad would have to take his turn and that could be up to three years wait, providing they accept him. I don't think he wants to try. He might be recognised coming and going. Anyway, it seems like an eternity to him."

"Three years!" I exhale. "I didn't know it was that long. No wonder so many pay the people smugglers and head for Australia in a leaky boat. So what can he do?"

"He'll have to keep his head down and find a job here. One day he'll be able to sneak back to another part of Afghanistan. It's his brothers I'm really worried about."

We all look at each other and feel utterly helpless.

It's not right, Lord. This lovely young woman should be finishing university about now. Instead she's a widow. She's had two babies and one of them died in her arms. And this generous young man, risking his life to be honourable. Now his family is in desperate trouble and he's cut off from them, maybe forever. He didn't have to rescue her. But he chose to leave home and go out of his way for her and the baby.

It's not fair, Lord. How long does this sort of suffering, this evil, have to go on?

What's that you say? You understand? You left your home and went on a rescue mission too? And the rejection was painful? And evil will be around for a bit longer because you've got plans to do some more rescuing?

Righto, Lord. But these three Afghans need your help—right now! What's that? That's our job? That's what you put us here for? Well, okay, Lord, but help us to help them. We're right out of our depth on this one.

Heather rises. "I'll get Mariam down to the UN again and tell them she is being hunted. They may speed things up even more. In the meantime, we'll have to keep her out of everyone's sight. But they can't be cooped up inside this little house all the time. I've told Afzal to be doubly sure not to let anyone in when they're in the back garden, especially when I'm out teaching."

"Can you really rely on your *chaokidaar*, Heather?" I ask, recalling the funny look he gave us.

"We're in a corner with Afzal," she says in a worried tone. "I just keep hoping he does the right thing. I wish old Abdul was still here; he was so trustworthy. Not much more we can do now but pray."

We head for the door. "See you tomorrow at the English Centre, Heather," Janna says. Afzal gives us another of his curious half smiles as we leave.

*

It's two weeks later. I'm trying to analyse why we get hot water in the front garden of our rented house and only cold water in the guest bathroom. There's another phone call from Heather. She talks to me briefly.

I turn to Janna. "I know why Afzal was giving us that silly half smile."

"Why's that?"

"He's fallen for Mariam."

Janna gasps. "How do you know?"

"Heather says to come round and she'll tell us more. She needs some male support."

Afzal opens the gate with an even sillier smile. Heather fills us in. "Mariam has been very withdrawn this last week, and finally I've found out why."

"Afzal," says Janna.

"Yes. He's trying to get romantic with her. She hasn't been going outside when I'm not here because he hangs around her, much too close. When she takes a shower he stands below the bathroom window and sings love songs to her. Now he's tapping on her window during the night."

"But he has a wife and family back in his village," I respond with growing alarm. "It's absolutely not fitting, and it could be dangerous for Mariam. We'll have to act promptly."

Heather nods. "But Afzal has us in a corner. He knows that if something happens to her there is no way we can drag the police into the situation."

"Why didn't Mariam speak up?" Janna asks.

"She says she doesn't want to cause us any more trouble."

"Well," I assert, "Mariam is in our care under our roof. It's his job to protect her, and he's not doing it. He'll have to go!"

"Old Abdul has recovered," Heather adds. "He would be very happy to have his old job back. You'll have to talk to Afzal, Grant. It needs a man."

*

I confront the *chaokidaar* and he doesn't deny his actions, but he's angry at losing employment. That in itself is a big loss of face.

His countenance grows black. "You cannot send me off like this. It is unjust."

"Yes, we can, Afzal. It's our responsibility, and it's been your responsibility to protect our guests, but your behaviour is totally unacceptable. According to our contract we can give you immediate notice, along with an extra month's pay."

He sets his jaw. "I will go to the courts."

"As you wish, Afzal Jhi. It is your right. But it may not be good for your honour if your family and friends in the village find out the truth."

The last thing we want is for him to open a case against us. I'm depending a lot on bluff and it seems to be working. My experience in the courtrooms of the Frontier is helping me carry it off.

Afzal sulks back to the gate. The funny half smile has gone.

We're very worried. Will there be a knock on the gate by a clerk from the court? What if he spreads false stories around at the mosque, or lets the cat out of the bag about Mariam? That would soon reach the ears of the Taliban network. A week passes, then two weeks, but there is no sign of any legal action or any unusual house-watching by strangers.

To give Heather a break, Janna and I have the Snow Princess and Salma to stay in our house for a while. Mariam has become like a daughter, Salma like a granddaughter. We laugh and cry and pray together. She's becoming more relaxed and her English is improving, and she teaches us some Dari.

One night Mariam has a dream about her teeth. "My two crooked teeth were replaced with two lovely straight teeth," she happily announces. "God is showing me he is doing something new in my life. He's giving me a new heart for my old sad one."

*

Five months have passed since the cross-border escape. Jawad's family has sold his shop. They had to, to pay off the jailers to release his brothers. We assume Mariam's cousins were also released after the prison keys were sufficiently greased.

On the phone Heather's voice is filled with excitement. "I'm at the airport, Janna. Their plane has just taken off. What a thrill for her mother when they all meet in Stockholm." She releases an emotional lung-full of relief, and then pipes up cheerfully, "So get ready, Janna! Tonight we're celebrating in the Arizona Grill at Jinnah Market."

That night we put in our orders at the Arizona Grill. "I've got to tell you something," Heather announces in a confidential tone. "After I put Mariam on the plane this morning I went direct to the English Centre. When I got home old Abdul told me that three serious-looking men with beards came to the gate this afternoon." The Grill's music is loud and we lean forward to hear more. "He said they only asked one question: 'Tell us, old man, is there a young Afghan woman with a baby in this foreigner's house?' Abdul knew I'd put her on the plane just a couple of hours before, so he told them, 'No, Sirs. *Bilkul hee nahi!*—Absolutely not!' Then they left."

We are stunned and we look at Heather in amazement. "Our prayers have been answered," says Janna quietly. "What impeccable timing."

Heather is gazing through the window. "I can still see her the night we went to the roof of my house and counted down the seconds to the new millennium. Mariam was so happy. It was as though she was counting down to a new life."

The steaks sizzle onto the table. I raise my Coke glass to propose a toast. "In her new life, may the Snow Princess find her real Prince, one who's charm doesn't come from the barrel of a gun." There are three loud "Amens".

THIRTY-SIX

THE THROAT CUTTER

ISLAMABAD, 2000

"Teacher! Teacher! You must come! Daoud's throat has been cut!" They bundle me down the steps and into a rusty taxi.

I'm shocked. "What happened? Who did it?"

"We'll tell you on the way."

Daoud is a particularly cheerful refugee. Like most of my Afghan students, he is in his twenties, attends English class for an hour each day and works hard for another ten. When I'm near his boss's electronics repair shop, I always drop in.

My cheery student shares a spartan two-room flat with his mother and sister. They are entirely dependent on him. Together they crossed the mountains to escape the Taliban.

Two years ago black-turbaned gunmen appeared on Daoud's Kabul doorstep and ordered the family to hand over the house. Daoud's father resisted and they riddled him with bullets. "Out! Get out, and don't come back," they ordered the traumatised family.

"Please! Oh please, let me grab some things," Daoud's mother pleaded.

"Go now or we will shoot you all," the bearded leader warned.

The evictors did not see the heavy gold bracelet Daoud's mother was wearing under her sleeve. The yellow metal provided funds for a guide to lead them across the mountains to Pakistan. To avoid the Taliban's Khyber checkpoints, they travelled on goat tracks, and only at night.

As our taxi weaves dangerously through the traffic, one of Daoud's friends fills me in. "One more minute, the doctor said, and he would have been finished. They got him to the hospital just in time, Sir."

Knowing that clan vendettas and blood feuds go on and on in Pashtun society, I ask the obvious question. "What was the argument about?"

"It was a kite, Sir!"

Now I get it. Passions rise fast in the kite-flying season. These days the afternoon sky is full of brilliantly coloured paper diamonds swooping and diving to gain advantage over each other. The objective is to sever the string of your opponent's kite and eliminate it. As the malfunctioning paper bird drifts to the ground, the first to seize it is the esteemed new owner. Regardless of busy road traffic or the risk of falling from flat-roofed houses, the sky-staring kite runners compete with each other for the honour of claiming the next prize. Daoud is an expert combatant and has liberated dozens of kites from the control of their owners. It seems that someone couldn't take a beating and has pulled a knife on him.

The taxi runs another red light in our rush to the hospital. "We don't know exactly how it happened, Teacher. His boss just rang and told us to get to the hospital fast. It's something to do with his motor bike as well."

Now I'm wondering if it really *was* Daoud's bike. I'd never seen him with one. Did he "borrow" it from someone else, and they caught him and handed out some retribution?

We rush through the paint-peeling, phenyl-fumed corridors of the hospital, looking for the emergency section.

I inwardly gasp when I set eyes on my student. Daoud is weak and ghostly pale. He has a blood-weeping bandage around his neck and a drip in his arm. A doctor enters. He's sporting the two mandatory symbols of his elevation above the rest of us ordinary mortals: a white coat and a stethoscope. "Cut right through the jugular. He's lucky to be alive. It's a clean cut and we've stitched him up."

Groggy Daoud sees that I'm in the room and wants to communicate. "Teacher," he whispers. "Left shop on boss's motorbike … to get parts. Ran into kite string. Didn't see it. Hardly felt it. Blood spurted everywhere. Over clothes … over motor bike … onto road. Turned back to shop. Grabbed my throat."

"He collapsed on the steps," one of his workmates chips in. "Luckily there was a taxi parked close to the shop."

Immediately I understand what has happened. The kite enthusiasts increase the cutting power of their kite-strings by coating them with a mixture of glue and powdered glass. Today has been very windy and obviously a taut string was angled across the road. With the speed of the bike, it would have scythed through Daoud's flesh like a high-speed band saw. No wonder the doctor said it was a clean cut.

Perhaps this is why the Taliban have banned this kite madness in Afghanistan. Maybe these anti-music, anti-TV fun-haters have saved some lives. However, they've also deprived the men and boys of something to take their mind off the country's woes and destruction.

I offer to pray. Daoud readily agrees. Unlike many Westerners, Muslims are God-conscious and always ready for a blessing through intercession. "Thank you, God, that Daoud made it back to the shop and there was a taxi nearby. Bless him with full healing and an awareness of your goodness and love to him." All present join in the final "Ameen", and, according to the local custom, we lift our open palms toward our faces as if to draw in the blessing.

I pause a moment as a sobering thought flashes through my mind. *Your body was sliced too, Lord—not with one, but with thirty-nine gouging lashes. And you didn't turn back to the shop until every drop drained to the ground. Thank you.*

*

I doubt that this accident will take away Daoud's passion for kite flying and the struggle to be the last survivor in the sky. But he is the lucky one. In makeshift camps outside of town, countless refugees never have the time for this neck-wrenching recreation. Theirs is also a struggle against elimination … foodless elimination from the human race.

THIRTY-SEVEN

MRS BAITTO

2000

A bevy of unkempt beggar girls shouts at Janna from across the bazaar street: *"Baitto! Baitto!"* They are not demanding money and they are not being rude. In fact, the greeting is spoken with endearment, waves and smiles. Janna is known in this forgotten section of the community as Mrs Baitto.

It all started with a couple of scruffy ten-year-old beggar girls collecting bits of paper in our street. On a steamy summer day, the raggedy pair hear the sound of water running inside our walls. They kneel and squint under our high steel gate. Janna, hose in hand, is watering our small front lawn.

"MemSahib! It's very hot, MemSahib! Can we have a drink?"

"They were dirty ragamuffins," Janna explains to me as we drive to an evening staff meeting, "but they were such nice girls. There was something about their eyes. I was going to fetch glasses, but they took the hose and helped themselves."

"Who are they?"

"Afghan refugees from just over the border. They belong to a small tribe known as the Pashai. During the Russian invasion they fled over here."

I'm navigating through the predictably unpredictable traffic. "And where do they live?"

"They have a camp several miles out of town."

"So how do they survive?"

"The men try to get day labour and the women cut grass for their goats."

"Ah, yes." I lean on the much-used horn. "I've seen women with sickles and huge bags of grass on their heads."

"The girls pick up bits of scrap paper. I found out they get two rupees a kilo for that."

I park the Toyota outside Heather's house. "That's a lot of scrap paper for one piece of *naan*."

We sit for a moment while Janna continues, "And, of course, many of them beg. Anyway, these two girls whipped off their shawls and asked me to spray their heads to cool them down."

From her tone I suspect there is something more to my compassionate wife's story. "And?"

"Their hair was so dirty. I went in for soap, but then I decided to go all the way and took out a bottle of shampoo. They loved it. Their names are Zora and Zubi and they are cousins."

*

A few days later, Janna is driving past some young Pashai scavengers attacking the huge metal refuse bin at the end of our street. Islamabad is a purpose-built capital, like Canberra, and by Pakistani standards is pretty up-market when it comes to handling rubbish. In most cities, reeking mounds grow on the streets until a truck and shovels occasionally appear.

Janna recognises Zora and Zubi. They have climbed up into the putrid container and are tossing out anything remotely edible or useful. Squatting on the ground below, a bunch of barefooted urchins are sorting through the showers of blessing. Some morsels are eaten on the spot and some are bagged for the goats. There are vegetable scraps, stale pieces of bread and morsels of curry mixed with mouldering rice, paper and worn-out plastic shoes. It's all being consumed or conserved amidst a buzzing cloud of flies.

Disgusted, Janna pulls over and watches the rubbish scavengers from a distance. A mortifying thought bursts into her brain. *What if they were my kids? Or what if I were one of their mothers? How would I feel? I have to help somehow.*

"Somehow" turns out to involve groups of needy women and girls descending on our gate.

A couple of Pakistani neighbours complain. "Why do you let those grimy animals hang around?"

"One day those cunning Afghan women will cut your throat with their sickles and then rob your house."

"Don't you realise that some Muslims in our neighbourhood pay the baker to cook up *naan* for those beggars each week?"

Janna is not deterred. "That's good, but I want to do more than just pay someone to cook bread for them. They're not animals. They're people."

So she continues to sit with them under the trees, talks with them, learns their names and listens to their stories. She discovers that they have been living on the plain outside town for years. They've built rough huts from mud, stones and thatch. They thought they could return to Afghanistan after the Soviets were ousted, but then the ethnic mujahidin groups started fighting for pre-eminence, and now the Taliban have rolled in. They have no idea when they can go back home.

When the weather turns cold, Janna buys jumpers in the second-hand bazaar and cheap plastic shoes to separate the refugees' feet from the mud. Our own kids are all working now and they send some funds, and other friends in Australia join in. The numbers grow, and the banging on our metal gate is incessant. If I'm in my home office, the demanding, steel-on-steel sickle-taps wear me down.

Even Janna is feeling the pressure. "Soap! Grant, the thing they want most is soap."

"By the look of some of those grubby faces," I say, "I'm not surprised."

"It's not just for personal use. They wash their clothes in plastic basins, in cold water from their well, with no soap at all. They are just like all women: they want their family's clothes to be clean (what they have of them). But they are so poor that even a couple of rupees for a bar of soap is out of their reach."

*

"I want a whole carton of soap," Janna announces to the shopkeeper, and she squeezes him for his best deal. He is sympathetic and takes the very minimum profit. That was the easy bit. Distributing it proves to be a much bigger challenge.

The eyes of twenty-five Pashai women light up when Janna comes through the gate with a plastic bowl full of soap. She starts handing each woman a cake. Fear electrifies the group: will the bowl empty before they get their turn? There is a surge of grabbing hands. Janna's presence becomes irrelevant. The bowl goes in the air. Janna is knocked to the ground. She squirms to avoid the dirty, trampling feet. Above her, women are shrieking, fighting and lunging. The few bars of soap that hit the ground immediately disappear.

A sympathetic hand reaches down and pulls the shell-shocked soap-supplier to her feet, and she staggers inside for a cup of sweet, black tea. "There was no malice intended," Janna points out to me, "but soap is like gold to those women."

"And you'll have another bunch tomorrow," I say. My administrative mind is whirring. "Look, Janna, you're doing a wonderful thing, but those women are coming at all hours, every day. They are reducing you to a frazzle. You don't even have uninterrupted time to prepare for your English conversation classes." She nods wearily. "Why don't we tell them to only come on Friday, the day of prayer? Now that I'm director of the Centre, that's the only free day for me. I'll help you with a bit of crowd control."

"Okay, we'll try it. You can make sure the men don't hang around. This is just for the women and girls."

"And," I add, "what about getting them all to sit down? That will control the surge. If anyone stands up they miss out."

*

Friday finally comes. It's been a tough week, repeatedly saying to about one hundred desperate women and girls, "No! Come back on *Jummah*. No, not today. Only on *Jummah*."

"*Baitto! Baitto!* Sit down! Sit down!" Janna shouts. "No sit, no soap!"

At first it falls on deaf ears. Then a wrinkled old matriarch at the front of the throng sits down on her haunches. Slowly the rest follow suit. When latecomers arrive, Janna shouts, "*Baitto! Baitto*!" It works and becomes standard procedure. After a couple of weeks they sit without being told, and Janna is given a new name: Mrs Baitto.

*

"The women have invited me to drink tea over at their camp," she announces.

I'm concerned. "Is it fitting that you go there alone?"

"Perhaps you should take me over, and you can sit with the men and boys."

We arrive, and according to custom the men take me aside. The women seat Janna in the best of their ramshackle shelters. In our respective circles we are generously plied with hot chai in cracked cups. Janna holds their babies, listens to more stories and inspects their goats. They insist that she return.

*

Over the months my compassionate wife continues to "baitto" her sickle-wielding friends at our gate, and to drink tea with them in their dilapidated shacks. She gives basic medical advice, prays with the sick and dying, and consoles the pubescent girls who are afraid of their impending marriages. Over time they change from a herd of jungle animals fighting for soap to orderly, seated rows of people who are respected and loved.

I know that development gurus might say that Janna's program is only band-aid stuff, that it's not benefiting them in the long term. I disagree. There are fewer colds and winter diseases because they have plastic shoes and second-hand sweaters, and are encouraged to wash their hands before eating. Fewer infants die because Janna shows them how to mix up oral rehydration fluid from salt and sugar. There are fewer glassy-eyed depressed women because someone cares, someone listens, someone prays. There are even a couple of boys going to school because their families haven't wasted their money on multiple drugs prescribed by greedy doctors when all they need is a Disprin.

I've seen self-esteem grow in the eyes of these displaced, hardworking grass-cutters because Janna treats them as God sees them: as precious people.

*

Is it any wonder that after several years, when we finally leave, they hug Mrs Baitto for a long time, and weep, and even kiss her feet?

THIRTY-EIGHT

BLOOD ON THE CEILING

MARCH 2002

"The grenade bounced along the floor towards us. It was like a slow-motion movie. The screaming, the smoke, the smell! And then the bump, bump, bump. It stopped right in front of us. We froze, waiting for the end."

Janna and I are debriefing one of our teaching colleagues. The dark-haired southern belle is in a state of shock. Janna reaches for the teapot. "Have another cup of tea, Abigail. Let's start from the beginning."

Abigail's hand shakes as she adds the milk. "Well, when I arrived at the International Church for the morning service, everything was normal. As usual there was a good crowd from many different nationalities: people from embassies and non-government organisations as well as Pakistanis. There were about eight of us from the English Centre."

She takes a deep breath. "Then this noisy guy bursts in from the back shouting *'Allah O Akbar'*. How he got past all the security I'll never know. He starts throwing grenades among the people. There are huge explosions, five or six of them. There is smoke and dust and this awful smell. People screamed. We all hit the floor. We tried to get some protection from the chairs, but you know how flimsy they are." Her genteel lip quivers.

"Go on," Janna says in an encouraging tone.

"Then the grenade bounced along the floor and stopped right in front of us. 'This is it,' I thought, 'that thing is about to explode like all the others.' I'm ready to die, but I wasn't thinking about that. Everything stood still as we lay there, totally mesmerised by that ugly metal ball that was about to blow us to pieces. Funny, though—it was at that very moment that I felt God's presence enfold me. And the grenade just lay there. It didn't go off."

"They say it was an old Russian one," I add to break the ensuing silence. "Then what happened?"

"The al-Qaeda guy pulled the pin on another grenade and blew himself up. His head hit the lights and fell back onto the floor. There was blood on the ceiling and bits of flesh all over our clothes, and shattered glass everywhere. I saw Ahmed dying in Sam's arms. He looked so peaceful. Everyone was stunned. A few were limping out or helping others to get out. I felt sick and weak. I just followed them." She dabs her eyes. "I'm so thankful that grenade was faulty. I guess there is more for me to do before I go."

Indeed there is. Quietly spoken Abigail will end up in Afghanistan as the support director for a number of key projects. The Afghan women will love her because she wears black, their favourite colour.

*

The suicide attack happened four months after 9/11 and after the US invasion of Afghanistan. I was leading the family service in another church. Stoney the Crow, my ventriloquism puppet, was helping me share the story of the Good Samaritan with the kids. Someone with a mobile phone came in and whispered to a couple of the leaders. Just as Stoney was about to ask the crucial question, "And who is my neighbour?", he was interrupted by the pastor.

"Please excuse me, friends. There has been a bomb in the International Church on the other side of town." He raised his voice above the swell of murmuring. "Do not be alarmed. After we sing one song, please quietly go home."

I put the crow back in his bag, and soon Janna and I were on our way to find our wounded staff in the Shifa Hospital.

*

It seems that al-Qaeda is out to create havoc and terror among anyone who looks like an American. Osama bin Laden is incensed that President Musharruf of Pakistan has opted to support the Americans in their "war against terror". Bin Laden says it's a war against his Muslim brothers and President Bush is a murderer.

Five people died in the shrapnel-spewing attack and forty were injured. It has traumatised members of my staff, blown the eardrums out of others and sent one local helper to his grave.

We are thankful that four of our colleagues were absent for the day. They had driven up the mountain to visit the Murree Christian School. But unknown to anyone, the school is secretly under surveillance by al-Qaeda operatives. They plan to make another deadly visit in a few months' time.

THIRTY-NINE

DO I KNOW YOU?

2002

Yesterday I told my Afghan students that today's English lesson was one they would not forget, and I am not going to disappoint them. In this culture educators are highly respected. The students all rise when the teacher enters.

"Good morning, Teacher," chorus the twenty-four eager male students.

"Good morning, gentlemen. Please be seated."

"Mr Lock, you promised a surprise for us today," enthusiastic Anwar chimes in.

"That's right, but let's do some work first. Your homework was to prepare a few sentences about a difficult time in your life, using the past tense. Who will be first?"

"Me, Sir!" Irrepressible Anwar raises his workbook. He is about twenty-two, the average age of the class. "'We hid our radio behind the bricks,'" he read. "'We listened to the BBC. If the Taliban found it we would be being shot.'" He frowns slightly. "Is that correct, Mr Lock?"

"It's fine. The last part needs some work, but I can understand what you're saying. Who will be next?"

"'They burnt my sister's school and took my older brother to fight for them. We were frightened. We ran to Pakistan.'"

"That's good. Next."

"'At Mazar-i-Sharif, the bodies of our relatives lay in the streets. The dogs chewed their meat. We was afraid to go out. We buried them at night and—'"

There is a knock. My identical twin brother goes to the door and invites me in. "Welcome, Mr Lock, we have been waiting for you."

All the Afghan jaws drop. "Look! There are two Mr Locks. *Gup-e-jalehb!*—Amazing!"

*

Thirteen years ago, on our first home assignment, our three kids pleaded for more staff to keep Murree Christian School going. "We have teachers and boarding staff from all over the world, but no Australians. Can't someone come and help in our school?"

Their prayers were answered from an unexpected quarter: their Aunty Ann and Uncle Barry.

"You know, Ann," Barry said, "we could do that boarding parents job for a year."

"Maybe, but what about the farming business and the cattle stud?"

"Colin and the other two men could handle the cropping. But you're right—we couldn't run the stud by remote control, not even for a couple of months, let alone a year. But I reckon it would be good for us to do some voluntary service."

"I know the boys would benefit from the cross-cultural exposure, but I really can't see how we could do it."

Over the weeks God kept working on them.

"Everyone will say we're crazy, Ann, but I'm really convinced we should go. We could make a difference."

"Yes, I'm starting to feel that that is what God is saying to us. Look, we would never have done it while Dad was alive, but couldn't we sell the stud? Prices are on the rise again."

"Let's talk to Mum about it."

The two-day dispersal of Kimbolton Beef Cattle Stud was a huge success. It had to be—with low grain prices and some drought years in the 1980s, negative cropping incomes had dragged the bank balance deep into the red.

It was some of the hottest February weather on record, and some of the hottest bidding as well. I wish I could have been there. Enthusiastic buyers came from all over Australia to get a share of Kimbolton's progressive genetics. With inseminations from the best sires in America, progeny from our own Melbourne Supreme Champion, embryo transplants from top cows, and computerised records of objective measurements, this was a sale not to be missed. Every available room in Kimba was booked out months in advance, and hundreds of vehicles and twenty-two light aeroplanes brought eager buyers from every direction to the two-day sale. It was a tribute to the respect the Lock family had gained in the beef cattle industry.

The following February, Ann and Barry, with their boys, Joshua, Greg and Phillip, arrived at the international school to do twelve months as "middle boys" boarding parents for Grades 4 to 6. The twelve months extended to twelve years, and now Barry is welcoming me to my own Islamabad classroom.

*

Eager Anwar is the first of the flabbergasted students to recover. "Sirs, we are to be too much confusing," he blurts out. "But which Mr Lock is our teacher?"

I shake my brother's hand and we are having trouble containing ourselves. "Thanks for looking after my class, Barry," I laugh and turn to address the class. "Gentlemen, please welcome my twin brother, Barry. Didn't I tell you that I would surprise you today?" Nods and sounds of agreement emanate from the group. "And my wife has sent a bag of Australian cookies. Let's break for ten minutes and you can talk to my brother."

Anwar pumps Barry's hand. "I am Anwar from Kabul. You are to be too good at tricking, Sir."

*

In his boarding administration job, Barry regularly comes down to Islamabad on official business. It only takes about an hour to drop the 5000 feet from the cool Murree Hills to the roasting capital. My students are not the only ones who are sometimes confused.

Once in a government office Barry was confronted by an animated Pakistani in a three-piece suit. "Ah, Mr Lock," he said, enthusiastically pumping my brother's hand, "it is so good to see you."

"Excuse me, Sir," Barry responded, "but do I know you?"

Like a garage roller door, a pall of affronted amazement descended over the man's face. "Know me, Mr Lock? You are my neighbour!" As Barry explained the reason for the confusion, the roller door lifted and my enlightened neighbour laughed.

Likewise, when I attend board meetings up at the school, some of the staff have difficulty. Once I was crossing the schoolyard on the way to a board meeting when I was approached by a flustered junior high girls' boarding parent. "Barry, John is really sick. It's giardia again. Can we put off the meeting about students' tickets and visas for the cultural convention in India?"

She must have wondered why the normally efficient boarding administrator was looking a bit vacant. I paused, long enough to savour the moment but not to produce undue embarrassment. "I'll tell you what," I said, "perhaps you should talk to my brother about that." The statement was followed by jaw-dropping, then realisation and then laughter.

It wasn't hard for Barry to swap places with me for my English class, but I'm truly glad I wasn't in his shoes when the counterfeit cricketers paid a visit to his school.

FORTY

COUNTERFEIT CRICKETERS

MURREE CHRISTIAN SCHOOL, PUNJAB PROVINCE, 2002

Al-Qaeda's training is meticulous, the deception perfect—but something goes wrong with the timing. The date is Monday, August 5, 2002. The time is ... 600 seconds late.

*

Four sportsmen carrying cricket bags arrive at the main gate of Murree Christian School. The army cricket ground is just nearby, so why are they coming here? The armed guard steps forward.

"What is your business?"

The athletic young leader raises his bag and squeezes the trigger of the automatic weapon concealed inside. A local man conversing with the guard gets the same treatment. The terrorists step over the bullet-riddled bodies and the guns come out. But the bags are not yet empty. Inside are clips with hundreds of rounds of ammunition. The intruders' bodies are wired with explosives, to be detonated in the dining room packed with students and staff taking break-time refreshments. The yard between the gate and the dining room should be thick with students and staff, coming and going, talking and playing. It will be like shooting fish in a barrel. The blood that flows today will make a statement throughout the world: "Out with the foreigners, the hated Americans."

But the terrorists already know that many of the students are not from the United States. For the past two months they have lived near the school and have regularly patronised the Jhika Gali village tea houses, where the high school boys quaff chai and joke around. Not all the accents are like those on CNN. There's Finnish, Australian, English, German, Canadian, Sri Lankan, Pakistani and others.

It matters not that their parents are toughing it out on the hot plains, serving and training the Pakistani people in fields as diverse as medicine and vehicle mechanics. They are all puppets of the American government and they are there to spread lies and propaganda. Hasn't Osama bin Laden warned about the Americans? He should know; he worked with them during the Afghan war against the Soviets. No, the Americans are not to be trusted. They support the rogue state of Israel, and decadence pervades their society. Capitalism and communism have failed. Sharia law is the only answer. And has not bin Laden supported a fatwa that permits the killing of women and children in violent jihad to oust the Americans? Now that the Twin Towers have been destroyed, it's time for Pakistan to be cleansed. One masterstroke at the international school will change everything. Eliminate half of the two hundred children and staff and the families will leave, and their governments will call the others home.

First take out the two ill-equipped guards and then head for the dining room, shooting staff and students on the way. Once inside the dining room, detonate the vests and be rewarded with eternal honour and the company of many dark-eyed, full-breasted virgins. Nothing can prevent success.

*

If the four murderers had arrived on time, the schoolyard and dining room would have been brimming with targets, but now the students are back in their classrooms. It's a grey, rainy day and there is only one class outside. The teacher, James, has worked in Afghanistan. He is the only staff member who knows what a Kalashnikov sounds like. It has a death rattle all of its own.

"Quick, kids! Run to the classroom! Let's move!"

The insurgents fail to see the last students disappear into the elementary building.

"Where are the children? The yard should be full of them."

"It's because we arrived late. All our planning, all the watching, and then we have to arrive late!"

"Shut up, you two! Stay focused on the plan. Take out the other guard first, and the duty policeman wherever he is, then head for the dining room."

The team moves forward. Unlike in the movies, they do not run. They are disciplined professionals.

They spot a visiting mother, lower down in the yard. Bullets whiz around Juliet and through her hair. She runs screaming toward the high school building. There is pain. Dark blood spurts from her hand and wrist. She makes it to the entrance of the high school. But the big wooden doors are shut. The alarm has been raised and the lock-down practices have been implemented. Most staff and students are under their desks.

Her hysterical screaming and banging with bloody fists do not open the doors. Juliet runs to a side window to attract attention. That's risky. It brings her back into the view of the attackers, but they are moving away from her and toward the dining room. There are only three insurgents now. A jammed gun caused one to retreat and join his colleagues somewhere outside.

*

Barry halts his conversation with Sadiq, the Pakistani maintenance manager, and steps outside the hostel dining room to check on the noise. He expects to reprimand recalcitrant boys detonating firecrackers. Instead he sees cat-like cricketers moving towards him—and they have guns.

He rushes back into the dining room, shouting to the kitchen staff and the remaining students. "Raise the alarm! Lock down and hide!"

More bursts of gunfire. They take out the other security guard who runs round the corner into a hail of bullets.

Barry knows that the door to the main entrance of the four-storey hostel is still open. It has to be shut. But the twelve metres of windows between him and the main door are in direct view of the approaching gunmen. He does a running crawl, keeping below the level of the sills, and slides the bolt. But will this old door hold? The security committee slated it for replacement, but it hasn't happened yet.

Now to run downstairs to warn anyone in the basement … Good, there's no one down here. The next thing is to hide.

Another burst rattles from the Kalashnikovs.

That's getting close. I'm not going back up there … Oh no! I can't believe it. The basement door won't lock.

Barry frantically scans the room. Stacked along one wall are four large rolls of carpet.

*

Hysterical Juliet is finally let into the high school. She falls to the floor clutching her bloodied hand to her chest. Staff rush forward. Although she's lost a lot of blood, she is not dying. But out in the schoolyard others are.

Like a frightened animal with nowhere to go, Parveen, the staff house-cleaner, shrinks into the corner of the locked bathroom. The worst part is listening to the moans and gurgling gasps coming from the path outside. "Hold on, Babar!" she calls out. "Hold on!" But he can't hear her. *Oh, why did he insist on going out to help the guard when it's only four months to his wedding day?*

In the classrooms the drumming of racing hearts amplifies the prayers of the two hundred terrified students and staff. They are all praying that the murderers will not come their way, or anyone's way. Some even pray for their enemies.

From the musty interior of a large roll of carpet, Barry hears cricket boots and rifle butts pounding the old door upstairs. If only it had been higher on the security priority list. More muffled blasts of gunfire, and glass shattering. Are they inside? Are they methodically searching for the staff and students? Will they come down here? Where is the army? They are only just across the road. Why don't they come? Will there be long rows of small coffins surrounded by weeping mothers and grieving fathers? He resists the thought. Where is Ann? Is she safe?

*

The insurgents are getting rattled. It's all gone terribly wrong. Nobody is in the yard. The doors are locked on classroom buildings, dining room and hostel. No students or staff are visible from the windows. The international statement in blood is not happening. Now the one policeman assigned to the campus has somehow shown up and is taking pot-shots with his ancient gun.

"The army will be on its way soon," shouts the young leader. "There is no honour in becoming a martyr for nothing. Let's get out of here!"

⁂

Since the bombing at the International Church in Islamabad, the school's security has been tightened. When our kids were living and studying there a decade ago, there was no need for lock-down drills and an armed guard at each gate. But things have changed. As deputy chairman of the board I've expressed concern about the walls. It might be nice to see the mountains, but this is Pakistan, and other schools, particularly those with female students, have much higher walls. I'm glad they are being raised.

⁂

Two months before the attack, Barry was sent by the school to a three-day seminar dealing with security in the event of kidnapping or terrorist attacks.

"Do not worry, Mr Lock," the lecturer, a retired army officer, laughed patronisingly. "Your school is the safest place in all of Pakistan. It is surrounded by military establishments. The army, then the police, would be there in no time. There are only a couple of roads in and out, and they would be blockaded in minutes. Terrorists could not escape, so they wouldn't even think of planning an attack."

My brother was not impressed. *In every country of the world people tell you what you want to hear, but it seems to be an art form here. Is it written in the terrorist's handbook that all terrorists must depart on a public road? And what if suicide bombers came, like at the Islamabad Church? They wouldn't be worried about a road block, would they?*

"Sir, I have a question."

Colonel Confidence stands tall. "Yes, Mr Lock?"

"Sir, why should a terrorist leave on a public road? If I was attacking the school, I'd run through the forest at the rear of the property, climb over the back fence, dump my weapons, put on local clothes and simply walk out on the mountain trails."

The lecturer scoffs at the challenge to his experience, but that is exactly what happens.

*

The terrorist leader waves his hand. "Head for the back fence!" Moving purposefully, they stalk behind the elementary boarding block, firing into the windows at any hint of a target inside. Then they move downhill to the fence.

*

It is nearly an hour since the first phone calls were made. Now the schoolyard is bristling with top brass from the army, police and special forces: braided caps, epaulettes, little canes under their arms, and many underlings milling around. The roads are sealed off, the school is surrounded and helicopters clatter overhead. But like the attackers, they are too late—far too late. They find a cricket bag of explosives dumped near the back fence, but no sign of terrorists except for their lethal legacy: six bodies in six pools of congealed blood.

*

Miraculous stories from Pakistani workers spread throughout the campus.

Ijaz feels an invisible hand grab his collar and jerk him into the safety of the maintenance shed, just as the attackers turn his way.

In the forest at the back of the campus, another invisible hand grabs agile Hamid's ankle. As the annoyed garbage man falls, a stream of lead flies over his body.

Half-crippled Latif fears for his life as he hobbles toward the back fence. He can hear the attackers approaching but there is no way he can climb the six-foot mesh barrier. Two men in white *shalwar kamiz* appear and hoist him over. He turns to thank his saviours. No one is there.

*

The police have put the word out, and the locals in a mountain village are suspicious of three exhausted men sleeping in their small mosque. A crowd gathers.

The local policeman raises his rifle. "Who are you? What are you doing here?"

The insurgents pull the pins on their grenades. “Stand back. We don’t want to hurt you. We are only against the Americans. We don’t want to kill Muslims.”

“But you have already killed Muslims. We heard it on the radio. You are murderers. You will be punished.”

“Stand back, I tell you! Stand back!”

The crowd parts and the three walk half-backwards down the path sloping to the Jhelum River. Wading through shallow water, they assemble on a large, flat rock. There are two explosions as they blast themselves into the next life.

What will they report when they reach the judgment gates of Paradise? “We were unable to kill any *kafir* Americans, just seven Pakistani Muslims: four at the school and ourselves. But we did kill two ‘Sweepers’: those Pakistani Christians.”

Why didn’t they use those grenades to blast their way into locked classrooms? Why were they ten minutes late? It’s known only to God and the angels who attended school that day.

*

Janna and I drive up the mountains to the shell-shocked campus.

“I just don’t understand it,” weeps an elementary teacher, “it’s so horrible!” Janna nods, encouraging her to go on. “Who could sink so low, Janna? Who is it that trains young men to shoot children and bomb churches?”

My wife doesn’t know it, but in four months’ time the finger of suspicion will be pointed at the man who drove her up to the school today: her husband.

FORTY-ONE

THE UYGHUR REUNION

ISLAMABAD, 2002

"They dragged me into their office," sobs Hamida, "and they grabbed two of my young boys. 'Do you love these nice little boys, woman?' they sneered. 'Of course!' I said. 'Well, if you don't bring your husband back, you will never see them again!'"

Hamida is fine-boned and cultured, and looks too young to have four sons under six. Janna serves green tea, then takes the baby and fusses over it. A friend of Hamida's interprets her Uyghur into Urdu for us.

"So what did you do?" Janna asks, feeling the young woman's pain.

"I travelled west to —."

I don't quite catch which Central Asian country she mentions, but it's not important.

"I found Abdullah but I came back alone. We had a plan. I told the authorities that I searched everywhere and couldn't find him. Allah be praised, they believed me and I got the two boys back." An eclipse of determined relief sweeps across her face.

"I did nothing for months. I knew they were watching. But we had our plan."

Her four round-faced boys silently sip green tea on the *toshak* cushions in our living room. Abdullah, her husband, sits beside them. He is swarthy, looks educated and is intensely proud of his disintegrating heritage.

He takes up the story: "We are Muslim Uyghurs from western China." For our benefit he adds, "There are Uyghur Christians, too, from way before the time of Genghis Khan. We want to keep our traditions but it's so hard. Han Chinese from the East are drowning our culture, our religion and our language. Tens of thousands of them are moving in to dilute our identity. They even want us to change our Uyghur names. We protested. I ended up in jail." His slightly almond eyes are full of stories: stories of sadness, resolve and urgency.

Janna gives me a what-are-we-getting-ourselves-into look. I'm getting worried. It would be good to hear the other side of the story because he's now saying something about a mini-Tiananmen Square event. That's serious. No wonder he ended up in jail.

"And then ...?" I prompt.

"I escaped during a prison transfer. I crossed the western border and laid low. That's when Hamida came and we made plans to meet in Pakistan. She secretly sold our house to get false passports made."

I don't doubt the black-market passports for a moment. In this part of the world, manufacturing illegal documents is a well-honed art form. Recently a printer quietly drew me aside in the bazaar and told me he could provide me with whatever document I needed at any given time. "Mr Lock," he boasted, "by tomorrow I could even supply you with your own death certificate."

Hamida's eyes plead with us. Their interpreter continues in Urdu, "We want to go to Australia. We have relatives in Australia. They sent the papers, but we need your help to fill them in. Our English is very, very weak."

We drink more cups of Janna's cardamom-infused tea while we work on the documents. Finally they are finished. The muezzin's intruding call to prayer is amplified through the neighbourhood. It's Friday and everything is closed. All the men have gone to pray in the mosques.

I'm feeling politically uncomfortable, but how can we not show compassion to this family of wanderers who are guests in our home? Is not showing kindness to sojourners a tenet of all three Abrahamic faiths? Pakistanis themselves are masters of hospitality. I look at this harassed family. Although we cannot vouch for their story, at least the UN should look at their asylum request.

I make them a promise: "Today is the day of prayer, but on Monday I will take all of you, and the papers, to the United Nations High Commission for Refugees. They will work it all out." We pray for them and then they depart, much relieved.

On Monday I will keep my promise, but only for five of the six. You can't keep a promise to someone who has disappeared into thin air.

FORTY-TWO

VAPORISED

It's dark—just before the first call to prayer. Uniformed men storm into the Uyghurs' rented room. The flashlights locate Abdullah. They grab him as he rises from the floor. He doesn't resist. Hamida huddles in a corner, protecting her brood. She nearly lost two of them before. She screams as they toss the families' few belongings in every direction. Abdullah, so close to a new start, remains silent. In the flashlight's glow, Hamida glimpses the bitter resignation written on his face as he looks at her in despair.

A ransacker grunts with satisfaction. He waves a small booklet in the air. "*Idhar hai!*—Here it is!" They evaporate into the darkness with their victim and his passport.

"Be strong, Abdullah," Hamida shouts into the night. The reunion has been all too short. Now Abdullah no longer exists.

*

Monday morning, and a dented Morris Minor taxi, a collector's item in the West, pulls up at our gate.

I look out the upstairs window. They are early. It's amazing how they fit so many into one of those things. There's Hamida and one, two, three, four boys, and the interpreter … but where's Abdullah?

That's the question everyone will soon be asking.

More weeping from Hamida. More sweet tea. The blank-faced boys sip in silence. The loss of their now-you-see-him, now-you-don't father has left the little guys stunned and glassy-eyed.

I take Hamida and her sons to the UNHCR and explain their situation.

The interviewing officer gives a knowing look. "I fully understand," he surprisingly confides. "My mother is Tibetan." He leans back in his chair. "I've studied the minorities in western China. Do you know that the Uyghurs were the dominant power 1200 years ago? Their art, culture and medicine left a big mark in Central Asia." He's staring at the ceiling.

His thoughts are obviously influenced by the state of his mother's homeland. "They say the Uyghurs had sixty-two different kinds of musical instruments."

His gaze drifts back to me and the reality of the moment. "Did Hamida see what kind of uniform they were wearing?" Hamida shakes her head. "I've got some good contacts in the police force. We'll start with them. We have a right to know where he is and what he is being held for. In the meantime we'll fast-track Hamida and the boys. She's now a woman at risk. Can you bring them back tomorrow with more passport-size photos? Four each."

We head to a photo shop. The camera flashes; the boys look bewildered and it clearly shows in their photos.

"The police know nothing about this guy," the UN officer says next day as we hand over the photos. "We're checking out the army and security agencies, but it doesn't look good."

*

Ten days pass. Nothing. Another week. Still nothing. Who were the abductors? Whose uniform were they wearing? Where *is* this guy? The government wants to know. The UNHCR wants to know. The army and police want to know. Above all, distraught Hamida wants to know.

Somehow Amnesty International hears about the vaporised Abdullah. They ring me from London. "The Pakistani government say they don't know, but *someone* must know who grabbed him," asserts the Amnesty representative. "Mr Lock, please try and recall. Is there anything more you can remember? Anything at all?"

I rack my brain: "I'm sorry, but I don't think so." I repeat what I know and finally direct the Amnesty enquirer back to the UNHCR official. I desperately wish I could help further.

FORTY-THREE

MEET ME UNDER THE BRIDGE!

Next day I get an unexpected phone call. The heavily accented voice on the crackly line resonates with urgency. "*Pool kay nicheh, mujhey milna hai!*—You must meet me under the bridge!"

"What bridge?" I involuntarily blurt out.

"The Islamabad overpass bridge."

"Who are you?"

"I am mujahid. I am freedom fighter."

The hair stands up on the back of my neck. I hide the quiver in my voice. "What do you want?"

"You are to be Mr Grant?"

"Yes."

"Your friend is in trouble—too much trouble."

I try to act dumb, but my gut immediately tells me he's talking about Abdullah.

"What friend?"

"He gives me your name. I escape."

"Escaped from where?"

Silence. Then: "Two days. He only has two days. He tell me, ring Mr Grant."

The mujahid bit doesn't help me to think clearly. Has Abdullah been kidnapped? Is this some precursor to a ransom demand? Flashes of espionage movies fly through my brain: agents in trench coats; impassive chain smokers watching from conveniently parked black sedans …

"I will not meet you under the overpass bridge, or any other bridge!"

There's a long pause and heavy breathing. "*Too aana hai*—You have to come."

More trench coats. Knife blades between the fourth and fifth ribs. Rags soaked in chloroform. "I will not meet you under the bridge," I repeat. "If this is so important, you come here, to my house."

More heavy breathing, then a resigned sigh. "*Taheek hai*—okay. What address? Quickly!"

I hurriedly oblige. As I'm repeating it, the line goes dead. More shadowy trench coats and guns with silencers race through my imagination. I'm in a cold sweat.

I look towards our high gate, wondering if the mujahid Voice will materialise. Already I'm regretting that I gave him my address.

*

An hour passes and it's nearly dark. A battered taxi pulls up. The Voice has arrived. The taxi doesn't leave. This is going to be a short visit.

We exchange brief greetings. I offer him a chair and water. He accepts the former and declines the latter. He looks like Bin Laden's nephew: unwashed *shalwar kamiz*, long black beard and *pakoal* headgear. He perches his wiry frame on the edge of the chair. He's both alert and composed, like one who is often tested and always survives.

"I am mujahid. I am not afraid. I fight in Chechnya." And he recites the mujahidin's mantra: "*Allah O Akhbar*—Allah is greatest."

I too am sitting on the edge of my chair. My mouth is dry. Mr Boffin, our friendly Siamese cat, saunters in and leaps onto the knees of the interesting visitor. The freedom fighter flinches, but only slightly, and Mr Boffin casually settles in his lap.

His black eyes drill me. "You are friend of Abdullah?"

Not knowing the implications, I'm not sure whether to answer, but weakly I say, "Yes."

"Abdullah say to ring Mr Grant. Very important. Two days only."

"Well, where is he?"

"Abdullah be in compound with prisoners."

"Which compound?"

"Intelligence compound. Secret compound." The Voice smirks with contempt. "I escape over wall."

I don't doubt it. He is tall, lean and muscular. But now I'm getting excited. He'll tell me the location of the compound and Abdullah will get help. I reach for my pen in expectation. "Where is the compound, Jhi? Where is Abdullah?"

"I don't know."

My jaw drops. "You don't know? But …"

He reads my thoughts. "I don't know. Very dark—I walk many hours. Very dark."

I lower my pen in disappointment and he starts up again about the two day thing.

"*What* will happen in two days?" I demand.

"They take him to Chinese border. Get money."

Now it's all starting to make sense. A uniformed group has abducted Abdullah and plans to hand him back to the Chinese, no doubt for a healthy reward. It's totally clandestine, that's why the Uyghur disappeared without trace. And if Abdullah's stories are true, there are those in his country who will be pleased to prevent him from raising a human rights storm in the West.

The Voice abruptly stands. Mr Boffin falls unceremoniously to the floor. The mission is completed. The message has been delivered. He has fulfilled his duty.

The taxi door slams three times before it catches, then disappears into the polluted evening gloom.

I ring the UN officer.

"You say he mentioned an intelligence compound?"

"Yes."

He sighs in resignation. "If that's army intelligence, they are accountable to no one, not even to the government."

*

Years later I run into Hamida's relative in Australia. I learn that a European country granted Hamida and the boys asylum. She started a new life without Abdullah, for whom she risked everything. He is back in jail in his precious Uyghur homeland.

*

After the Voice leaves, Janna and I feel uneasy. The intelligence branch is very powerful in Pakistan. What if they find out about the mujahid's visit? Will they want to interview us? Will they feel vulnerable if they find out we suspect a border deal?

"I have no regrets," confides Janna. "It's only right to help the needy who come to our gate, whoever they may be." I nod in agreement.

Then another unexpected sojourner arrives. He comes from the land of the "weapons of mass destruction".

FORTY-FOUR

ONLY KAFIRS ASK QUESTIONS

ISLAMABAD, 2002

I wish that big kid would stop tapping on the window while I'm reversing out of the hardware bazaar. Tap, tap, tap, tap. It's acutely irritating, but I won't look directly at him. It's much harder to disengage from a beggar once you make eye contact.

Tap, tap, tap, tap. He's certainly persistent. But he hasn't seen my to-do list for today. I've got a director's report to prepare, then there's my class, and I have to summarise the student assessment tests. "This better be quick," I mumble as I relent and wind down the window.

He's small but must be in his twenties, with an intelligent face.

Why is he swaying? Drugs maybe? They're easy enough to get here in Pakistan. No, couldn't be. He's too alert for that. Whatever! I'm in a hurry.

I glance downwards. Even though they are stabilised by a crutch under one arm, his legs are all wobbly. I know that unscrupulous beggar kings break the legs of babies so they look grotesque, but this is clearly polio. His voice has a desperate yet confident tone.

"Sir, I need your help."

I'm surprised he speaks in English, good English. I'm not to know that he is fluent in five languages and has taught Arabic and Islamics in between his university studies.

I pull out a generous five rupee note and thrust it through the window. He gives it back. That's irritating. I don't have time for his ungrateful negotiations.

A whisper quietly reverberates from the deep portals of my brain: "Come on, Grant, help him." *How can I deal with every beggar who comes along,* I argue with the whisper, *especially when I'm running late?*

I can't believe it. I must be crazy. I'm pulling out the ridiculous amount of 300 rupees. *There, that's super-generous. I've never given a beggar more than ten rupees, so that should help him. Okay?* The Whisperer is not impressed. "You are only trying to silence me so you can get on with your precious little program. Can't you see he needs a friend?"

Oblivious to the conversation in my head, the man thrusts the 300 rupees back. "It's too much, Sir!"

That's weird. Three hundred rupees is three days' pay for a skilled workman. Any self-respecting beggar would have rapidly disappeared around the corner, smirking at the gullibility of the easily duped foreigner. Yes, this guy is definitely different.

"Okay," I say, "get in. Come home and have lunch with me."

"Thank you, Sir. My name is Wurzan, and I come from Iraq."

Over lunch he tells us his story. "I am a Kurd from Halabja, the town that Saddam Hussein gassed last year." I remember the incident. It was labelled as the biggest gas attack on civilians in history. "Saddam sent his brother, Chemical Ali, to pay back the Kurds for resisting his army. They buried thousands in mass graves and then they tried to blame Iran." His face hardens. "But it was genocide."

"Is that why you left Iraq?"

"No! The main reason was that I asked too many questions."

"About what?"

"About life and about our religion."

Janna and I wait for him to enlarge.

"I couldn't do the things my friends could do, so I did a lot of reading. Questions kept coming up. My father is a teacher and a very religious Muslim, but he couldn't answer them." Wurzan reaches hungrily for his fourth piece of *naan*. "My father took me to the local religious leaders the Maulvis. They were not happy. They told me that it is wrong to ask questions about our holy religion. It shows a lack of faith. Only unbelievers ask questions. I told them I was not an unbeliever, I just wanted to explore the truth. 'But you are too young to be challenging our learning,' they said, 'come back when you have grown up, and after you have read these.' Then they put a heap of books in front of me. They were surprised that I had already read half of them. On the way home my father told me that I had embarrassed him and dishonoured him. 'Only *kafirs* ask questions,' he said."

I take up our guest's concern. "I've often wondered why people can't ask questions in Islam, Wurzan. It claims to have the answers for life, yet it seems oversensitive about people wanting to scrutinise it. And it's particularly sensitive if a Muslim investigates another religious system. That isn't the sign of a confident religion; it's a sign of insecurity and control."

Wurzan nods. "Young people are told to be quiet and just accept everything. But in the university, my lecturer encouraged us to explore and evaluate."

"What university studies did you complete?" Janna asks.

He sets his jaw. "They wouldn't let me finish. They threw me in jail and made sure I stayed there during the final examinations."

"But why?"

"I was a student of law and I was asking questions about human rights in our country."

"When Saddam Hussein is running things, is that a good idea?"

Wurzan lifts his shoulders and takes on a maturity beyond his years. "Mrs Janna, in 1948 Iraq voted for the Universal Declaration of Human Rights in the United Nations." He continues in barrister-like fashion, "My question is this: why don't the citizens of Iraq have the freedom to participate in our society? Many young Kurds in university are asking this question. Why should we be treated worse than animals?"

I can't help but admire the pluckiness of this young Iraqi intellectual. His question is one that most dictators would not want to hear, let alone one as repressive as Saddam Hussein. "You're right, Wurzan. Along with Iraq, many Islamic countries voted for the Universal Declaration of Human Rights. But do you know that they're now trying to amend it?"

"Why is that, Sir?"

"Because it doesn't line up with Islamic sharia law. Sharia law severely restricts religious and gender freedom, as well as freedom of speech."

"Which you are finding out the hard way," Janna adds. "So tell me, Wurzan, how did you get out of jail?"

"My relatives arranged it, but I was frightened. I knew I would always be watched. If Saddam could kill five thousand Kurds with gas, he could easily deal with me."

"So you got out."

He nods. "I came via Iran, and I have already been to the United Nations here to apply for asylum in a Western country."

I can see that this young refugee doesn't let the grass grow under his unstable feet. "Well, Wurzan, we wish you well in the West. At least you'll be able to ask questions more freely."

"Thank you, Sir."

"But there is one question that many people in the West are asking, and it's a question Muslims never ask."

He raises an eyebrow. "And what is that?"

"Is there intelligence behind everything, an intelligent creator?"

He gives half a laugh. "But anyone can see that there is creative intelligence behind everything. Why don't they accept that in the West?"

"That's easy. It's because they might have to ask the next two questions."

"And what are they?"

"If there is an intelligent creator, what is that creator like? And secondly, where do I fit in?"

"But, Mr Grant, they are questions I too am asking."

I look at my watch, then rise. "I have a class in twenty minutes. I can give you a lift into the city if you like."

"And why don't you come back for a meal next week," Janna offers. "You could do with a bit more flesh on those bones of yours."

He gives an infectious smile. "Thank you, Mrs Janna. Your cooking is so delicious."

*

The lonely Iraqi visits us every week and we become family for him. He occasionally rings his mother but never talks to his father. Janna and I accept his invitation to travel across town and drink tea in the mud room he shares with five other refugees. His asylum application goes well until the medicos look at his X-rays and detect tuberculosis. That means an extra six months for us to ask each other questions, to laugh and to eat together.

But someone with a notebook is watching those wobbly legs come and go. And the things written about us are not very helpful.

FORTY-FIVE

TRAINING TERRORISTS

DECEMBER 2002

It's one of the most time consuming and frustrating things to do in a foreign country, and yet the most necessary. Whether you are a visitor or a long-term contributor, you can't exist without it. That little visa stamp is absolutely essential. Without it you feel naked, vulnerable and unwanted. You are a misfit, an interloper, an alien. You are a criminal, a trespasser. You don't belong. You can have the vaccinations, learn the language, understand the culture, know somebody important, have the best intentions. You can even have a PhD from Oxford, Harvard or Beijing. But all that is for nought if you don't have that little mark in a little book called your passport.

*

I'm worried. I've been going back to the visa office for nearly four months now. We've never waited this long for our annual visa renewals before.

"Is there a problem?" I ask the sleepy lackey behind the front desk.

He's vague, as usual. "You'll have to talk to the officer in charge."

I wait my turn. He is affable, but there is no progress. "No, Sir, it's not ready yet. Please come back again in two weeks."

But something is radically wrong. This delay is definitely more than just bureaucratic lethargy. He is hiding something. I'm hearing new phrases such as "Your case is being decided".

The next time I visit I'm steered into a different part of the visa office and told to wait. I start chatting with a junior officer. As soon as Adeel learns that Janna and I enjoyed ten years in his home city of Peshawar, we are bosom buddies. When no one else is around he speaks quietly to me.

"Mr Lock, I know you are waiting for your visas."

"Yes, we are," I reply with a spark of hope that someone, at last, knows something about it.

"You are not going to get them!"

I can't believe my ears. "Not going to get them?"

"No, Sir."

"What's the problem?"

There is no answer. His face assumes a pained expression; he has already said more than he should have. Another official returns to the room. Adeel leans forward. "Go to the Ministry of Interior, to Mr Mohammad Jazeem. He wears a green turban."

Fortunately I know Mohammad Jazeem. He is the one who hands over your passport after all the visa work is completed. Two visits later, the green-turbaned official seems particularly genial.

"Ah, Mr Lock, you've come for your passports. Sorry about the long delay." His fingers shuffle through a drawer and he pulls out two booklets. What a relief. I haven't seen those blue covers with their gold embossed kangaroo and emu for four months. We are about to become people again. I feared the worst, but Mohammad Jazeem is so friendly I'm sure that the assertions of my contact in the visa office are unfounded.

On the other side of the grimy window, Mr Jazeem flicks through the pages of my passport. "I just need to draw your attention to one thing." He finds the relevant page and points to an entry. "Mr Lock, I am obliged to notify you that you and your wife must leave Pakistan within fourteen days. Otherwise you will be illegals."

My stomach is a cold, heavy stone. I open my mouth, but the words are slow in coming. "But … we have been serving the people of Pakistan for twenty years."

"I know, Mr Lock," he replies apologetically.

"And now we have to leave? Why?"

"I don't know why. The intelligence and security department has made the decision. They don't give reasons and they cannot be questioned, even by the minister himself."

There are several stop-arguing-and-get-moving coughs from the queue behind me. I don't hear them. My knees feel weak, but permeations of Pakistani culture are rising indignantly within me. "Sir, we have our biggest religious festival in a few days. Then we will have to pack and say farewell to many Pakistani friends. It's not right that we leave without saying goodbye to them. Only fourteen days! It's not reasonable, Sir."

There is nothing more important in Pakistan than religious festivals and friends. Mr Jazeem makes a suggestion. "Write a nice letter to the Deputy Director and make an appointment. Ask him for a one-month extension. I think he will grant it." He closes the booklet and adds an afterthought, "But don't ask him to reverse the decision because he does not have the power."

I take the passports with clammy hands and drive home slowly. One half of my brain is racing; the other half is totally numb. As soon as she sees me, Janna knows the outcome.

"It looks like we're a big threat to Pakistan's national security," I say, and try to force a laugh. But my mouth is dry.

"Grant, I told you we are being watched from that shop over the road," Janna fumes in exasperation, "but you don't seem to worry."

"We can't stop anyone from watching us, and we have nothing to hide. Yes, we've had Pashai women at the gate and regular guests, but there's nothing wrong with that."

"But it's only happened since Wurzan has been coming. He is so obvious with his wobbly legs."

"Perhaps those stories of us being Indian spies have resurfaced."

"Or was it something to do with the Uyghurs and that scary mujahid who visited you?"

"We'll probably never know, but we need that extension. Fourteen days is ridiculous after the time we've been here."

Just when all avenues appear exhausted, an unknown Pakistani comes up with a solution. I meet him outside church after a worship service but I've never seen him before. He looks a suave, smooth type. My mind has already labelled him as "Oilcan Harry".

"Mr Lock, you don't have to leave. I can help you."

My mind immediately forms the question, *So what's in it for you, my friend?* But I merely raise an eyebrow. "Yes?"

"It's quite simple, "continues Harry. "All you have to do is marry a Pakistani girl."

My jaw drops. "But I'm already married!"

He is totally unfazed. "No matter. No matter at all. The important thing is that she is a Pakistani. Then the government will let you stay."

I'm starting to twig to this "altruistic" guy's motives. "And I suppose you have someone in mind. Your sister, perhaps?"

He nods but then, too late, realises that I've seen through his scheme. I don't know if he's looking for money or for a family connection to get him to Australia, but I verbally get stuck into him. "My friend, what about my wife?"

He huffs and puffs. I glance at Janna chatting to a group of women a few yards away. "You'd better not mention it to her. She has a very heavy handbag."

"Forget it," our selfless hero mumbles. "I think we should just forget it."

"That's a good idea, my friend, particularly since we've just come out of church. I don't think you were paying much attention in there."

That was probably a bit rough on him because there were times during the service when I wasn't paying much attention either. I was mulling over our visa problems. I concluded that I'm thankful there is one kingdom where you don't have to fill out countless forms, wait in long queues, pay money or marry into it. You just receive it as a gift. And the stamp in that cosmic passport is shaped like a heart, with one word underneath: "Forever."

*

The Deputy Director kindly gives the extension and we celebrate Christmas with confused feelings. We sell or give away our belongings and start packing for the shipping company. I hand over my director's job and we find a new home for our precious Siamese cats. It's a heavy-duty grieving process as we farewell our classes, the staff and the school's watchmen with their shotguns and metal detectors.

*

As the giant wheels of the 747 clunk into their housings, we are holding hands and looking down at the roofs of Islamabad. Only last year I told Janna that I enjoyed Islamabad so much I could just about retire there one day. Now we've clearly been shown the door.

Cruising southward at 30,000 feet, I scan the wrinkled sand dunes of the Thar Desert. I'm trying to spot my plantation just outside Mithi. I've heard that the trees are now twenty feet high. Glimpsing that plot would bring some satisfaction, a sort of sedative to mollify the pain of departure. But it doesn't come into view.

In two minutes we will cross the border and be out of Pakistan. I slump back into my seat. I should be feeling thankful for twenty years of opportunities to make a difference, but right now I'm just feeling unwanted and betrayed.

*

While recovering in Australia, we receive an email from a close friend in Islamabad.

> Janna and Grant,
>
> I was talking to a man who has links with the intelligence and security department. I told him that we need you back, and asked if you should reapply for a visa from Australia. "Don't even think about it," he said. I asked him why not, and he gave the craziest of answers. "Because they made friends with miscreants and enemies of the state. They taught terrorists how to blow up churches and schools," was what he said.
>
> So it looks like they picked on you to impress someone that they were on the job. It's sad we can't get you back.
>
> You'll be missed greatly.
>
> Andrew

We stare at each other for a long moment and then start to laugh with incredulity.

"Well, Janna, it's clear our time in Pakistan is finished."

She's missing the Pashai women and girls, our colleagues, our students and our cats. "We must be meant to be somewhere else," she half-whispers, "but where?"

"Yes, where?" I echo.

We would like to see the answer written in the sky. And when it finally does come, it's not unlike that.

*

Back in Australia, we talk with the leaders of our organisation. There is a possibility of work in a college for Aborigines in the Northern Territory, but our hearts are really with Muslim people.

"What about teaching English to Afghans in Kabul instead of Islamabad?" one of the committee suggests. "So much international communication, trade and education is in English. Afghans need it to re-enter the international community."

"That was our first thought, Leigh," I respond, "and we like helping Afghans, but we're really concerned about current security and stress levels in Afghanistan. They haven't found Bin Laden yet, and with America's attention on the new war in Iraq, the Taliban is regrouping."

"We've had enough of terrorist attacks over the last year," Janna says. "I think we should find a quieter environment for a while."

The committee nod in unison. "Right, let's look at other alternatives," declares the chairman.

*

Three months later Janna and I are driving to speak to a support group. The decisions have been made and the tickets have been purchased. "Don't say Egypt, Grant," Janna says suddenly. "Just say we'll teach English somewhere in the Middle East."

I glance at her. "But I thought we decided that Cairo was the right place, and the tickets have already been bought. Why can't we share that with people?"

She doesn't give an answer.

A week later, in predawn blackness, I'm being stirred from the luxurious embrace of deep sleep. "Oooh. It's still dark."

Janna digs me again. "Grant, wake up! Wake up!"

She has about twenty per cent of my fuzzy attention. "What is it?" I'm drifting back into restful oblivion.

She shakes my arm vigorously. "I know where we're going!"

"You what?"

She reaches for the light. "I know where we're going to serve next."

I sit up in bed. She now has one hundred per cent of my attention."You'd better tell me."

"I feel excited!"

"I can see that. You're just about bubbling over. Tell me what's going on."

"I don't care if it is Cairo, Kabul or Coober Pedy, I just wanted to be sure and I wanted an excitement about it. That's what I've been praying specifically for over the last ten days."

"And?"

"I just woke up with this tremendous excitement, and now I'm certain because the name is written across the inside of my head."

"Well, come on. Tell me."

"You'd better talk to the committee, Grant, and cancel the Cairo tickets, because we're going to Afghanistan. We're going to Kabul!"

TALIBAN COUNTRY

AFGHANISTAN

2004–2008

SEPTEMBER 11. COALITION ENTERS AFGHANISTAN

1999 | 2000 | 2001 | 2002 | 2003 | 2004 | 2005 | 2006 | 2007 | 2008 | 2009 | 2010

LED BY THE TALIBAN | HAMID KARZAI PRESIDENT OF AFGHANISTAN

FORTY-SIX

THE RETURN OF THE BLUE-EYED BOY

KABUL, 2004

Janna is almost in tears. "Learning languages is not my thing, Grant. I really don't care if they are postpositions or post offices, conjunctives or conjunctivitis. I just want to speak it. Why do we have to have all that grammatical jargon?"

"Different people learn in different ways, you know. Why don't you talk to the supervisor and try an alternative approach?"

"First Urdu, then some Sindhi, now Dari." She pulls her headphones off, closes her books and buries her head in her hands. "It's all too much. I wish I had Mr Boffin here to help me."

It was a crystal clear day when we flew from Dubai, across Iran and on to Kabul. From high altitude we flew over what appeared to be a continuous vista of scrunched-up brown paper. Barren mountains gave way to barren mountains. Somewhere down below, twenty-five million people were surviving, the majority of them rural. But from up there it looked empty and not worth having, though plenty of would-be conquerors had tried to get it: Darius the Persian, Alexander the Great, Genghis Khan, the British Raj, the Russians. And now the Americans with their NATO allies.

Janna studied the crinkles. "Apart from a few bits of green in the cracks, what is there to fight about?"

I quote a famous real estate slogan: "Location, location, location. Afghanistan's always been a conduit for traders and conquerors. Part of the old Silk Road from China passed through here."

"But that's all history now."

I flipped to a page in the *Time* magazine I'd been skim-reading. "This article says that if Afghanistan ever settles down, they could make a fortune in a modern version of the Silk Road. India, South-East Asia and China all want gas from the colossal fields in the countries just north of Afghanistan. International energy consortiums would love to pipe it out through Afghanistan, and, of course, they would pay handsomely for the privilege."

"They might end up paying more than they bargain for," laughed Janna. "Apart from kidnapping people for ransom, the locals could take pipelines hostage as well."

"It also says that there's an absolutely massive copper deposit near Kabul, and the Chinese are keen to develop it, providing President Karzai can bring unity and security to the country."

"And until he does," Janna realistically summed up, "the big money is in the opium poppy and the heroin black market."

Our jet's wheels screamed and smoked as they struck the Kabul tarmac. We had arrived in Afghanistan. Damaged and shot-up aircraft lay rusting on the side of the runway. The signs of prolonged warfare were all around. It was easy to see why Afghanistan is rated the second poorest country in the world. But what can you expect; there had been war of some kind for a quarter of a century. It was one thing for the Afghans to fight the Soviet invaders for ten years, but it was harder to muster up sympathy for them when they spent more than the next decade fighting each other. However, regardless of apportioning blame, the reality was that this was a deeply wounded and fragmented nation, and, as usual, it was the little people, the poor, who had suffered most.

That's why we had come.

*

Afternoon dust storms suffocate the city with its thousands of damaged or destroyed buildings. Men, not horses, pull the carts. Sidewalk shop keepers use pre-weighed stones in their scales in lieu of proper weights

Four million jammed-up souls. Refugees returning from Pakistan. Drought-driven rural dwellers; fatherless families. Vagrants from insecure villages and the unemployed from umpteen regions. At crossroads, hundreds of desperate men wait hopefully for a day's work. UN vehicles roar through town. Helmeted troops patrol in Humvees. Watchful helicopters hover overhead.

Hope is in the air. The Taliban have run to the mountains, and girls are back in school. Rebuilding is everywhere, and poppy-primed mansions rise from the ruins.

At our first briefing the executive director of our new international team greets us warmly. "Pakistan's loss is our gain," tall, clear-eyed Harri comments. "As you know, your first five months are totally dedicated to learning language and culture. To serve the Afghan people well, that's vital. Then you'll join our EFL project and as planned, Grant, you'll take over as project director. The English teaching team is really looking forward to your joint experience and input, and that includes our regional branches."

"And what is the current security situation, Harri?"

"You'll have your first real briefing on Thursday, but it's fairly quiet now. However, we've seen this sort of thing before."

"Meaning?"

"Well, this organisation has been serving the Afghan people for forty years, through both violent regime changes and quieter periods. We just don't know if this more hopeful atmosphere will last. After all, the Taliban and al-Qaeda are still out there in the mountains on the Pakistan border. Anyway, while it's relatively quiet, we can get on with our training and development work."

❋

They say that Kabul has the highest content of air-born faecal material in the world. You try not to think about that as shovel-wielding men flick dark, turbid fluids from their shallow toilet pits onto the fouled, dusty roads. While being mindful of your step, it's more inspiring to keep your eyes focused on the mountains. Beyond the local stony monoliths, the distant Hindu Kush is peaked with snow. During winter, the white bounty will delight my wife as it blankets these polluted streets with purity.

"May Kabul be without gold but never without snow," the locals regularly quote to me. They stoically bear the bitter winter and frozen pipes, hoping there's sufficient precipitation to replenish the water table and the wells this ancient city depends on.

*

With another three grinding months of language learning ahead of us, an unexpected and welcome email arrives from Pakistan.

> Janna, and Grant, we've just heard that you are in Afghanistan. In a few months we are retiring and returning to the States. Do you want Mr Boffin and Missy back?

The letter comes from our cat-loving friends in Islamabad. They kindly took our two Siamese cats when we left Pakistan.

"Of course we want them back!" Janna springs up and down. "We could see some of our friends as well. Almost everyone is flying now since they had those kidnappings on the Khyber Pass road."

"I think you're forgetting we lost our visas for Pakistan, and they'll probably never give us another one."

"Not even for a short visit?" Janna can almost feel Mr Boffin's comforting cuddles. "We won't know until we try."

It turns out there is only one difficult question on the application form. "Have you ever been refused a visa for Pakistan, and if so, for what reason?"

After much procrastinating, I finally write "Yes" and "No reason was given."

We have told the truth, though I reckon we have no chance. But for the sake of blue-eyed Boffin, I return the forms to the shabby Pakistan Embassy and hope for the best. After three weeks the visas are inexplicably approved. But will they really work for people who allegedly trained miscreants to blow up schools and churches? We are going to find out.

*

Our plane descends through the clouds over familiar Islamabad. The serious Pakistani immigration officer studies his computer screen. Is he checking a blacklist? We are trying to look relaxed. As he peers into the screen, his hand slowly extends toward the all-important stamp. That's positive. Finally he thumps it twice and hands us our passports. "*Khoosh amdehd.* Welcome back to Pakistan, Mr Lock."

Relieved, we head for the luggage carousel. Deep down I'm still expecting a big, hairy hand to grab me by the shoulder and say, "*Idhar aao, Janaab*—Come this way, Sir." But it doesn't happen.

A ring of determined taxi drivers accost us outside the terminal building. Once they realise we know Urdu, their ridiculous prices return to bargained normality.

In the back seat Janna exhales with relief. "Our names were not on their list."

"If they ever were. But I guess we'll never know. I'm thankful we can at least do a short visit."

*

Back in the air, heading westward to Kabul, my happy wife is delighted on two counts. Below are the inspiring Hindu Kush Mountains, and in the carry-box on her lap are our two Siamese cats.

Mr Boffin and cream-coloured Missy soon adapt to Kabul. Janna's Dari proficiency seems to pick up in direct proportion to the amount of time Mr Boffin spends on her lap.

"He is such an amiable, understanding cat," she purrs. "He just knows I need some stress relief."

"Or perhaps he knows the days are getting colder," I suggest.

She raises a book to throw at me. "Get out of here!"

The gate bell rings. It's our good friend Heather, who moved over from Islamabad more than a year ago. "Sorry I couldn't meet you when you arrived," she apologises. "I was back in Canada on home assignment."

It's so good to see her and to hear the latest about the Snow Princess.

"Mariam and Salma are doing really well in Sweden," Heather reports. "Now I'm working with a whole group of Kabul widows."

"Whereabouts?" inquires Janna.

"It's a garden training project, only half an hour from here. Hey, Janna Jaan," she adds, using the colloquial term of endearment, "too much of those language books will drive you bonkers. You need a bit of face-to-face practice as well. What about coming out and meeting my widows?"

"I couldn't think of a nicer thing to do, Heather. I'd love to."

FORTY-SEVEN

BEFORE THE FALL

2004

If they can't find work they might as well enjoy themselves. Like Roman citizens at the Colosseum, scores of unemployed Kabuli men perch on broken-down walls surrounding the vacant allotment. There is no bread, but there are circuses, of a sort. They are here to cheer the winners and to remain silent for the others. However, it's not in their collective power to give the thumbs up or down. That is the prerogative of three Afghan policemen who are about to administer the weekly tests for aspiring Afghan drivers.

Regardless of whether we own a car or not, our development organisation insists that we all have local licenses in case of emergencies. Since the suicide-vested Taliban are creeping back into town, this is a good idea.

Thirty cars wait their turn. All the potential license recipients are males, except for one.

"I don't know how I'll go," says Janna. "You've been down here to practise, Grant, but I haven't made the time."

It's true. Two days ago I slipped out of my project office and came down here with cheerful Ali from our logistics staff. The dusty square was silent and empty.

"I really don't need to practise," I told him, but he disagreed.

"Idea good, Sir," he insisted in broken English. "Only one chance, day of test."

"But, Ali, I've got an HC Class Australian license." I waved the important piece of plastic in the air. "I've driven everything: motor bikes, cars, big trucks and buses."

He was impressed, but I didn't stop there. "I've driven bulldozers and loaders back on the farm, and twenty-metre spraying machines as well. So, whatever it is, it should be simple. Just tell me what I have to do."

Okay, blowbags Grant. Did you tell him you haven't driven for the last nine months since you arrived in Kabul? Sure, you don't need a vehicle now. Your office is only ten minutes walk away and there are usually plenty of those old Russian taxis cruising the streets. But did you tell him your eye sight is fading because you've got Stargardt's disease, and that your central vision has been declining for five years now? But brag on if you wish. Just beware. Pride comes before a fall.

"Well," Ali explained, "see you white lines, in middle of block?"

I'd already wondered about the two parallel white lines about three-and-a-half metres apart. They extended for twenty-five metres then took a ninety-degree turn for another twenty-five metres, like a right-angled boomerang. "Yes, I see them."

Ali pulled up at the end of the lines. "You reverse down, and around corner, and out other end. Must not touch lines." He has the common Afghan habit of forgetting to use the article in his English.

"That's all you have to do?"

"*Baleh*—Yes. It proves Sir can drive."

"A piece of cake," I replied.

"You have cake, Sir?' Ali asked with interest.

"No, Ali. It's just an English saying. It means that it's very easy."

I took my position behind the wheel and adjusted the mirrors. No problem. After reversing a four-wheel trailer behind a long-grain truck, this little exercise was definitely a piece of cake. I reversed through the right angle successfully.

"*Tabreek*—Congratulations!" said Ali. "Now pull around and have another practice."

"What?" said Big-head. "Who needs another practice?"

"Most people do it few times, Sir."

"I just did it, didn't I?" I looked at my watch. "I've got a donor report to finish today, Ali Jaan. So what's next?"

He shook his head.

"Surely I'll have to drive around a few streets to show that I can han dle the traffic?"

"No, Sir. That's all."

I couldn't believe it, but it helped explain Kabul's chaotic traffic and its inventive drivers. By simple observation I have deduced that there are two crucial, unofficial traffic laws. The first is "The Law of Space". If there is a space in the traffic, regardless of where it is, you can move through it or fill it. But it is subject to the second law, "The Law of Inertia". Since inertia is a combination of mass and velocity, if another vehicle has more weight and/or speed than your vehicle, then you must give way. With these universal laws in place, the mayhem works surprisingly well—providing, of course, that your all-essential horn is working.

"That's all," Ali repeated. "You've already done the medical check and the oral test."

*

We had a particularly smooth run with the medicals. Ali had told us that they'd check our eyesight and blood pressure, and there would be lots of health questions. "They even get you to pull up your trouser leg to see you don't have an artificial leg. There are a lot of mine-blast victims around these days."

Janna and I were directed to the tall, ramshackle Transport Department building in downtown Kabul. Half of the top floor was blown off during the fighting and hasn't been repaired. We joined the queue of men waiting for their medical checks.

The young, white-coated doctor looked up, rose quickly and almost bounded down the line to shake hands and embrace me. "Welcome, Mr Grant. Welcome." He led us to the head of the line and sat us down at his desk. He detected that I was having trouble recognising him.

"But, Sir, you know me!" he half exploded. "I'm Mustafa. I was in your English class in Pakistan, in Islamabad. You were such a good teacher."

"Ah, Mustafa!" Recognition filtered down through the fog. "It's great that you've returned, and have a job."

"Thanks to your English classes, Sir."

We traded the normal drawn-out questions concerning the welfare of our families, and then Mustafa took up his chart and began the medical assessment. "Okay, Mr Grant, what is your blood group?"

"A-Positive."

"And yours, Mrs Janna?"

"B-positive."

"Very good. That's all done. Now, just go into the next room for the oral traffic rules test. The police officer will talk to you."

"But, Mustafa, what about the blood pressure and the vision test?"

"No need for those," responded my ex-student. "You were the best teacher I ever had."

*

I don't know why, but the police officer was a bit irritated. He was standing before about sixty attentive Afghan men, wedged shoulder-to-shoulder into one small classroom. The grimy walls were covered with every conceivable road sign. Until the sardines could proficiently identify each one, they wouldn't pass the test. With a short cane resembling a conductor's baton, the frustrated officer was pointing at the signs and waiting for the corporate, sing-song response. This is where a good short-term memory would be useful, because in Kabul they will only see about five of those forty signs.

The officer came to the door and spoke curtly to us. He wanted to get this over. "I will ask you a few questions, and if you answer correctly, you will pass the oral test." We nodded. "Suppose your car reaches a crossroad and the light goes green. What do you do?"

"That's easy," I replied. "You drive through."

His face went slightly red and he repeated the question. I could see he was not happy with my preliminary answer, but in the interest of minimising future crossroad pile-ups, I decided to stick with it. "Green is for go, Sir. When the light goes green, I drive through."

His agitated moustache twitched and his face got redder. He and I were both thinking the same thought: *Good grief, how dumb can this guy be?*

He was about to rephrase his question when he changed his mind and blurted out in exasperation, "Do you have a driver's license from your country?"

I whipped out my Australian plastic. "Yes, Sir, and so does my wife." Until now he had hardly acknowledged Janna. He didn't know how to respond to an applicant of the fairer sex. Afghan women don't drive.

He quickly signed our papers, gave us a "just get out of here" look, pointed his baton at another sign and continued conducting Kabul's traffic-trainee choir.

For me, the green light question will always remain on a par with other mysteries of the universe, like black holes, migratory birds and women's handbags. I turned to my equally bewildered wife. "Well, that just leaves the practical test next week."

*

Five days later and it's our turn to do the test. "I'll go first, Janna. I'll show you what you have to do."

Unlike my smooth practice run, however, things are going wrong. I turn too late. Now there's no way I can reverse around that right angle without running over the outside line.

I've failed, and I'm so embarrassed. As I get out of the car, there is total silence from the unemployed sentinels perched around the wall. At least they don't hiss and boo.

Ali pleads with the policemen for a rerun. The officer shakes his head. "Look at that line of vehicles waiting for their turn." He signals for Janna to start.

She carefully steers backwards, turns in time and perfectly completes the boomerang run. Springing out of the car, she dances around in child-like exuberance: "I did it! I did it!" It's a part of her character I love, but it is seldom expressed in this cultural environment. If Afghan women even laugh in public, they are reprimanded for improper conduct. But here in the dusty testing ground the assembled males are caught up in the success of the only female applicant, and they clap and cheer. I'm proud of her too, but I'm wishing I could become invisibly small and just disappear, along with my big mouth.

*

A week later I hand Janna a card with her photo and Arabic writing. "Ali gave this to me at the office today. Congratulations! It's your Afghan driver's license."

She's justifiably chuffed. "And when do you do your next test, Grant?"

"I don't need to."

"Why not? Won't they give you another try?"

"I don't have to." I wave my Afghan license in front of her.

She explodes. "Hey! That's not right! You didn't pass the test! How come?"

"Ali said he had a word with them when he picked yours up and they had pity on me."

She turns on her heel and huffs off. "But you didn't even pass, Grant. Boy, they sure got it right when they said this country is a man's world."

It won't be long before she gets another reminder of that.

FORTY-EIGHT

IT'S A MAN'S WORLD

2004

Janna hears the grunting before she turns the corner. When she does, she is disgusted. A man squatting by the side of the street is defecating where everyone can see him. But in fact, no one can see him at all; he's wearing a traditional *shalwar kamiz* suit.

Apart from being one of the world's most comfortable garments, this loose fitting garb also converts the entire country into a men's toilet. Drop the baggy shalwar trousers and the long kamiz top covers all. No doubt rural relatives have more convenient places, but the town dweller is often caught a long way from home. Even if there is a rare public toilet nearby, the choice is easy. The side of the road is to be preferred to the stench of the ever-increasing piles inside the often unattended building, which seems to be more frequented by the up-market wearers of Western blue jeans. The road is the answer for the more traditional dresser, and if it is bare of bushes, no problem—thanks to the versatile *shalwar kamiz.*

My Western wife is disgusted by the sight and sounds of the constipated squatter, who takes absolutely no notice of the foreign female. That's the operative word: female. Even with the same style of clothing, it's a totally different story for women. How they manage is often a mystery, but they are certainly not permitted to answer the calls of nature in a blatantly open way, as is the case for the more exalted gender of the species.

Over a period of time Janna learns how they survive. On a bus trip the males will all pile out and do the *shalwar kamiz* trick by the side of the road. The well-covered women remain sedately seated; they stopped drinking the night before. They will travel in a modest, albeit dehydrated, fashion. No male will be offended, embarrassed or dishonoured. It's a man's world.

*

Janna recalls a stressful time in a busy Hyderabad bazaar.

"I've gotta go, Mum—now," Maria announces with heavily punctuated urgency.

"Right now?"

"Yes, Mum. Right now! Where do I go?"

The question is already taxing her mother's brain. There may have been a teenage boy squatting by a well-watered wall a hundred yards back, but females don't do that. "Maria, it will only take ten minutes to get back to the St Philip's compound," Janna says.

"That would be nine minutes too long, Mum," responds her twelve-year-old daughter with conviction.

What to do? Where to go? A kindly-faced Sindhi woman emerges from the nearby cloth shop and pauses to deposit coins, the result of a well-haggled discount, in her money purse. Janna steps forward. "*Muaf keejeeay*, please excuse me, but my daughter needs a toilet. Right now!"

Although taken aback by the foreigner's abruptness, the woman immediately comprehends the gravity of the situation. Women look after each other; that's the way it is.

"Quickly! Follow me!" She slips down a side alley. "My cousin lives down here." The relative is equally accommodating and leads Maria directly to the toilet. When my thankful daughter reappears, the kindly cousin is pouring tea for her unexpected visitors.

*

"It's all very well for you Westerners," an Afghan points out to me. "Your countries are developed, and educated. You can afford sanitation, and you know about disease."

"And that's why we're here," I respond, "to help your people build some facilities in their yards instead of using the streets."

It's true that in the West fancy bathrooms have almost become a shrine for us. But you don't have to have a *Better Homes and Gardens* bathroom to beat flies, smells, giardia, diarrhoea, cholera and hepatitis One of the reasons why people are poor is because of the vicious cycle of poverty, ignorance, disease, doctors, medicine and funerals. It's all money that could be used for education, more nutritious food or building a cycle-breaking toilet. But when you have to pay back the loan, you are stuck. Meanwhile, the flies still buzz around with their filthy feet, and the unwashed hands keep the pharmaceutical companies in business. As an Afghan proverb says: "Every rock strikes the feet of the poor."

*

Our organisation of international professional volunteers, along with our Afghan colleagues, is continually changing the lives of Afghans, at least the ones who want to help themselves. The ones that just want a woe-is-me handout are bypassed. Our people have helped locals to build thousands of cost-effective, appropriate toilets. We supply the cement and supervision, and they provide the labour and the mud bricks for the walls. In addition, to break the ignorance cycle, selected locals are trained to teach hygiene to their fellow-villagers. Our team is credited with building the cheapest and best household toilets in Afghanistan, and the women love them.

But for some women, a decent toilet is the thing furthest from their mind.

FORTY-NINE

I SOLD MY BABY

2006

Peering through the mesh of her faded blue burka, a distraught young woman waits for our Kabul gate to open. My wife recognises the shapeless shape. "Come in, Leena. Do come in." The visitor throws back the all-covering garment from her face and Janna gasps. "Leena! You look terrible. Whatever is the matter?"

"I had to do it. There was no other way."

"What do you mean?"

In a stoic attempt to restrain her feelings, Leena takes a deep breath. "It's my Shanzi." And as if she can't believe she's done such a maternally reprehensible thing, she whispers, "I sold her. I sold my own baby daughter!" Like a flood-burst dam, the emotion pours out. Her bony frame pulsates with gasping sobs as she falls into Janna's outstretched arms.

*

People agree that when the Taliban took over Kabul back in 1996, the rains stopped. In the middle of the Taliban drought, Leena's family arranged her marriage. The girl had never been beyond her village, five hours north of the capital, but the new groom declared that Kabul was the only place to get work. So the couple moved from a rural village to an urban village.

The two places had much in common. Both had mud-brick houses, were without electricity and depended on community hand-pumps at the end of the street. That's providing the hand-pumps were sucking water and not air. Without good snow and rain, the water table had sunk to an all-time low. There are thousands of hand-dug wells in Kabul and many need to be dug deeper to follow the receding water table. That's where Sadiq found work. It was dangerous, with cave-ins and all, but it paid.

The money came in, the babies arrived and the Taliban ruled the city with an iron hand. The day they beat him up, Sadiq was walking home in the dark.

The boss had promised a bonus if he finished the job that day. That was why he was warily striding along in the blackness, and that was why his young wife was waiting and worrying. Sadiq knew it was a gamble. It was risky to be out after the curfew, but he needed the money. After all, Leena was expecting twins in a few months. She was a good wife. She worked hard on her embroidery. At least that covered the ever-increasing rent. They already had one boy and one girl. What a blessing, and what an honour, if the twins are boys.

A Toyota Hilux roared up the long, empty street. There was no place to hide, no trees, no parked vehicles—nothing but nine-foot-high walls. He threw himself into a deep roadside drain, but it wasn't deep enough. He was caught in the lights of the Taliban vehicle. The black turbans sprang out and surrounded him. A flashlight stunned his tell-tale, almond-shaped Hazara eyes.

"Get up, you Hazara animal!" Sadiq received help from a steel-capped boot. "Don't you have any respect for the Taliban curfew? Where are you going?"

"To my home, Sir."

"And why are you out so late?"

"I dig wells. The boss said I had to finish it today."

"You are lying, Hazara pig. You are up to no good."

"Look at the mud on my hands and my clothes. I tell you, Sir, I am a well digger."

The kidney blow from behind dropped Sadiq to his knees. The previously silent patrol leader stepped forward, stroked his beard and made his judgment. "You work for the Northern Alliance. You are spying on the Taliban. Now the Taliban will teach you a lesson."

"No! No! I am not a spy," shouted Sadiq as the rifle butts rose in unison.

The Taliban has an underlying hatred for Sadiq's ethnic group. Hazaras are from the North, and the Northern Alliance is the only remaining force that prevents the Pashtun southerners from conquering all o

Afghanistan. Furthermore, Hazaras are Shias, and Shias are not counted as real Muslims by serious Sunnis. And the Taliban are more than just serious Sunnis—they are fanatical. "We are here to establish sharia law," they declare, "and to show what real Islam is like. We have honoured Allah and he has given us victory."

The Taliban patrol left Sadiq a battered mess. He will never lift another shovel or think straight again. The rifle butts and the heavy boots did their unforgiving work. In their rented mud-brick room, mangled Sadiq now sits on the floor, propped against the wall. When he is not shouting garbled abuse at the children, he withdraws into an aimless stare of comatose depression.

"At least you have a husband," the widows tell Leena. But that's arguable. Apart from the two older children, and the twin infant girls, she also has a dead man's mouth to feed. Between them and starvation are the embroidery skills she learnt from the mother she hasn't seen since her wedding day. Apart from being the young Hazara woman's stitching critic and embroidery buyer, my wife is now her proxy mother.

*

Janna opens her arms to the sobbing woman. "Oh, Leena, come inside. You poor thing."

Over green tea and biscuits, the under-nourished mother unloads her sad story.

"*Madar-e Jaan*, there was no way out. My milk has gone. I have nothing more to give." Her faded *shalwar kamiz* hangs loosely from her coat-hanger shoulders. "The twin girls weren't growing, just crying all the time. Then there are the three others to feed. I have to stitch all day. My eyes get so sore, and my head pounds, but I can't stop. Sadiq can't even think straight; he doesn't realise that we are four months behind in our rent."

"But Leena, where is Shanzi now?"

"I met this woman in the bazaar. I had to go to the tailor's shop to get my tablecloths edged with a machine. She was ordering a new outfit. She's Hazara and her husband has a good job. She was pleasant enough, but she seemed sad, like me."

Janna notices the woman's name is not mentioned—it probably hurts too much.

"She took Shanzi out of my arms and cuddled her for a while and asked me about my family. 'So this is Shanzi, one of the twins?' she said. 'Yes,' I said, 'and her sister Shenaz is in our room with Rosa, my seven-year-old daughter.'

"The woman obviously loved babies. She told me she has one child, a five-year-old boy. She said that her husband is a good man but he is disappointed with her because he wants at least one more child. Because he has a son, he doesn't mind if it's a girl or a boy, but she is not able to have any more. Now he's talking about finding a young girl to take as a second wife. She said she couldn't bear that."

"So what happened?"

"Two weeks ago she visited me and offered to buy Shanzi. She said they would give her a good life, and if they had Shanzi her husband agreed not to take another wife. It would mean a good future for Shanzi and one less mouth for me to feed. I was so torn. It was awful, but it was our landlord who made up my mind.

"Your landlord?"

"He said if I didn't pay him the four months rent owing, he would throw us onto the streets or come and take Rosa for his third wife."

"But Rosa is only seven years old!"

"It is not uncommon here," Leena declares blankly. "Anyway, I got just enough money to pay off all the back rent." She stares out of the window with tear-glazed eyes. "It ripped my heart out to hand over my little Shanzi and take the money. Sadiq didn't even notice she was gone." The grieving woman pauses a moment. "*Madar-e Jaan*, will you pray for me?"

"Yes, dear Leena, and I will check the embroidery you have brought You do such good work."

*

On her next visit, sad-faced Leena receives a surprise. Janna points to a large object on the floor.

"This is for you, Leena Jaan. Go ahead, have a look at it."

Leena pulls away the cloth. Her cheerless eyes light up and her hands go to her mouth. "Oh, *Madar-e Jaan*, it's a hand-operated sewing machine." She runs her work-worn hand over the smooth metal as though it were twenty-two-carat gold, and she flicks open the bobbin cage with dexterity. "My mother had one of these. Is it really for me?"

"Friends in Australia have paid for this, Leena. You can edge your own tablecloths without paying the man in the bazaar."

"And, *Madar-e Jaan*, I will make clothes for other women. And I will earn much more money. And I will send my children to school."

*

I've just arrived home from a long day of meetings at our organisation's development office. We are having an in-depth review of our micro-hydroelectric program for villages in remote mountain areas.

Janna is excited. "Grant, you should have seen Leena when she lifted the cloth and saw the sewing machine. It was the first time I've ever seen her smile."

"But does she know how to maintain it?"

"Absolutely. She showed me all the correct oiling points. Her mother taught her well."

I'm personally amazed at how these resilient Afghan women somehow keep their desperate families going. I give my compassionate wife a hug. "I'm really proud of the way you are empowering these embroidery ladies."

"I love to do it. It gives me so much fulfilment."

"Even with all the amazing lies they spin to get you to pay more?"

"They can be pretty creative," she laughs. Then she whispers, "I wonder if I would tell lies if I were as desperate as they are?"

"Interesting question. How many do you have on your list these days?"

"Sixteen, and about half are widows. It's not just the money, though; they really need someone to listen to them. I always get out my best china. They love that."

"Well, I'm sure that the $50 sewing machine is going to make a huge difference to Leena's life."

"Yes, and she told me that when she makes enough money, she will buy Shanzi back."

I grimace inside. "I reckon she'll do well to just look after the rest of her family. Anyway, I doubt if Shanzi will ever be for sale again."

"Of course not, Grant. Leena knows that. But she'll always be Shanzi's mother, and there will always be an aching emptiness in her heart." She pauses. "That's what mothers are like."

I detect the hurt in Janna's voice. Our kids are now spread around the globe and we seldom see them. Like Leena, Janna feeds on memories.

It helps to have good friends like Heather. "Come on, you two, I'm taking you out to the Korean restaurant. I've got things to share with you about my latest project."

And that's where we all meet the Charmer.

FIFTY

THE CHARMER

2006

As we head for the tables in the modest Korean restaurant, Heather recognises an Afghan who was a former project colleague. Pervez is sitting with a well-groomed expatriate whom he introduces as Omar Bayer. The silver-haired gentleman rises. He's only average height, but the kind of man who fills a room with his presence. I figure he's a young sixty-eight.

"I would be especially honoured to have you join us at our table," he says. We make a polite refusal but he is adamant. He adjusts Heather's chair as we sit. I perceive that our velvety table-host knows how to look after ladies. He's already making Janna and Heather feel special.

"Where are you from, Mr Omar?" I ask.

He responds in a smooth, cultured accent. "I am from Istanbul, Turkey." He inquires about our Australian background, and then turns to Heather. "And may I ask where you are from, Heather?"

I'm having trouble working out where this gentleman fits into the scheme of things. I'm envious of his charm, and, hey, it's almost criminal to have that much hair in your late sixties.

"My roots are in Terrace, a small town in British Columbia," she responds. Her blue eyes shine. "And if I'm in Canada at the end of summer, I always drive the grain trucks down at Red Deer." Heather has sparkle enough to catch the attention of any man, including Omar.

"My dear girl," responds the Charmer, "what brings you all the way from Terrace to Afghanistan?" He listens attentively as she elucidates her dream.

"There has been so much hurt and bloodshed in this country. I want to reverse that in a small way. I want to build a place of employment and hope for war-weary Afghans. It will be a peace-filled Family Park where women and broken families can come and enjoy God's goodness and creativeness." The Korean barbecued beef is set down on our table.

"It will be an attractive walled garden with trees and tables, a children's playground and a tea house. I'll employ the poor to help me build it and I'll train widows to help in the vegetable garden and the small restaurant." She beams, "I've already got a good foreman lined up, and some initial funding."

Attentive Omar wants to know more. "And where will this Family Park be constructed, Heather?"

"It will be in the Bamian Valley in the Hazarajat Mountains. That's where the Taliban blew up the huge Buddha statues in 2001."

What is it about the Taliban? I know they can't abide the worship of idols, but the Buddhists left centuries ago. Why is it that twenty generations of Muslims managed to live under the shadows of those ancient cliff-face giants without knocking them down? Oh, of course—they weren't real Muslims. They needed to be shown what Islam truly is by the Taliban, the "Students". Well, Students, you successfully destroyed two giant slabs of your own country's history. I've climbed up those two thousand-year-old cliff stairs, viewed the rubble fifty metres below and mourned the ignorance of it all. Afghans used to spread blankets on the heads of those rock giants, share chai and laugh as they enjoyed their panoramic picnics. There's not much to laugh about now. Go for it, Heather. Make a place where the smiles can return, even if only for an afternoon.

Surprisingly, our table host seems to know something about Bamian. He clears his throat.

"I studied archaeology, including the old Silk Road. Not many know that the Buddhists in Bamian were the first ever to use oil in paints. They used it to paint murals on the walls of their cave monasteries and chapels." We are impressed. "When Genghis Khan invaded and his grandson was killed, he ordered that every living thing in the valley, every man, woman, child and animal, be exterminated."

Heather almost jumps out of her chair. "You're right, Mr Omar, and that's where my Family Park is going to be built, right below the ancient fort of Shahr-e Zohak, the old Red City. That's where the grandson died. The governor's given me five acres right beside the river."

The Turk looks pleased with himself. Heather continues, "Do you know that the Taliban tried to do a Genghis Khan on the Hazaras in Bamian? It was a slaughter. Their plan was to ethnically cleanse the

Shias and replace them with Sunni Pashtuns." She sighs. "There are widows everywhere."

And there's the rub for this country. If it's not tribal allegiances keeping them apart, it's the two major branches of their religion. The majority Sunnis say the Shias are not real Muslims. The Shias disagree and look for comfort to one of the few majority Shia countries in the Muslim world, neighbouring Iran. And although most despise the presence of foreign troops on their Afghan soil, almost everyone agrees that if they leave there would be civil war again. They'd have to decide who would be king of the mountain—or should I say "mountains", because there are great swathes of relationship-restricting, communication-crushing mountains in this country.

"So when can you start work on your Family Park, Heather?" Janna asks.

"As soon as the governor finishes the paperwork. She's really keen to get it moving."

Omar raises an eyebrow. "She?"

"That's right. Habiba Sorabi is the only female governor in all Afghanistan. I'll have her formal approval next week, but then I'm stuck."

"Stuck?"

"Absolutely! I can't move until I find an architect, a good architect, not one who only knows how to wave his university degree in my face."

We settle into enjoying the beef and *kimchi*, then Omar speaks up in his creamy voice. "I may be able to solve your problem, Heather."

"You know of a good architect, Omar?"

"My dear Heather"—and he elevates his shoulders—"I *am* an architect." Heather looks stunned. "And I'm impressed that you want to incorporate traditional Afghan styles into the park. I love that sort of challenge."

You'd better watch out, Heather. Omar Bayer is as smooth as silk. Is he really an architect? And if he is, is he any good? I hope he's not just setting you up.

Omar immediately addresses our unspoken concerns. "I come from a large family of Turkish architects. My grandfather was famous and my uncles are well known. I graduated with the highest marks in the entire Academy of Fine Arts in Istanbul. I've worked all over Europe and I've just been honoured by the Russian government for my work in their country."

This sounds too good to be true, but the impressive resumé begs an obvious question. Our straight-shooting Canadian friend immediately fires the query across the bow of the self-assured Turk. "In that case, Mr Omar, why are you here in Afghanistan?"

He smiles. "You must call me Omar, Heather Jaan. I have several projects running for the Turkish government, but I really came back to repair my mother's grave."

"She's buried here in Kabul?"

"Yes, she died here when I was five." His voice drops. "I loved her very much."

Omar has our full attention. We all look at him, waiting …

FIFTY-ONE

GO TO HELL

"I was an only child," the architect explains. "The doctor told my mother that if she had another baby, she could die. But she got pregnant, here in Kabul, and she started haemorrhaging. My father took her to the hospital in a horse carriage. She always kissed me goodbye, but this time she didn't. So I ran after them, cursing and throwing stones. I really was a difficult child."

"But Omar," I interject, "your parents were Turkish. What were they doing here in Kabul?"

"During the Second World War my father was a medical professor at Kabul University. My mother taught Turkish at the embassy next door to our house. I often went there to have fun. I remember playing with King Nadir Shah's son, Zahir Shah. I was very bad, and I beat up some of the Afghan boys. I was so uncontrollable they would lock me in the stair cupboard. It was pitch black and it always seemed like a lifetime."

"A bit rough for a five-year-old," Janna says.

"They didn't know what to do with me, Janna Jaan." Omar stares at his fork. "Nannies seldom survived more than two weeks. They just ran away."

"So your mother went to hospital, Omar?"

"Yes, and I desperately wanted to see her, to talk to her. My father took me as far as the hospital garden. 'Don't move from here, Omar,' he told me. 'Look up at that window. Your mother will come and wave to you.' I despised him. He never spent any time with me. Finally she came and he was beside her. She only gave me a small wave and then disappeared. I didn't understand how weak she was. It was her farewell to her only child, I suppose. I was so angry that I started hating her as well."

We see hints of pain in Omar's controlled face.

"Then I shouted and swore at the empty window. I told my mother to go to hell, to die and go to hell!" The architect's voice falters. "And she did die, that same night. I was only five. I felt so abandoned. I remember walking behind the coffin and cursing her for leaving me. She was buried here in Kabul, in the Turkish Cemetery. I remember it all so clearly. I was so angry—I jumped up and down on her grave and cursed her. She had deserted me. As I said, I was a difficult child."

A tone of penitence melds with the grief in his voice. "I have recently repaired her grave. I've repaired all the graves."

I'm starting to understand why Omar has come back to Kabul. But is he still bitter deep down, or has he dealt with that somehow? "What did your father do after that, Omar?"

"He took me back to Turkey and left me in Ankara with my mother's extended family. I hated it. I spoke mostly Afghan Dari, like the kids I played with, so I hardly understood them. I felt just like an orphan." Omar straightens up and forces a smile. "But enough of all that. I am boring you with my terrible childhood."

We politely disagree. As we all rise, Heather puts the question. "Well, Omar, are you interested in designing my Family Park?"

The award-winning architect is clearly captivated by the challenge of building something with hope and tradition in Bamian's death valley. He turns to the enthusiastic woman from Terrace, raises his hand to his chest and makes a small bow. "My dear Heather, I am at your service." She beams. He smiles. "We must meet again to discuss the plans."

Take care, Heather. He's a lot older than you, but there's a big hole in your heart since your fiancé died suddenly a couple of years ago. There's a lot we don't know about our silver-haired charmer. Is he married? What about family? Why is he living in a cheap guest room above the restaurant when he says he has a house in Kabul? And why does he keep glancing at the door?

I resolve to find out.

FIFTY-TWO

THE SWEETHEART AND THE SETUP

The Turkish architect has joined us for a meal. Daoud, his Afghan driver, wove his way through the soccer players in our wide street and is now drinking tea with our *chaokidaar*. Inside, we welcome our guest. Looking dapper in a fashionable black shirt, he effusively thanks us, particularly Janna.

Omar, you are just too smooth with women. This evening we want to hear your story; we want to meet the real Omar.

We begin on common ground.

"Yes," he smiles, "Heather took me to Bamian and showed me the site for her Family Park. She's an engaging young woman. I'll meet with her again soon to present my draft drawings."

Janna serves her mouth-watering lasagne. "I understand you are in Kabul on your own, Omar. Are you married?"

That should get the ball rolling. There's so much we don't know about our elegant architect.

"I've actually been married three times, Janna."

The hostess's eyes widen. "You have three wives?"

"No, but I've had three marriages. And four divorces."

Janna pauses. The guest's plate of steaming lasagne is suspended in space. "Three marriages and four divorces? That's not possible!"

He gives a wry smile. "I married one of them twice!"

Janna places the plate in front of him. "Oh! Well, who was the first?"

Omar senses that Janna is an empathetic listener. "Faheem was my first real girlfriend. It was love at first sight. She was lovely, with big brown eyes. For several days I watched her on the university bus, and I knew she was watching me. 'We can be good friends,' she told me, 'but we cannot fall in love.' But we did."

He pauses. "I didn't know she was dying."

"Dying?"

"She had incurable tuberculosis. We were so in love we ignored it. We made plans to marry after university, and to work together. She was such a beautiful person."

Omar's face softens. "In the end I had to carry her up the stairs to classes. She was only eighteen when she died."

There is silence as the unguarded softness retreats behind the smoothly controlled Omar mask. "I cursed God because he had taken my mother, and now Faheem. I made a vow never to be hurt again. I would be a robot, with no feelings. I decided to live only for money, alcohol and sex, and the US army base was just the right place to be."

Janna raises an eyebrow.

"In the holidays I worked as a draughtsman at the US army base. There were a lot of very lonely American army wives and they wanted some company. I was there for them, and I became their gigolo. I also arranged a useful partnership with the manager of the base store. He stole imported American goods, like Jack Daniels, and I black-marketed it on the streets. It was big money. After that I just bought my friends. Then Mouberra came along."

"Was she your first wife, Omar?"

"Yes, but I didn't want to marry her. It was all a big setup." Again Janna raises an eyebrow for clarification. "Mouberra rang me and insisted I meet with her for coffee. Then she dropped the bombshell.

"'You have to marry me Omar,' she said. She was a good-looking girl but I hardly knew her.

"I laughed. 'And why do I have to marry you, Mouberra Kamaal when you are already engaged?' I thought it was just a practical lark.

"'Because I'm pregnant,' she said.

"'Well,' I joked, 'these things happen. But what's that got to do with me?'

"Then she looked me in the eye and said, 'You are the father!'

"I stopped laughing. 'That's ridiculous, Mouberra,' I told her. 'I've never been near you.'

"'Two months ago at the New Year's Eve party you had sex with me Omar Bayer,' she said. I told her she was crazy because I couldn't even remember talking to her. 'Of course you can't,' she said. 'You drank so much alcohol you went into a coma and they carried you off to hospital. But before that you took me to an upstairs bedroom and you are the father of my baby.' I still didn't believe her. My friends and I agreed that I was so drunk that night, I was incapable of anything."

"So what did you do?" asks Janna.

"Her father was a big politician and an architect. 'You will marry Mouberra,' he insisted. 'It is your duty to protect her honour.' I thought I'd get out of it by leaving for a while. For two months I was all over Europe designing offices for the Ministry of Tourism. But when I got back they had everything ready. I had to go through with it."

It's getting dark and I rise to switch on the twelve-volt lights that operate from our solar-powered batteries. We only get "city power" for a few hours every second or third night.

"Was it a boy or a girl, Omar?" inquires Janna, who loves babies.

"Neither," growls Omar. "There *was* no baby. There was no pregnancy. It was all a big setup."

Well, Omar, it looks like chickens coming home to roost. The guy who was deceiving American husbands and robbing the American army stores was himself deceived. Somebody decided you were a good catch: handsome, brilliant and already launched on a high-flying career. The more you talk, the more I like you Omar, but it's hard to feel sorry for you.

"When I found out, I was furious. I threw her out of the house, but her family and my family leaned on me and we reconciled. Mouberra and I thought it might help if we started a family. That was the first time I ever had sex with her. When the baby arrived I was in a hotel room with another woman. I didn't even go to the hospital. He was a handsome boy, but he grew up to be wild and lazy and mad about girls."

Like father, like son, Omar. You might have taken some short cuts, but I don't think you could ever be called lazy.

"I took her and the boy to Germany where I worked with a brilliant professor. Mouberra didn't like it when I fell in love with his daughter. Finally we had to leave because of my son's lung problems. When we got off the train in Turkey, Mouberra dumped the boy in my arms and said, Here's your son, Omar, and I want a divorce!' Then she picked up her suitcase and walked out of the station."

Mmm. Looks like you got trumped in the divorce game, Omar.

"So that was your first divorce, Omar," Janna remarks.

"Yes, but she came back again and we remarried. It only lasted three months and we divorced again. So it was my second as well. My uncle and aunt helped look after the boy. One day they introduced me to Artemis. She was a blonde, and gorgeous. She had a stunning figure, and I soon had her in my bed."

FIFTY-THREE

THE SMITH AND WESSON

Janna serves the dessert and Omar is on to wife number two. "After we married she studied architecture, though she didn't really understand the subject."

"So she worked with you, Omar?" I ask.

"She hardly came to the office. Then she got pregnant and produced my second son. I loved that boy so much. I called him Melek. It means 'king.'"

Hooray for little Melek! At last you've mentioned the word "love", Omar. Up until now it's mostly been "hate". I hate my father. I hate my mother. I hate my wife. I hate everyone. And God gets a big mention on your hate list as well. If it's not "I hate", it's "I want". I want that woman, I want that car and I want to be part of the elite.

"Artemis just stayed home, drank and played cards with her friends. I really adored my second son Melek and I played with both my boys a lot more. But I couldn't sit through those long, boring card games with her friends. Then I won some big contracts and I became famous throughout Europe." The master architect gives a sad sort of smile as we start on the syrupy roly-poly pudding. "I had seven cars but the Jaguar and Porsche were my favourites. There were movie stars, and alcohol, and plenty of willing girls in my hotel apartments. Artemis became an alcoholic and a gambler. I grew to hate her."

No wonder, Omar. You're flying high in downtown Istanbul while she's in Ankara mothering two fatherless sons. I reckon you drove her to be what she became.

Omar folds his napkin and is half talking to himself. "My driver knew about it. My friends knew about it. Everyone knew about it except me."

"Knew about what Omar?" interjects Janna.

"For six years Artemis was having an affair with a man I thought was my friend. She betrayed me! I was absolutely livid!"

Janna opens her mouth to challenge his double standards, but thinks better of it.

"I decided to kill them both. I drove to Ankara and bought a Smith and Wesson for $300. I was so angry. All night I sat in a bar drinking whisky, going over and over how I would make them pay. Believe me, Janna, when I woke up and looked in the mirror, my hair had all turned grey.

"Artemis confessed. I grabbed her by the throat and pushed her against the wall and thrust the barrel of the gun into her mouth. I was about to pull the trigger when little Melek came running through the door. He was so happy to see me that he didn't see the gun. He just ran to me shouting, 'Daddy, Daddy!' I couldn't go through with it, but afterwards I beat her up. Then I found my so-called 'friend' and whipped him with my pistol. He was on his knees with blood pouring down his face and head. 'You were never around, Omar!' he screamed. 'I felt sorry for her and then we fell in love.' The truth hurt and I didn't want to hear it. 'Shut up! Shut up!' I shouted, and I beat him all the more. I nearly killed him."

Omar looks at us in silence. We see a glimmer of embarrassed remorse in his eyes. "That was the end of my second marriage. I was not in a good position in the divorce court and I had to find a huge amount for the settlement.

"I hated everyone and I hated God. Then my father phoned me. 'Omar, come over and stay the night,' he said. 'I want to see you one last time.' I was puzzled. How could he know I was planning suicide? He met me at the door and his face was grey. 'I will be dead in a week,' he said. 'I need to talk to you.' It was another blow for me, but at least he opened up about the early days and how my mother died here in Kabul. Six days later, at the funeral, I didn't even get out of my car. Life seemed hopeless. Meaningless. I just sat and stared as the coffin disappeared from view. I decided I would be next, and I planned my suicide. I woke up in hospital. I hadn't taken enough sleeping tablets with the alcohol. I tried again. Berna found me on the floor. She was a very caring young woman and helped me to start afresh. Later she became my third wife."

Well, Omar, I'm inwardly agog at your self-absorbed, roller-coaster life. But then, it's all in keeping with your chosen mantra: me first and to hell with everyone else. But I'm also puzzled at myself. I don't understand why I'm not feeling more anger and disgust at the way you've walked over all those people. How you've wiped your egotistical, shiny shoes on them, kicked them into the gutter and marched on to fulfil the next conquest, whether in business or in bed. Is it because deep down I've shared those thoughts and, but for the grace of God, might have been right behind you? Or is it that, despite your profligate selfishness, I can sense your absolute loneliness?

"Things were more stable with Berna," the Turk continues. "Business boomed and we started contracts in southern Russia. And then they found the tumour."

I am thinking that nothing more could surprise me with Omar, but as he goes on, I'm compelled to revise my assumptions.

FIFTY-FOUR

THE LAMA OF ELISTA

"'The news is not good, Mr Bayer,' the doctor told me. 'The tumour is cancerous.'

"Berna was right. The occasional pain was something serious after all. But I wasn't too worried. I asked him when he could operate. 'I'm sorry,' he said, 'but it's not possible to operate.' I'd heard of people living with cancer for a long time, so I asked him how many years I had. 'Not years, Mr Bayer,' he said, 'you only have a few months. It's in your pancreas.'

"I went all weak. I couldn't believe it. I had just signed a huge contract in southern Russia, and I had to get started. 'There must be something you can do, doctor. There must be something.'

"He just shook his head. 'You should put your affairs in order right away. There's nothing anyone can do now; it's too advanced.'"

"But here you are, Omar," I say. "You're sitting right in front of us. What happened?"

"I went into complete denial, Grant, just like I did with Faheem when she was dying from TB. I went to Volgograd and got everything moving. It was an exciting project."

"But what about the tumour?" Janna inquires.

"The Buddhists at the temple dealt with it."

"The Buddhists at the temple?"

"In Kalmykia. I was returning their stolen statue."

The story is getting weirder than ever, but the teller promptly addresses our stunned looks.

"Grant, there's a monastery in Elista, the capital of Kalmykia on the Caspian Sea. The Kalmykians are descendants of Genghis Kahn's troops and they converted to Tibetan Buddhism centuries ago. Well, I was about to come back to Turkey from our Russian office in Volgograd. Nicola, my Russian secretary, took me to an antique art shop. My wife was getting interested in Orthodoxy, so I selected some ancient icons for her. I was looking at a beautiful little Buddha statue when another customer sidled up to me and said quietly, 'I wouldn't buy that if I were you.' I asked him why not. 'It's stolen property,' he whispered. I asked him how he knew. 'It looks just like the one that was stolen from the monastery at Elista,' he said.

"'That's nothing to do with me,' I said. The craftsmanship was exquisite, so I bought it anyway.

"That night I was fast asleep when the light went on. I sat up in bed and I saw a man. I was frightened; I thought he was a thief. 'Omar Bayer, I am waiting for you,' he said in a strange accent. I was terrified. 'Waiting for me?' I whispered.

"'I'm waiting for you in the temple at Elista,' he said. Then he disappeared. It was scary, yet so real. The amazing thing was that it seemed like he was speaking but he communicated all this without talking. Next morning I told Starislov, my translator, about the man who visited me in the night. 'We're going to the Buddhist temple at Elista,' I said. He told me it was only a dream and I should take no notice of it. 'I don't care, we're going,' I said. 'We have to pass through Elista anyway, and the man is waiting.'

"My driver parked the Mercedes near the temple and we met some of the young monks. They weren't very interested in us until I produced the Buddha statue. Then they got really excited. 'The Lama predicted that today two men would come with the statue,' they said, 'and he is waiting.' Then they rushed us into the inner room.

"He stood there with outstretched arms. As soon as I saw him I recognised him from the vision, except he was totally blind. 'You are my karma brother from a previous life,' he told me—whatever that meant. We Muslims don't believe in a previous existence, but he claimed he was a priest in his former life and I was a bandit. We talked and Starislov translated.

"Somehow the Lama knew I had a tumour. I told him I only had a couple of months to live. 'Do not worry about the tumour, Omar. You will have a long life,' he told me. He ordered me to lie down on the floor. Then all the priests started chanting and making this loud 'Oom' sound. One of them reached inside my body and pulled out the tumour. They mixed it with soil and burnt it, and put the ashes under a big statue of the Buddha. 'You can keep the small statue, Brother Omar,' the Lama said. 'Just come back and bring me a transistor radio.' I didn't keep the statue, but I sent my driver back with the radio. There was something spooky about the place, and I never returned.

"But I was totally healed. My doctor couldn't believe it. There was absolutely no trace of the tumour. Berna was amazed."

After a contemplative pause the Turk continues, "I suppose you could say that just as the sand was running out of the hour glass of my life, the glass was turned."

"And how did that affect you personally, Omar?" Janna asks.

"I just carried on, Janna. Business kept booming and life was so sweet."

Why isn't there more conviction in the architect's voice? I reckon things have radically changed since then, and I'd like to know how.

"Tell us about it, Omar."

FIFTY-FIVE

THE MASK

"Business was rewarding in Russia, and so were the Volgograd women. I also had a very nice private relationship going with Nicola, my young secretary."

I'm expecting a superior male smirk on the face of the debonair architect, but all I monitor is vacant emptiness. The mask is dropping.

"Over the years my company was chosen for more awards and bigger contracts. Young Melek, my favourite son, joined me in the Russian office."

Out in the street, a pack of scavenging dogs sets up a barking battle. It breaks Omar's concentration and he looks at his watch.

"Ah! I must be getting back to the guesthouse soon." He launches into generous appreciation of Janna's cooking. "To return the favour I will take you both to the Serena Hotel for the best steak in Kabul," he promises magnanimously.

It sounds a lot like the Omar who buys his friends. Janna gives an affirming smile. "You're always welcome, Omar, but there is still some coffee in the pot. It's not that late yet." She tops up his cup and passes the Anzac biscuits. "I've been thinking, Omar. Why do you live in that room above the Korean restaurant when you rent a house in Kabul?"

The Turk gives an embarrassed cough and lowers the mask a little more. "It's because they keep plaguing me at my house, Janna."

"Who is plaguing you?"

"My subcontractors. They want their money."

"But I thought that things were going well with your three projects here in Kabul."

His face slips a little more. "They were, until my two American partners left Afghanistan—with all the money."

*

Here we go again. Everyone's out to make a quick killing from all the development funds pouring into this country. The international contractor subcontracts to the Afghan contractor, who re-contracts to a local Afghan builder. By that time the money is getting very thin, and so is the cement in the concrete. With a bit of luck, the local building inspector is related to the contractor; if not, a handy bribe will convince him that underneath the paint everything is up to specifications. He probably paid a lot to get his inspector's job so he has to recoup those costs along the way. Anyway, Allah has put this money before him and how can one resist the Almighty. And he is honour-bound to consider his family. Now that he has this good job, they all look up to him, and its one's duty to care for one's family.

So the report is signed. Everyone is happy. The accountability process is working. The building is ticked off on some international donor's checklist. Another school built. "Hooray!" Another clinic erected in the mountains. "Three cheers!"

Unfortunately, in a few years the school or clinic will start to crumble. But then, it's not being used anyway, because it's hard to convince doctors or teachers to leave the city. "My family will not let me go," they say "It's too dangerous for doctors in the rural areas; if someone dies during treatment they shoot you." "If I can't find a position in the city, I'll drive a taxi until one shows up."

With such progress we are really winning the hearts and minds of the Afghan people—or at least the hearts and minds of those Afghan contractors who are building nice houses for themselves in the city, next to the mansions of the drug lords. Meanwhile, the poor carry on as usual with stoic resilience and continued deprivation.

I don't know if Omar's company is part of "the system". One wonders when two of the partners have flown the coop with a bag full of money. It has certainly left him in a difficult situation.

*

The mask is right off now. Omar's face is grim. "The payments to the subcontractors are overdue and now the Turkish government is delaying their instalments to me. The subcontractors think I won't pay them, that I'll flee the country as well. That's why they keep coming to my house." He straightens a little. "When it comes to money, I have always paid my bills. But they don't believe that, so I gave them my passport."

"You gave them your *what*?" I splutter. "But what if there's a medical emergency or a security evacuation and you have to leave?"

"I am a man of honour." His eyes are filled with proud self-belief. "I told them to keep it until the debts are paid. I am not going anywhere." I look at him, dumbfounded. Then he pauses, and in a tone of quiet resignation makes a confession. "Actually, Grant, I'm in deep trouble. Deep financial trouble."

"But what happened to all your success and profits in Russia?" Janna asks.

The maskless Turk looks very lonely, and very embarrassed. "Everything went wrong in Russia. My world fell apart. It's just as I was told in the vision twenty years ago."

We've had a few visions and dreams of our own, Omar, even though in the West they're not taken very seriously. So why are you calling this "the vision" and not "a vision"?

Janna and I respond in unison, "What vision, Omar?"

FIFTY-SIX

THE BEAUTIFUL EYES

"I had to find water. My lips were cracked and my tongue was like swollen sandpaper. The desert sun was burning into my brain. Then at the bottom of a dune, I saw a pair of big gothic gates. I tried and tried, but I couldn't get inside. My strength was gone. Suddenly they swung open and a bearded man was standing before me. He had long hair and the most beautiful eyes I'd ever seen. They were the sort of eyes that look right inside you.

"'Do you want water, Omar Bayer?' the man asked.

"'I am so thirsty,' I replied. He invited me in."

The Turk closes his eyes to conjure up the details of the vision. "It was an impressive building, like a Roman stadium, with many people moving around. It was filled with a beautiful white light. I can't really describe it. There were voices all around, and I didn't feel thirsty any more. 'You will never be thirsty here,' the man with the beautiful eyes said. People gathered around, welcoming me.

"'Who is this man?' I asked them.

"A woman spoke up. 'He is Jesus,' she said.

"The man spoke to me again: 'Omar, come with me.' It was wonderful to hear him say that. I started walking with him. 'I have work for you,' he told me.

"'What work?' I asked.

"'I want you to build fine houses for all these people,' he told me.

"'Certainly, Sir,' I said. 'Let's work out an agreement.'

"We stopped walking. He said nothing—just turned and looked at me with those eyes.

"'But you know I am a businessman, Sir,' I said. 'And I always require an advance payment. After that I will start the work.'

"There was sadness in his voice, and his beautiful eyes seemed to x-ray my soul. 'Omar,' he said, 'you cannot come any further with me. You are not ready. All you think about is money.' I opened my mouth but I couldn't say anything. 'Businessman Bayer,' he said, 'you will lose all your money. You will lose your wife and your two sons. You will lose everything and you will go to prison.'

"Then I woke up. I knew it was more than a dream. Berna wanted to know every detail. I can't believe I just ignored it. And now it's all happening."

The lonely architect rests his head in his hands and stares vacantly at the floor. For so long his mask of self-confidence has been held in place by the glue of professional brilliance and charismatic selfishness. Now it lies wrinkled at his feet. It seems that twenty years ago the same mask was removed by the man in the vision, but Omar couldn't live without it. He turned and walked out through the doors, back into the desert. Better the mask than the beautiful eyes.

"What did you do?" asks Janna.

"I ignored it all. I was consumed by my good life, my business and my Russian women. But four years ago it all started to fall apart."

"Four years ago?"

"It was the middle of summer and most of the staff were on vacation. Melek had gone back to Istanbul for a couple of weeks while I kept the office going in Volgograd. Berna rang. She was hysterical.

"'It's the business, Omar! You have to come back to Istanbul at once!'

"'Stop blubbering, woman,' I told her. 'Melek is with you, isn't he? Let me talk to him.'

"'Melek left this morning with the cheques,' she said.

"'What cheques?' I shouted. I was starting to get alarmed.

"'Melek and your partner, Rahool, told me I had to countersign them so they could pay the subcontractors.'

"I breathed a sigh of relief and I told her that was okay because the subcontractors were due for their next instalment. 'But Omar,' she sobbed, 'they didn't pay the subcontractors. They cashed the cheques and took all the money!'

"I started sweating and shivering at the same time. Melek had rung her as he was boarding the plane. He told her he wanted to make a new start. Berna rang the bank straight away. The cheques had been cashed. The account was empty. Almost US$2 million gone! I nearly blacked out with rage. Berna was still babbling on the phone about Nicola, my

Russian secretary and mistress. I told her that Nicola was still in Moscow, on holidays. 'No, she's not!' Berna said. 'She left with Melek this morning. They got married two days ago.'

"I was livid. Deceived by my own son, my favourite son. Deceived by the people who worked closest to me, my partner and Nicola. I swore I would never forgive Melek—never forgive any of them."

Omar pauses and I break the silence with a question. "Did you go bankrupt, Omar?"

"Almost, Grant. We had to sell nearly everything to pay the subcontractors. I kept blaming Berna, but she'd had enough of my selfishness and unfaithfulness and divorced me. Soon after that she became a member of the Orthodox Church."

"But didn't you recall the vision?" Janna says.

"Berna tried to talk to me about it, but I was so bitter I just dismissed it and left it buried in the past."

Omar leans forward in his lounge chair and takes a draught of lukewarm coffee. "That was only the beginning. A year later my new secretary told me that Melek was ringing from Florida and wanted to talk. All the anger erupted inside me. I refused to speak to him, but finally she convinced me. 'He has some good news for you,' she said.

"On the phone Melek was very apprehensive. 'Congratulations, Father,' he said. 'You have a grandson and we are naming him Omar, in honour of you.'

"'Honour, Melek!' I exploded down the phone. 'When you betrayed me! When you swindled me of everything! Did you honour me then?'

"He said he had done wrong and couldn't bear it any longer. He wanted to reconcile with me, to work something out. 'Please forgive me, dear *Baba*,' he pleaded.

"I yelled at him, 'I will never forgive you, Melek! I wake up every morning thinking about how you and Nicola cheated me. There is nothing you can ever do to make me forgive you. You are not my son! I never want to speak to you again. Choose another name for your boy. As far as I'm concerned, you are dead.' Then I hung up on him. He tried to ring back but I refused to take the calls.

"That was just after 9/11 and the Taliban were ousted in Afghanistan. I moved here to Kabul and went into partnership with two Americans.

There was a lot of money to be made. Huge amounts of construction funding poured into the country and my partners had all the connections."

So it's not just about your mother's grave, Omar. As usual you are following the money trail. And it seems you haven't learnt to find good partners. They keep running off with the money. Is it because you are so full of yourself that you just can't make good personnel decisions? Or are you so bombastically brilliant that they can't work with you, and grab the money and run?

Omar's face is drawn more than ever. It's obvious there is more bad news to come.

"Then Mouberra, my first wife, rang. My oldest son had died of a brain tumour. 'Please come back for the funeral, Omar,' she pleaded, 'out of respect for our boy. And there's not much room left in your family plot; you'll have to decide what to do.' But I wasn't going back to bury a wild boy who couldn't hold down a job and was in and out of engagements like a yo-yo. 'I am not coming back, Mouberra,' I told her. 'Put him in my father's crypt. I know there is room there.'"

"Didn't that stir you to ring Florida and reconcile with Melek?" Janna asks.

"I was still too bitter, too angry, and then it was too late."

"Too late?"

"Artemis, my second ex-wife, rang me. I hadn't spoken to her since I beat her up for betraying me. Her speech was very slurred—she always had a bottle of raki nearby. As soon as I heard her voice, the hair on the back of my neck stood up. I knew it would be about Melek. 'Our son is dead, Omar,' she said. 'He crashed his car in Florida in the middle of the night.' I could hardly breathe. Deep down I really loved Melek, but the pride and bitterness had gripped me so much I couldn't admit it. Anger controlled my life. I hated it, and yet I fed on it.

"'Omar,' she pleaded, 'you have to be here for the funeral. He really loved you.'

"I refused. 'I am not leaving my work for someone who cheated me.' I hated them all and I didn't want to see any of them. I didn't want all those memories and faces and failures to confront me. 'Listen, Artemis,' I shouted, 'I am not leaving Afghanistan. You can bury Melek in my grave—I won't need it. I will die here in Kabul and I'll be buried beside my mother!'"

Was it just another outburst of bitterness, Omar, or were those words prophetic? You're in deep trouble with another lot of subcontractors. And if you think your honour is important, wait until these honour-intoxicated Pashtuns finish with you if you don't pay them soon.

Omar's eyes meet Janna's gaze. "It was my fault that Melek died. I cut him off. I drove him to alcohol, and to the car accident. I wished him dead … and now he is."

Well, Omar, you seem to be changing. This sounds like genuine penitence, genuine self-awareness. It's taken you a lifetime, but something is happening to you.

"But surely you remembered the vision then, Omar?" Janna asks. "About how you would lose everything including your sons?"

He looks a bit ashamed. "You won't believe this, Janna Jaan, but despite the reminder of all those tragedies, the vision never entered my head. Not until I heard the Chinese singer."

FIFTY-SEVEN

THE CHINESE SINGER

"On one side of the room," explains our Turkish guest, "sitting cross-legged on a *toshak*, was a young Chinese man with a round face and a colourful little circular cap. He picked up a thin-necked stringed instrument and started to quietly sing in Chinese. It was just a small gathering and they invited me to join them for tea. We put our cups down and just listened. As he sang, his face filled with delight, and tears started flowing down his red cheeks. Then I started to weep too. I was embarrassed but I was unable to control myself. I couldn't understand a thing he was singing, but my spirit could."

Omar fingers a silver ring on his right hand. "This is the ring of the Sufi Dervishes. I studied with their master for years. I've had associations with Buddhists, and the Masonic Lodge, and I even went to a Catholic Church for a while when I was a teenager and stole coins out of their fountain. But I had never experienced anything like that Chinese singer."

He pauses as a pair of noisy American choppers pass overhead, probably closing in on a tip-off about where Taliban may be hiding. If someone fires a rocket or a Kalashnikov at one of them , they'll get a mouthful of heat-seeking retaliation from the other. The Turk takes another sip of coffee while the second aircraft clatters past.

"I asked them what the young man was singing about. Someone said he was singing to Jesus. Then I remembered the vision, and I remembered what the man with the beautiful eyes told me. It had taken two decades, but I realised it had happened just as he said. Like a fool I'd ignored it all. He gave me a wake-up call but I just kept going my own selfish way. I lost my money, my wife, my sons, everything, but I still didn't look inside myself. I didn't want to. *I* was never the problem; it was always someone else's fault. As I listened to the singer, I realised that hate and anger had become my masters. I buried my head in my hands and sobbed. I looked at the radiant face of the young weeping man with the oriental guitar. His tears meant fullness. My tears meant emptiness. I wanted what he had. I wept for a long time and I could feel something happening inside me."

My belt radio crackles. Omar glances around like a man coming out of a trance. "Oh, I am so sorry. It's very late. I have talked too long and I apologise for boring you." We genuinely assure him that is not the case.

I excuse myself from the room as our security officer makes his scheduled radio call. "Yes," I respond, "we're all in and okay at House 23. Good night. Over and out."

I turn the volume down as he continues to checks on the homes of our colleagues. We all carry radios and mobile phones and we run a "buddy" system as well: if you go out you inform your buddy before you go and when you return. If there is no positive input from the radio, the phone or the buddy, our security team puts its emergency plans into action. It could be a crisis, a kidnapping or someone who has foolishly violated all our security protocols.

I return to the lounge and Janna is handing over a packet of her Anzac biscuits for the Turk to take with him. He gazes at us with relationship-starved eyes and thanks us profusely. All evening Janna has noted the loneliness in his voice. As he puts his shoes on at the door she speaks up. "Omar, you really must come back for my birthday party next Friday. We've invited a group of friends. I insist you join us." Omar is visibly delighted.

As I accompany the architect to the gate, a cloud comes over his face. "Please forgive me, Grant, but the sub-contractors are continually after me. Are you able to loan me $300? It will help keep them off my back." I gasp internally. "I will return it in ten days' time, when the Turkish government pays me their next instalment. It would be most kind of you if you are able to oblige."

Whoa! I wasn't expecting this, Omar. It's one thing to commiserate with you about your money problems, but it's another to get personally involved. Hey! We're volunteers, remember? We get just enough to cover our living expenses and that's all. We're not the cloistered, big salary earners who roar down the streets in their large vehicles or are flown out of the country to recuperate every twelve weeks. I don't know what to say to you, Omar—but I certainly wouldn't want to be in your shoes. It's true our monthly living allowance has just come in, but if I loan some of it to you, will I get it back in time? We'll need it in a fortnight. You're a brilliant architect, but I perceive you're very erratic in financial management. Maybe those dollars would grow wings and we'd never see them again. It's risky. Very risky.

I look down and see myself opening my wallet and handing over the money.

"You are so kind, Grant," Omar says. "I will be forever grateful to you. Do not worry, I will repay you." He hugs me warmly. "Thank you for a special evening. It will be an honour for me to join you for Janna's birthday celebrations."

Omar's driver emerges from his extended tea-drinking session with our watchman, who swings open the double-steel gates. The Turk slips into the back seat, Daoud reverses out and they disappear into the Kabul night. I'm left standing on the edge of the darkened street, wondering if one of the smoothest operators I have ever met has just conned me as well.

*

Ten days later, as promised, Omar returns the money. But his Afghan creditors have less trust in him than I do, and they are closing in. In the meantime I am trying to keep a secret.

FIFTY-EIGHT

THE SURPRISE

NOVEMBER 2006

Janna is ecstatic. We've just picked up our second daughter from Kabul airport. Maria will be the only one of our three children to attend their mother's sixtieth birthday party. At least, that's what Janna thinks.

The sitting room door opens and the bearer of the tray enters in front of me, announcing, "The tea is ready."

Absorbed in Maria's family updates, Janna's peripheral vision assumes it's her husband who is carrying the tray. But it's not his voice. She looks up, sees her son beaming at her and screams in unbelief. "MATTHEW! What are *you* doing here?"

Matthew savours the look of total surprise on his mother's face. "I simply flew from Vancouver to Los Angeles, and then I travelled with Maria."

"You mean you were out at the airport all the time?" She leaps up and hugs her son while Maria and I smirk at each other. I'm not very good at surprises, but with Maria's conniving we've pulled it off.

"I just waited in the airport until you took Maria away in a taxi," Matt grins. "Then I got one for myself."

"And Angela? Is she hiding too?"

"Sorry," Maria explains. "She's still in Indonesia. She couldn't leave her teaching. But, Mum, two out of three ain't bad."

Janna grins. "But how did you know how to get a taxi and find us here?"

"Dad supplied all the information I needed. And Mum, I came to Kabul long before you ever did, remember?"

"Matt, I'm too excited to remember anything. Hold on. It was for your physiotherapy placement."

I help refresh her memory. "It was when the Taliban were in control."

"That's right," confirms Matt as Maria pours the tea. "Down at the soccer stadium they were executing adulterers and cutting off the hands of thieves at half-time. TVs, radios, cameras—everything was banned here."

"But Matt," Maria chips in, "I remember you sent us some photos."

"Well, I did sneak in a few shots when no one was looking."

"Yes, I remember now. The street photos were all white," says my snow-loving wife.

"Don't remind me," Matthew says. "It was so bitterly cold. No gas, no electricity and fuel was super scarce. They put a charcoal heater under the table and a blanket over the top. Then we all sat around it with our hands and legs underneath, soaking in the warmth. I've never been so cold in my life."

"Okay," announces Janna, "I want to see the latest family photos." She beams at Maria and Matt. "This will be such a special birthday for me."

Defying statistical probability, our three children have all married class-fellows from their days at Murree Christian School in Pakistan. Congenial German Jan-Mark Seewald came to Angela's rescue at her first high school woodwork class. Quiet Zambian-raised Canadian John Barham made his move years later when Maria was teaching in South Korea. Karolyn Gustafson, a sparky Canadian, clicked with Matt from Grade 3. Now our kids are scattered all over the globe. Maria is right—two out of three ain't bad.

Matthew draws me aside. "Dad, after Mum's party, and before I go back, I want to ask you some questions about what's going on over here. Is Pakistan really harbouring the Taliban on their side of the border?"

"Matt, when it comes to the war against the Taliban, Pakistan is the elephant in the room. And the elephant is playing a double game."

My son's eyes widen. "We definitely have to talk more, Dad."

FIFTY-NINE

THE ELEPHANT IN THE ROOM

The day before Matt and I plan some talking time, there is another nasty security incident in downtown Kabul.

The suicide bomber doesn't look like a Taliban insurgent. He's wearing an Afghan police uniform, just like the rest of the officers clambering into the already overloaded police bus. It's morning rush hour. Honking vehicles creep through the fumes. Hustling pedestrians pack the footpath. Nicotine-starved Kabulis are buying their morning fix from a cigarette barrow. The bus pulls away from the curb. Sardined inside the doomed vehicle, the counterfeit cop reaches into his pocket and activates the detonator. The explosion rips through muscle, minds and metal.

Amid the smoking mayhem, a bewildered, blood-soaked boy is screaming, "*Padar-e Jaan! Padar-e Jaan!* Father! Dear Father!" But his father's cigarette barrow has disintegrated into splinters, and the dismembered vendor is dead.

*

Matt loves Afghan kebabs, so I take him to a nearby restaurant and put in an order. Next door is a busy little butcher's shop that supplies the meat. It's an open-air classroom for veterinary students. The display of saleable body parts is amazing. Western cookbooks don't have recipes for fat-tail sheep testicles, but here nothing is wasted.

The aroma of freshly baked *naan* and charcoal-grilled kebabs sensitises our taste buds. Turbans and baseball caps, blue jeans and *shalwar kamiz* gather round the tables, discussing what Kabul men discuss. On a nearby table there is a serious chess game in progress. Further away a Nike cap just sits and stares. An unwatched TV in the corner gives a snowy replay of Champions League soccer. Men with families eat in a separate area, where well-covered daughters and wives are away from the prying eyes of unrelated males.

"This sure brings back memories," says Matt, who was a connoisseur of sizzling mutton *karahis* in Pakistani tea houses. "Dad, it was a great birthday party. It was so good to meet your friends. That Turkish man sure is an interesting character."

"Omar? I'm glad you spent time chatting with him. Underneath the facade, he's a very lonely man, with some huge problems in his business." The waiter brings a pot of green tea and our talk quickly turns to the weak central government's problems with the re-emerging Taliban.

"You know, Dad, people still don't understand the Taliban and where they came from in the first place."

Smoke spirals up from numerous cigarettes as we discuss the subject. It's no surprise that people ask questions about the Taliban. They seemed to appear from nowhere. They took over most of the country from the various ethnic mujahidin groups who pushed out the Russians and then proceeded to fight among themselves. The Taliban come from the biggest ethnic group, the Pashtuns, and they belong to the biggest Islamic group, the Sunnis. Over a period of years, many Pashtuns were indoctrinated and trained in extreme mosque schools in refugee camps over in Pakistan.

Matt is fiddling with the saltshaker. "They are so brutal. Half the people they killed in yesterday's police bus bombing were ordinary civilians."

The Taliban operate on a mixture of violent strains in Sunni Islam and Pashtunwali, the strict Pashtun tribal lore. There is a strong nationalistic component and an emphasis on intense jihad (violent struggle). They say that Allah has cursed their country because Afghans have drifted from pure Islam and have become soft, and the Taliban shows how it really should be done. When you add the criminal elements that join them, unemployed men desperate for work and opium drug lords, it really is a complex movement.

Matt raises the drug issue. "Some say the Taliban should be commended because when they were in power they outlawed the opium poppy. Did they really do that?"

"Yes, but only for a while, when they were seeking international recognition as a valid Afghan government. Since their resurgence in the last few years they have encouraged it again, and they take a healthy cut from the multi-billion dollar industry."

"But I thought that strict Muslims aren't supposed to take drugs."

"That's right, Matt, but they conveniently decree that because the heroin is for the decadent West's consumption, it's okay to grow it. Unfortunately, drug addiction is now escalating here in Afghanistan." I point with my chin. "I've been watching an in-house example just two tables away." Matt turns his head a little as a smarmy-looking character joins the spaced-out Nike cap. Smarmy has something in his hand. He leans forward and talks confidentially to the wall-gazer.

Matt nods slowly and changes the subject. "What everyone keeps asking is: with all the superior technology and fire-power, why isn't there more progress against the Taliban?"

*

Matt's point is valid. Everyone knows that after 9/11 the Taliban wouldn't hand al-Qaeda over, so the Americans and the Northern Alliance forced them back into the mountains. Of course, a lot of Taliban just evaporated into their Pashtun villages.

People in the West don't realise how extensive and inaccessible the mountain ranges are. They don't know that a century ago the British colonialists drew a border right through those ranges. Since then half of the Pashtuns are on the Afghan side and half on the Pakistan side. So the Afghan Taliban simply run over the border to their Pakistani Pashtun friends. It's a double sanctuary for them.

Matt and I discuss the history of Mortimer Durand's British demarcation of the thousand-mile border. Matt brushes away an annoying fly. "I know those mountains are rugged, Dad, but why doesn't Pakistan's army do more to hunt the Taliban down when they cross into their side?"

"Because they don't want to."

"They don't want to?" My son eyeballs me. "But I thought Pakistan agreed to join the USA in the war against terror."

"They did, and they shoot some up, but they actually want the Afghan Taliban to win. Pakistan is playing a double game."

"Really?"

"That's right. People in this region know it, but the Americans have been slow to recognise a vital component to the war in Afghanistan. Hey! Here come our kebabs."

The young waiter sets down a stack of smoking skewers and we tuck in.

Matt drops another empty metal rod onto the pile. "Mmm, these are so good. Now where were we? Oh yes—a forgotten component."

"Kashmir."

"Kashmir? What has Kashmir to do with Afghanistan?"

"Plenty." I top up our cups with green tea. "It's all to do with the continuing struggle between archrivals Pakistan and India. As you know, back in 1947 the British gave those two countries independence. India for the Hindus, and newly formed Pakistan for Muslims who didn't want to live in Hindu India. And between them was a little mountain paradise: Kashmir."

"I remember we drove through it on one of our holidays."

"Yes, but only the Pakistani part. Anyway, Pakistan said, 'We should have Kashmir because seventy per cent of the population is Islamic.' But the Maharajah, Hari Singh, said, 'No way. I'm signing up with India.' So the two sides fought, and they've been scrapping over it ever since, including a couple of major wars. Divided Kashmir has added great bitterness and hatred to an already touchy relationship."

"So what's that got to do with the Taliban in Afghanistan?"

I finish my last kebab and wipe my fingers. "In the big picture, Pakistan fears encirclement by India. They fear a pro-India Afghanistan would mean two borders to watch. They claim that Afghanistan is part of *their* backyard, and it's Islamic, not Hindu, so India should keep out. But India has had good relationships with Afghanistan, particularly the northern non-Pashtuns. And India knows that if the Taliban and al Qaeda succeed, they will promote more Islamic terrorism in disputed Kashmir and in the rest of India. Access to regional trade, minerals and gas also comes into the equation. If the northern non-Pashtuns end up with greater control in Afghanistan, India would be in a happy position.

"So to avoid that, Pakistan wants the Pashtuns to come out on top. And they figure the best way to do that is by supporting the Taliban."

"That's right, Matt. The Americans give them a heap of money to buy armaments, but they're playing a double game. They promise to fight the Afghan Taliban, but they actually support them."

"But aren't the Americans aware of that?"

"It seems they are just starting to realise it. And now Pakistan is being stung by the nasty scorpion they have been quietly feeding."

"How is that?"

"Because they have a growing Taliban movement of their own, which wants to change things in Pakistan itself. So Pakistan fights their own emerging militant Taliban while covertly supporting the Afghan Taliban. It seems that the main drivers are certain members of their powerful army intelligence organisation, the ISI."

"That's pretty enlightening, Dad. So solve Kashmir and you solve Afghanistan."

Matt is partly right. It would make a huge difference. But we can't overlook the other big regional players such as Iran, China and Russia, as well as the West. Most are worried about the region's potential to produce more Islamist terrorists that threaten their national stability. And India and Pakistan both have nuclear weapons. There's a serious question being asked in the Pentagons of this world: what would happen if a militant Pakistani Taliban got their hands on a nuclear trigger?

With an armful of dirty plates, the waiter pauses beside us. "*Chund dega?*"

I translate: "How many more, Matt?"

"Same again, Dad. I'm just getting started. I ate thirty skewers of kebabs once, remember?"

"I sure do. It was in Chitral, and your future father-in-law wagered you couldn't do it."

Matthew smirks. "And then he had to pay for them all." He folds his arms and gazes over my head. "It's more complex than I realised, Dad. Do you think this war in Afghanistan is winnable?"

"It all depends on which war we are talking about. If it's the war against al-Qaeda, they've been dispersed but certainly not knocked out. If it's the war against the Taliban, it remains to be seen. They'll still be there when everyone else goes home, unless there is a political solution. Then women's rights, few as they are, would take another Taliban setback. If it's the war against the heroin industry, well, the north has been cleaned up, but in the Taliban south it's still going strong, producing ninety per cent of the world's supply. Despite all the international development efforts, there are just so many factors running against getting this country on track."

"Lack of security must be top of the list. Look at that police bus bombing yesterday."

"Not so fast, Matt. I reckon lack of security and corruption are equal number one. They feed on each other. In fact, if I had to pick one, I'd say corruption is the biggest problem."

He raises an eyebrow.

"Well, how secure are you if policemen, soldiers, magistrates and politicians simply look the other way, or change sides, all for the highest bidder?"

"Mmm. And all that black heroin money wouldn't help."

I nod. "Then there is the ethnic hatred between the groups. They just don't trust each other. The fact is, most Afghans want the foreign troops out, but they know that if they left today there would be another civil war tomorrow. Pashtun south versus non-Pashtun north, with a big fight over who would have Kabul. Then there's the weak central government and lack of a sound and fair judicial system, as well as a historically ineffective police force."

"But aren't they training up a heap of new policemen?"

"Yes, but that might be just producing some smarter crooks in better uniforms. Fortunately, there seems to be greater progress in building up a national army. But the big question remains: who can you trust?"

Matt leans back in his chair. "What about education? I've read that a lot of the police trainees can't read or write."

"Not surprising. The literacy rate is about twenty-three per cent for boys and much less for girls. And unemployment is running at forty per cent." As if to reinforce my point the tea house owner springs from his chair and drives off a persistent beggar. "Then there's the lack of rights for women and the ingrained culture of revenge and violence."

Matt takes a deep breath and exhales. "Doesn't it make you feel like you ought to just pack up and go home, Dad?"

"Occasionally, Matt." Another plate of sizzling kebabs appears on our table. "But when I see the delight of an old lady getting her first glasses, or Afghans we've trained building micro-hydroelectricity plants for mountain villagers, or Janna's embroidery widows making a go of it, I just want to be here to be part of it all. There's a local saying: *Qatra qatra, daryaa mehsha.*"

"Which means?"

"Drop by drop a river is made."

"That takes a lot of drops, Dad."

"Agreed, but think on this: in forty years, apart from all the training that's been done, our eye program has treated nearly four million patients."

"And that," quips Matt, "is a lot of eye-drops."

"Hey, we do a lot more than eye-drops. We're even into laser surgery now." We both laugh and get stuck into the next round of kebabs.

SIXTY

DEEP POCKETS

2006

The Levantine mandolin CD has started over again, for the third time. Mouth-watering aromas drift from the kitchen of the Lebanese restaurant in downtown Kabul. We are hungry but haven't ordered yet—we are waiting for the silver-haired architect. It's 9.00 pm. Heather, Janna and I are seated in the restaurant garden.

Heather looks at her watch for the sixtieth time. "Something's really wrong. He loves coming to this place. I'll phone him again." She punches in the numbers. "The guy sounds out of his brain. He needs to get out of that room. I've heard he's talked of suicide lately. Those subcontractors are really on his tail."

Heather's been ringing every twenty minutes. This is the fourth time. "Hello, Omar, we're still waiting for you. Is everything okay? You're leaving? Good. We look forward to your company. Yes, of course I have the money. It's right here in my bag." She signs off and looks at us. "He says he's coming, but he doesn't sound too good."

The fairy lights on the trees twinkle for another twenty-five minutes. The consul from the Australian Embassy settles at a nearby table. I go and chat to him for a while, just to kill time. As I get up to leave, he says, "The Ambassador really appreciated your meeting with us last week, Grant. Thanks. You and Janna gave our people some excellent insights into Afghan culture." He glances at his ever-present security guard. "I'm so envious that you can get out and rub shoulders with the locals." I return to our table and rejoin the wait.

Finally the narrow steel gate swings open and Omar steps through. We heave a sigh of relief. From our table we can see him raise his arms. An armed security guard frisks him, a mandatory requirement for all male guests. This is downtown Kabul, where the vulnerable UN workers, foreign contractors and cloistered diplomats venture out, but only to approved, high-security locations.

We rise to greet him. He is clean shaven, but pale and uncharacteristically dishevelled. I say, "Welcome Omar, we're so glad you came."

His usual self-assured charm has disappeared. He sits where he can watch the gate. "They are out there. They followed us. Daoud, my driver, is trying to talk to them. They would rather kill me than wait for the repayments."

We try to settle him with expressions of concern. Heather reaches into her purse. "Here is the amount for the preliminary visit, Omar. It's all I have right now. I hope it helps. I'll have more by the time you produce all the draft drawings." She hands him $400. He reaches for his pen and signs the receipt with a flourish. It's the only vestige of the former Omar we have seen tonight.

He looks a little relieved. "Thank you, Heather, you are so kind." He glances at the gate. "I have to give them the money but I'm not prepared to face them. They want much more than that. They have already made threats on my life. They could just grab me and take me away somewhere."

Heather picks up his genuine fear. "I'll do it," she says, and strides confidently past the Kalashnikovs, adjusting her head-shawl as she steps through the narrow gate.

Watch out, you subcontractors. Here comes the spunky, no-nonsense woman from Terrace, and her fluency in Dari is as good as yours.

In the still evening air her feisty Canadian voice drifts over the wall. "You should be ashamed of yourselves, victimising this old man. He's not a thief."

"Four hundred dollars is nothing, woman. He owes us tens of thousands. We know he has the money. He is holding out on us."

"Listen! You know his partners have taken the money. They were bad men. Omar Bayer is an honourable man. He will repay you in time. He gave you his passport, didn't he?"

"Yes, but maybe he has another one we don't know about."

"I tell you he isn't going anywhere. He's doing work for me. That's where this money comes from, and there is much more to follow."

"Listen, woman! We have bills of our own to pay."

"Does not your Holy Book extol the virtue of patience? Be patient, and you will be paid."

There are a few slightly conciliatory grunts. Three car doors slam. An engine starts and we hear the vehicle roar off. Heather returns just as the mutton kebabs arrive, the ones Omar really likes. But the agitated Turk hardly eats. He pokes the food as though his enemies had covertly laced the meat with poison. He gives little attention to our one-way conversation.

We try to encourage him. "Omar, we know you can get through this. We're praying that you will find more work."

He settles a bit and starts nibbling. Janna passes him a packet. "Omar, you told us about your vision. This is about the man with the beautiful eyes." He takes the paperback, flicks at the pages offhandedly and slips it into his pocket.

I go to the gate to check outside. The subcontractors have definitely left. After Heather's chastisement they won't be back tonight. Omar visibly relaxes.

Yes, you can relax a bit now, Omar, even though it's not your style to be the penniless recipient of a meal paid for by a woman. You are used to being the lavish entertainer and wealthy host. Those days are gone. Now you are learning some humility.

With the help of a glass of red wine, Omar continues to unwind, and he makes a little speech. "I used to think money could buy friends. I was wrong." He looks around at us. "You, and your friends, are my real friends." He addresses Janna and me. "Thank you for inviting me to your birthday party, Janna Jaan. That was a very special time for me. You welcomed me like real family. I am starting to learn what really counts. In the vision he said I would lose everything. My sons are gone. I lost my wife, my houses, my cars and all my money. I have made many mistakes and now fear is my companion. Please keep praying for me."

We nod our heads as he adds an afterthought. "I have been spared. I'm just so thankful I haven't gone to prison." But Omar spoke too soon. The vision must be fulfilled.

*

Ten weeks later, in winter darkness, faithful Daoud is driving Omar home. It's mid-January 2007. The sub-contractors have been aggressive, but the besieged architect has managed to placate them with small payments coming through from his Turkish government jobs. The traffic passes the old Russian Embassy and Omar surveys the wide snow-covered roadsides.

"When I was a boy, Daoud, there were magnificent plane trees along the entire length of Darulaman Road, right out to the King's palace. Too bad the Russians cut them all down just so they could land planes near their embassy in the event of an emergency evacuation."

Daoud gives a grunt of agreement, and pulls up behind a long row of brake lights at the police checkpoint near Parliament House. He watches as the overcoated police, exhaling clouds of vapour, check each number plate. "They're looking for someone," he states casually, and lights up another cheap cigarette.

With flashlight in one hand and automatic rifle in the other, the policemen check each car and wave it on. This is normal enough in Kabul and Omar is nodding off in the warm back seat of the old Lada. A uniform shouts and directs Daoud off the road. "Out! Get out of the car!" he barks.

Omar stares through the foggy window at the teeth and moustache of the officer in charge. "Out! Get out of the car!"

Omar complies with dignity but inside he's shaking. The uniforms surround him.

"What is your name?"

Omar tries to bluff his way through. "I am Omar Bayer, a respected citizen of the Republic of Turkey. What do you want?"

"Show me your passport!"

"I do not have it with me."

The officer leans his face towards Omar's. "Sir! You know you must always carry your identification." Then, in a mocking tone, "Sir, I don't think you *have* a passport."

Omar's heart is racing, but he keeps up the charade. "Actually, officer my business colleagues are looking after it."

The officer ignores the comment. He turns to the Lada and orders faithful Daoud to drive on. Turning back to the lonely Turk, he sneers. "Sir, without identification you are an illegal alien. I think the commissioner of the Kart-e Seh police station would like to ask you a few questions." He waves his hand and the uniforms shove Omar into a dented Suzuki van. As it splutters into life in the chill air, Omar fails to see the subcontractor's car parked in the shadows. He also fails to notice the satisfied smirk on the officer's face as his fingers stroke the bundle of notes in his deep greatcoat pocket. For some, it's turning out to be a good night's work at the Darulaman Road police checkpoint.

SIXTY-ONE

NUMBER 17

2006

The Vilayete prison is not a pleasant place, particularly in the middle of a Kabul winter. The cold is less noticeable when you're jammed into a tiny cell with seven South Africans who failed to make their fortune smuggling opium. The cell is bare. The night toilet is a depression in a corner, and the air stinks. Omar takes the shallowest breaths possible and resolves that he will never lie down in that cold muck. It's only for one night, surely. He wraps his arms around his body, leans against the wall and dozes intermittently.

For five more nights the Turkish architect squats or leans against the cell wall. The days are long and the jokes are as dirty as the filth they are locked into at night. Despair pervades his being. He's losing track of time.

*

I answer my mobile. It's Gordon. "We've finally got a lead on Omar, Grant." I'm relieved. He's been missing for three weeks. "We'll check out the Kabul jails. He's in one of them."

"How do you know, Gordon?"

"An Afghan just rang me. All he said was, 'If you're a friend of the Turk, you'll find him in prison.' Then he hung up."

Tall, white-bearded Gordon has been around a long time. "There are a lot of prisons in Kabul, Grant. We'll try the Vilayete jail first. I'll pick you up at two."

If you have relatives or friends you stand a better chance of surviving in a Kabul prison; otherwise, it's stale bread and water. Janna is making up a pack. "I'll send some cheese and beef jerky—that's a bit of protein—and toiletries and a razor. I can't imagine Omar not wanting to shave.

And I'll cook a batch of those muffins he likes. You'd better take some cash, Grant; you know what jails are like here."

Gordon's little white car figure-skates between roadside banks of ploughed snow to our downtown destination.

"He's been moved," announces the obese officer in charge of the stark stone establishment. He withdraws a chubby finger from an ink-stained entry in his register and looks up. "And we have no record of where he was taken. Visit the Director of Security. He will know."

We skate back to a block of offices ensconced behind high walls crowned with snow-frosted razor wire.

❋

A Taliban suicide bomber would love to be where we are now, in front of a big desk in a large office decked out with gaudy plastic flowers. The suicide bombers' potential target rises to greet us. He's smartly suited and has a serious face; after all, identifying the insurgents in Kabul is a serious business. It's very hard to detect a suicide belt under bulky winter clothing. He orders green tea and we get to chat. He's business-like and looks too young. Perhaps the careers of his predecessors were unexpectedly cut short.

Gordon looks a little quizzical. "Your name sounds familiar, Sir. Do you have a brother by the name of Parwais?"

A crack appears in the director's stone face. "Yes. Do you know him?"

"Parwais was my Afghan counterpart in a solar cooking program we set up for refugees, up near Mazar-i-Sharif. He's a good man, a very good man."

The director's countenance is transformed. He grabs his phone and is soon laughing with his brother. "You'll never guess who drinking tea with me, Parwais! It's Gordon, from your time up in Mazar. He's right here, in my office!"

Softly-spoken Gordon has cracked the Afghan relationship code. It's the same as the DNA code; once you're into it, all sorts of possibilities open up. The director can't do enough for us. He makes a few more quick calls. "Your Turkish man is in Number 17 Prison. That's where we keep political prisoners. It's one of our better establishments."

We ask more questions. "No, he hasn't actually been charged. It seems he can't produce his passport. That means he's treated as an alien."

We explain Omar's predicament, but even with the Parwais connection we've gone as far as we can go.

"I'm afraid he can't be released until it's all sorted out," the director responds. "But take this, it will help you visit him." He scribbles on a pad and adds the all-important signature.

At Number 17 the officer takes one look at the magical marks on the paper and promptly arranges a visit with the Turk. I'm a bit disappointed that we don't get into the celled area. I wanted to compare the conditions with a couple of Pakistani jails I've visited. In Peshawar we took parcels to the inmates at Christmas time. In Islamabad it was a white South African who swore the drugs in his backpack were planted by others.

A security guard directs us to a corner of the snow-covered prison garden. We anxiously wait in the tepid warmth of the winter sun. Twenty minutes later a casually dressed prison warder appears with Omar. He has a beard, looks drawn and is a bit unstable on his feet.

"I am so glad to see you, Gordon and Grant!" There are big hugs all round. "It's such a relief to see someone I know. Thank you for finding me."

As we sit I ask the first question. "What happened, Omar? Where were you arrested?"

"The police were waiting for me at the Parliament House checkpoint. I'm sure my subcontractors are behind it. I was taken to the Kart-e Seh police station."

"Why? What did they say?"

"The station commissioner said that without a passport I'm an illegal alien." He looks a bit sheepish. "Perhaps it was foolish of me to give the subcontractors my passport after all."

"If you hadn't," Gordon chips in, "you might be dead by now. They want their money and they'd rather kill you than risk you skipping the country."

"That's why I gave it to them, to assure them I'm staying to work off my debts."

The dishevelled prisoner chews some of Gordon's chocolate. "The police station commissioner told me I was in serious trouble. 'This is a very bad matter,' he said. 'You owe a lot of money, and now you cannot show me your passport.' Then he changed and was really friendly. 'But we are very understanding here, and we want to help you,' he said. 'There are various ways of solving these problems, Mr Bayer. If you just make a small contribution of only US$100, I think we can overlook these matters.' But I didn't have $100, Gordon. I didn't even have one hundred Afghanis."

The former high-flyer looks at us ruefully. "There was a time when I gave $100 as a tip. Anyway, the commissioner wasn't interested in me after that. His men shoved me into a van and took me to the Vilayete jail."

It's amazing. How long will it take? Forever or never? For years the internationals have been training up Afghanistan's hope for civil order, the National Police Force. And here we are right in the middle of the capital, only a few blocks from Parliament House, and we have a police chief whose spots are yet to change. It would have been a good night for him: first the subcontractors' rent-a-cop contribution, then $100 from Omar. But how can there be change if it isn't modelled from the top? Perhaps they are having more success training the National Army, but it's still a terrible thing to fall into the hands of the Afghan police.

"We looked for you in Vilayete," Gordon is telling Omar. "Then we found you'd been moved here."

"They said I'd be their guest for only one night," the Turk continues "and then they'd release me. But I'm still here. At last a friendly warder agreed to ring you, Gordon." He straightens his shoulders. "They haven't even charged me yet. If I've done something wrong, they should charge me so that I can respond."

Come on, Omar. Pull your head out of the sand. Surely you know that in Afghanistan people can rot in jail unless there's money to swing their release. Even the Taliban grease the keys so that some of their incarcerated colleagues can rejoin them. And for the "lucky" ones who are charged, the case can drag on for a decade. It's no wonder some of the Afghan poor are saying that the Taliban's quick justice was better after all. Off with the thief's hand, whip the woman found outdoors alone, shoot the adulterer:

and just get on with life. Better than the same old snail's-pace corruption, favouring the rich, the powerful and the connected.

Omar is talking to Gordon. "At least this place has a mattress to sleep on. It's a hundred times better than that other filth-hole."

I pull out the bag of essentials. Omar spots Janna's muffins: "No one is getting any of those." He digs through the bag with delight, jubilantly waves the razor in the air and then spots the book I threw in. He slips his hand into the pocket of his jacket and pulls out the paperback Janna gave him at the Lebanese restaurant. Glancing at the warder some distance away, he cracks a smile. "They don't know this is a Bible. They think it's just an ordinary paperback. It has meant so much to me."

The warder grinds his cigarette butt into the snow and starts fidgeting. We get the message and rise. I've been thoughtless. All this time Omar has been looking uncomfortably cold. I take off the sheepskin coat Janna recently haggled for at the second-hand bazaar. Omar receives it gladly.

Snowflakes feather down on us as we hug goodbye. "You'll get more visitors now that we've found you," Gordon promises.

Clutching his bag of essentials and looking much warmer in my coat, Omar leaves with the warder. "Remember to contact the Turkish Embassy for me," he calls back. "They'll come and get me out."

*

The Turkish Embassy doesn't come, but within days the architect is released from Number 17. He's transported, in chains, to join serial killers and Taliban terrorists in the most notorious jail in Afghanistan, the dreaded Pul-e-Charkhi prison.

SIXTY-TWO

IN THE CHAIR

2007

They say history has a habit of repeating itself. In 1812 Napoleon Bonaparte arrived in Moscow. He had achieved his grand objective: to conquer Russia. He sat in an empty aristocratic Moscow house. The snow was starting to fall and he knew he would have to sound the embarrassing retreat. It had all been pointless. In his hand was a book that related a similar blunder by the Swedes a century earlier. Thirteen decades later, Adolph Hitler would do it all over again.

The Americans and NATO are hoping history won't repeat itself in Afghanistan. It did for the British during the "Great Game" of the nineteenth century, when they grappled with southward-surging Russia for ascendancy in Central Asia. About every forty years from 1839, they fought and lost a war with Afghanistan, three in total. Russia itself did the same in the 1980s.

When the Soviets pulled out, the Americans shouted, "Hooray!" They had spent millions on covert operations to see it happen. Then they went home. Senator Charlie Wilson suggested the American war committee spend some money on helping the Afghans build schools. The thumbs around the boardroom table all pointed down. "The Russians are out, we've won the war and we've spent enough. It's time to sit back and enjoy our pumpkin pie. We've liberated the people of Afghanistan and the bad guys are all sorted out."

Is there a pattern in there? Are we learning anything from all of this, except that history repeats itself? Yes, the suicide-vested Taliban are back and they are mingling with the crowds. Their roadside bombs are making a savage but effective statement. Down south in poppy country they are back in control and taking ten per cent for their trouble. They draw fighters from the ranks of the unemployed, those who hate the *kafir* invaders and those who are disillusioned by a weak central government that can't keep its promises of hope. And if they don't get enough starters from the hungry, the patriotic or the fervent, they recruit more at the point of a gun.

Now the West says, "Things are not going well. We need a review of strategy. 'Winning hearts and minds' is the answer." They are right, but is the slogan itself a bit suspect? Should "Winning hearts and minds" be changed to "Serving hearts and minds"? The term "winning" smacks of some kind of domination, some kind of suspect motive. "Serving" has a different tone and gets a different reception.

International Assistance Mission (IAM), the organisation that invited Janna and me to Afghanistan, has been serving Afghans and building their capacity for forty-five years. IAM and its workers have been respected by all but a few Afghan individuals. IAM has worked under the rule of King Zahir Shah, under the communists, the mujahidin, the Taliban and the government of President Karzai. All have been aware that IAM was not a protagonist in any of the conflicts, but was there serving whoever sought help, irrespective of caste, political, religious or tribal affiliation.

For six weeks I'll be sitting in IAM's executive director's chair, leading the organisation I've come to admire so much. It's the people in it that I admire: 120 expatriate professional volunteers and hundreds of Afghan employees and trainees. From community development in the far north to a new eye hospital in the Taliban heartland in the south from primary mental health in the far west to a community hospital in the middle of the mountains, I'm impressed with the way they serve We've trained Afghan engineers, community developers, mental health workers, physiotherapists, small business advisers, English teachers and more. IAM is respected by the Afghan people and the Afghan government because it is not associated with some conquering force.

I'm desperately hoping nothing goes wrong on my watch while Harr IAM's executive director, is overseas. I really don't want to have to handle a kidnapping or an evacuation of provincial staff in the event o local trouble. I'm encouraged that I have an experienced security team to work with. That means I can concentrate on leadership, and meetings, and my current regular role as project support director for our NOOR Eye Care Program. It's a far cry from my chase through the sand women's compound of Dr Ralph's desert eye camp at the Mithi hospital twenty years ago.

Noor means "light" and IAM's NOOR Eye Care Program is huge. IAM has trained nearly all the eye doctors and eye care workers in the country, and through them and our five eye hospitals we treat almost a quarter of a million people a year, including performing sixteen thousand operations.

"But Grant," I hear you say, "you know nothing about eyes." I don't need to. That's for the experts. My role is in organisational governance and I keep the communications open between our teams, the donors and the Afghan Department of Health. We are in the process of handing over several of our hospitals to the government. We want to concentrate more on training in future. It's pretty challenging. I was reluctant to take it on, but Harri insisted I was the right person. It takes me to regional hospitals around the country. I like that. I know what it's like to live out in the sticks and feel forgotten.

I've seen a spider-bitten teenager with a paralysed eye-lid receive back his sight. I've seen a grinning cataract patient after the bandages have been removed. He won't be a burden on his family any more; he will work again. And I've seen a desperately sad farmer carry his emaciated four-year-old from the consultant's room. The boy is a limp, wizened monkey with bulging eyes. "Your son is currently too malnourished for us to do anything for his eyes," he is told. "Feed him well and bring him back later." But how does a farmer get grain from dust?

The best thing is that Janna and I usually travel together. She does her member care work with IAM personnel while I visit hospitals and talk to the doctors and government people.

Travelling in Afghanistan does present risk, but optometrist Tom Little, a veteran of thirty years of optical service, helped us out with some pragmatic advice. "Take due care, Grant, but once you accept the fact that you could die out here, it all gets much easier." Tom lived and died by that same counsel. In 2010 he would be gunned down while responding to a plea for medical care from the elders in a remote mountain region. Nine others would die with him.

*

The six weeks are up and I greet tall Harri with his piercing Finnish eyes.

"Welcome back, Harri. I'm pleased to report there has been no major crisis, but I have worked out what IAM means." The volley-ball champion looks at me quizzically. "I thought it stood for International Assistance Mission, but with all the appointments I've had I now know what IAM really stands for 'In A Meeting'."

He gives a knowing look and we both laugh. Then we begin the debriefing.

I'm quite happy that Harri is now back in his chair. Soon I'll be even happier because a crisis is about to unfold.

SIXTY-THREE

BACK IN THE BARN

2007

Hans looks up from his mutton kebabs and into the barrel of an automatic pistol. "We are taking your wife, *khaareji* (foreigner). Do not move." Ignoring her protests, the face-covered gunmen hustle flabbergasted Helga out of the local restaurant and roar off into the darkness.

Maybe they'll ransom her themselves, or maybe they'll sell her on to a Taliban group. Whatever the plan, it's a good thing they are amateurs.

*

Late at night distraught Hans receives the first phone call. "Where are you, Helga?" he shouts. "Are you okay?"

She talks fast. "I'm okay, but I don't know where I am. Listen, Hans, speak only in German—they don't understand it. They can see I'm pregnant, and I've convinced them that I have to have special medicine or I'll become very sick. That's why they let me ring you."

The German electronics technician sitting opposite Hans doesn't look up. He rotates his finger in the air as he concentrates on his tracking equipment.

"Keep talking, Helga. Keep talking," says Hans.

There are angry Afghan voices behind her. "*Zoot, zoot!*—Quick, quick!" She rattles off her list and the mobile goes dead. The technician frowns. "Not long enough, but we have the general area. Let's hope she rings again."

She does, after she remembers another "essential" drug. Sickness lowers the retail value of their commodity, so the captors allow her to use her confiscated mobile again. Then Hans gets another short call giving details for tomorrow morning's drop. But Helga's medicine will arrive earlier than expected. At 3.00 am an explosion destroys the door of a suburban Kabul house, and a stun grenade erupts inside. Night-goggled

German troops overpower the disorientated kidnappers and escort dazed Helga to safety.

*

"Fortunately," Harri announces to our international colleagues assembled for a security update, "it was a happy ending. If those guys had been real professionals they would have done it differently. Probably taken Hans, not Helga, and they wouldn't have allowed any phone calls to pinpoint where they were."

David, our security leader, continues, "As expected, the Taliban are filtering back into Kabul. The main thing is to keep alert and focus on proactive strategies. Remember, most kidnaps happen after careful surveillance. So don't walk or drive to your project office at the same time or on the same route every day. Tell me, has anyone felt they are being watched?"

Janna raises a hand. "A guy in a black car sat opposite our house for a whole day. The next day I did what you told us—I recorded his number plate."

"Was he aware you did it?"

"He sure was. I walked over and stood right in front of his vehicle, pulled out my notebook and wrote down the number. He drove off and I haven't seen him since."

"Good work, Janna, and from now on I want you all to report to me if there is anything even slightly suspicious going on. There may be times you need to stay inside and work at home, and there may be demonstrations in certain parts of the city. Either way, we will radio you or ring you on your mobile phone."

*

Hooray for mobile phones! Afghans love them. Since most of the landlines have been destroyed, cell phones are a welcome electronic option. Once the sole domain of executives and cool young dudes, now mobiles are everywhere. And as the phone companies build towers beyond the cities, villagers can communicate with their urban-based relatives.

Even more than elections, the mobile phone is educating Afghans about democracy. Millions use their mobiles to record votes for their favourite performer in *Afghan Idol*, a very popular, albeit super-conservative, version of *American Idol*. Even the TV- and electronics-scorning Taliban are using mobiles big-time now, which is why they are sometimes the targets of missiles from signal-seeking American drones. It's also why in Taliban-controlled areas the mobile phone companies are compelled to switch off their signals at night, so the Taliban can get a good night's sleep, or aren't tracked when they lay their highly effective roadside bombs under the cover of darkness. If the mobile companies don't comply, the Taliban simply blow up their towers.

*

From the back of our security gathering, Eliza speaks up. "Just a reminder, everyone. Don't get caught out by the tyre-puncturing gangs."

"Tell them what happened, Eliza," David says.

"I was downtown yesterday, and you know how jammed up everything gets down there. A young man bangs on my window and points downward. Of course I didn't open up, but he kept doing it. Then I realised I had a flat tyre. Not a good place for a puncture. I had to get out to look, and of course there is a big string of cars behind me, all honking. The man offers to help me change it. That was a relief. When I went back to pull the boot lever, my handbag and computer were missing. I turned around and the 'helpful' man had gone."

There is a gasp of indignation from the team. "She was set up by a clever little group," David points out. "They stab the tyre, and while their diversion man does his thing, they steal what they can. Remember, if you do get out, lock the door behind you. Use your mobile phone and we will come and help, and it's okay to drive on the flat tyre for a while if you have to. Now, Heikki and Lisa have something to say about slashers."

The Finnish engineer rises. "Ladies, if you are in Mandai Market, carry your handbag under your shawl. We got caught last weekend. There was extra jostling in the crowd when two men started arguing, just in front of us. At the next shop Lisa reached for her purse and it wasn't there, just a slit in the bottom of her bag. Then we realised that the argument and the jostling was all part of a set up."

There are more gasps from the newcomers and nodding looks from the long-termers.

David wraps up the meeting. "Remember: don't drive too close to NATO patrols. They are targets for suicide bombers who could be in vehicles or on motor bikes. We're safer in taxis or our own old vehicles than in the high-profile UN Land Cruisers that roar around everywhere." He passes around a wad of papers. "We've covered a lot of ground today, but go over these revised checklists. For some this extra security will be new, but for others, well, we've been through it before. The Taliban are definitely on the way back and that includes criminal elements mixed up with the more fanatical ideologues. Some of our regional teams are only sending Afghan colleagues to certain districts and having to pull out all together in others. Times are changing, but there are still plenty of needy places for us to serve. And rest assured, if we think it's getting too risky, we will all evacuate from the country."

*

It seems the Americans didn't learn from their first Afghan experience fifteen years ago. Once the Soviets were ousted they promptly disappeared. Now, a decade-and-a-half later, we are in the middle of another similar chapter, and it's not going well. If only they hadn't rushed off to Iraq to start another war, they could have made a huge developmental difference here, while the Taliban were still back in the hills and hope for a new start was strong. It's fine now to talk about the importance of winning hearts and minds, but the gate has been left open, the "hope" horse has bolted and the Taliban are back in the barn. It's going to take a lot more effort to get galloping "hope" rounded up and to help the Afghans secure their barn.

*

The following month there is another nasty reminder that the Taliban are becoming bolder, right here in Kabul. Half a dozen expatriates are jogging in the early morning. They've chosen the safest part of town, on the hill behind the Intercontinental Hotel. They are probably the onl group who still go outside for exercise.

Like many, Janna and I have invested in an exercise bike. We got a bi buzz when we visited a family who started their generator and showe us how to play Wii Sports. Playing tennis in a basement was unexpected fun, and a brilliant application of technology.

The small jogging group is pounding down the hill track. Ahead of them, a boy in a *shalwar kamiz* steps out from behind a rocky outcrop. He raises his arm and releases a grenade. “QUICK! RUN BACK!” shouts athletic Dugald to the women who are out in front. Adrenalin surges into their veins. It’s fight or flight. The terrified women turn and sprint back up the slope as the old grenade bounces past them and over the embankment. But there is no explosion.

Dugald, a feisty Scot, chooses to fight. The slightly greying project administrator is angered by the unprovoked attack from a mere school-age kid. “Hey, you wee lad! What do you think you’re doing?” he shouts in English at the twelve-year-old. “Why aren’t you in school?” The boy can’t understand the foreign brogue, but he understands the tone, and it’s disconcerting. He fumbles for something under his *shalwar kamiz* while the foreigner reaches for his own missiles. The Scot hurls his first rock as a bullet zings well over his head. The boy appears unstable on his feet. *I’ll bet the Taliban have pumped him up with drugs*, surmises Dugald. Now his American companion joins him in showering a volley of rocks at the bewildered gunman.

The kid fires off two more ill-aimed shots, then takes a bruising hit himself. He’s dazed and confused. This is not the way his handlers said it would be. Those stone-throwing, shouting unbelievers are supposed to be afraid of him; after all, he is the one with the gun. Panic sets in. He turns and runs down the hill.

⁕

“I was terrified,” Joan confides to Janna when they meet to discuss the women’s embroidery project. “I sure went up that hill faster than I came down. The boy was so young.”

“The Taliban must have indoctrinated him,” Janna says.

Joan heaves a sigh. “Where did you say you bought your exercise bike?”

“In Electric Street. I’ll be down that way tomorrow. I’ll get the taxi to stop by and find out if they have any left.”

But when Janna does get a taxi next day, she won't be stopping anywhere. She'll just be trying desperately to get home.

SIXTY-FOUR

AFGHAN ANGELS

Today, in the Bush Bazaar, there have been some great bargains. Yes, it's named after George W., and if her timing is good, it can make a foreign woman's budget stretch a long way. The market has grown up around the surplus needs of foreign troops, particularly the big US base out at Bagram. If goods go past their use-by dates, they have to be tossed out. But why do that when a heap of Afghan traders will take them off your hands? We don't know, but perhaps some fall off the back of trucks on the way to the base and some might drift out of the army stores, just like they did back on Omar's base in Turkey.

It all ends up in several alleys of little shops stuffed with imported food and groceries. In Bush Bazaar, sometimes you can get huge tins of rolled oats at heavily discounted rates. So what if the use-by date is exceeded; it still makes great muesli. The tinned tuna is only a few months past the due date, so that's okay. Not like the tin Janna bought in the regular bazaar when we first arrived. It didn't smell right and we decided not to eat it. The cats supported the boycott; they turned up their noses and backed away. Out of interest I asked, "What's the use-by date on that tin?" Janna retrieved it from the garbage bin, read the label, gasped and then laughed. "It was supposed to be used by 1984. That's exactly twenty years ago."

Today's seldom-seen bargain is preserved fruit in large tins. Janna has chosen one of peaches and one of mixed fruit. With a load of bulging shopping bags on each forearm, and clutching the two big tins, she heads for the road. "I hope I don't have to wait too long for a taxi," she mumbles to herself. "I've got a member care meeting this afternoon."

But the taxi cupboard is bare. "There'll be no taxis down here for a while," another waiting shopper explains, nodding toward the roundabout. "There's a demonstration starting, and they won't drive through while that bearded bunch is there."

Surely there are taxis waiting on the far side, Janna thinks, and she staggers off toward the large roundabout. *I'll skirt around the edge and get one. It's Murphy's Law. It would have to happen when I've bought the most gear ever.*

On the island in the centre of the roundabout, an arm-flailing Pashtun is making a passionate speech about the foreign occupation. Angry fists are raised, and supportive shouts emanate from the crowd.

Janna rests her arms briefly and reaches for her mobile phone to call her IAM security buddy (me). "Grant, there's some kind of demonstration down here, near Bush Bazaar. Our security team didn't know about it and it seems that no one down here did either. I think I'll be okay. I'm just skirting well clear of them. I'll get back to you if I have a problem. There should be plenty of taxis waiting on the other side."

Disappointment. Still no taxis. Bathed in perspiration and exhausted, she lowers her baggage and sags to the ground in the shade of a tall stone wall. "If a widow came past right now," she murmurs as she massages her aching arms, "I swear I'd give her both those clunking great tins of fruit. I'd even pay her to take them away."

The first old Lada taxi appears, but before she can rise he's seen the demonstration and has done a U-turn and is gone. Another one approaches. Janna waves vigorously. He ignores her, and with a blue-black smokescreen pumping from his exhaust, vibrates back down the uneven road.

My buddy is getting worried. If taxis are high-tailing it like that, this is not a good place to be. The angry chants rising from the primed up mob are getting louder. There is a huge primal roar, the kind you hear when Manchester United scores a goal. Fear rushes through her body, and Janna feels the hair on the back of her neck rising. She's well used to avoiding the unexpected in bazaars, but mobs are unpredictable animals. It's just as well she doesn't see the wisps of smoke rising as they burn the invader's flag. As in many parts of the globe, if something goes wrong, you can always blame the Americans.

In the roundabout, the human lava flow bubbles and surges, uncertain of which road to engulf to vent its pent-up wrath. Finally it chooses. Janna's heart rate doubles. In the distance she sees the angry mob surging towards her. Anxiety intensifies and a panic attack is coming on. For years she never understood those sudden chest pains and the fear of passing out. But now she does. She speaks to her racing thoughts, holds her breath for a bit, then consciously slows her breathing. The attack comes under control, but fear is only periscope-depth below the surface.

She hauls her load from the shade of the wall to the base of a roadside tree. It's a better place to spot the next taxi, if there is a next taxi. Yes. Yes. Here it comes.

The alarmed driver pulls up by the tree, not for business but to size up the chanting mob charging toward him. Janna springs out and in her urgency uses Pakistani Urdu instead of Dari, but the meaning is obvious. "*Kart-e Seh jaana hai!*—I have to go to Sector Three!"

He shakes his head vigorously. "No, no! No foreigners today. Too dangerous!" He grates the faded vehicle into gear and is about to U-turn and retreat. That's when the Afghan angels intervene.

"They appeared from nowhere, Grant," Janna recounts to me. "They looked just like ordinary Afghans: khaki *shalwar kamiz* and black moustaches. The first one thrust his head through the driver's window. He didn't shout, he just commanded: 'You will get this woman out of here! You will take her to safety!' The driver argued. He could see the approaching mob and he didn't want to be caught with a foreigner. 'They could burn this taxi and it's not mine,' he shouted. But he didn't try to drive off. The second man pulled the back door open, pushed me in and tossed all the bags in on top of me. Then he slammed the door, banged his palm up and down on the roof and ordered, 'Go, go!' The driver dropped the clutch, spun around and we were out of there."

Janna exhales deeply. "I was terrified. I don't know what I would have done without those two men. When I looked back, they were gone." Her brown-eyed gaze drills me with conviction. "They must have been angels," she whispers. "Afghan angels."

I look at her with stunned relief as she pauses, then adds, "But on the way back I was in for another big surprise."

SIXTY-FIVE

ONE-WAY STREET

"That taxi driver and I were both glad to be clear of the mob, Grant, but then I started feeling agitated. He kept looking at me in his rear-vision mirror."

"Well, they all do that," I said, "You *are* a foreign woman, remember?"

"But he was doing it more than usual, like the young driver who gave me the nasty run-around last year—the one who thought all Western females are 'easy' women. Anyway, when we were well away from the demonstration, he finally spoke. He half-turned and asked, 'Are you a Christian?' I didn't know if it was a good idea to answer that, but I said, 'Yes.' He drove in silence for another five minutes, then turned and half-whispered, 'So am I.'

"I was surprised.

"'In Pakistan I was in a refugee camp,' he said, 'and I had a vision. That's when I decided to follow Hazrat Isa (Prophet Jesus).'

"I asked him if he met with any other Christians. He was shocked, and looked around as though someone might hear. 'No, no,' he said. 'If people found out I had chosen something other than Islam, I would be in big trouble. For a start, my boss would sack me and it would be hard to get work with anyone who knew.'

"I asked him how his family reacted.

"He clenched his jaw. 'They do not know,' he said. 'If they found out they would take away my wife and children. Then, if they couldn't convince me to return to Islam, they would cut me off forever. They'd probably beat me up, even kill me, and they'd do it all in the name of Allah.'

"'But,' I said, 'doesn't the Quran say that there is no compulsion in religion, that everyone can choose?'

"He shook his head. 'All that means is that you have a choice to come into Islam, but you don't have a choice to leave. It's a one-way street.'"

Janna passes me her empty cup: "Another one please, with plenty of sugar." I'm thankful she has made it back safely, but now I'm slowly shaking my head.

"You know, Janna, I find it quite amazing."

"What?"

"On home assignment in Australia, we hear Muslims claiming the virtues of Islam. 'It's a religion of freedom. It protects women, and Islam and sharia law are the answer for good community living.' If only someone would say, 'Show us an Islamic country where there is freedom, where women are treated as equals and where sharia law is producing a society that inspires the admiration of others.'"

"If there is one, we're yet to know about it," she says.

"I wish people wouldn't put their brains to bed in the West."

"Perhaps it's because everyone has to be so politically correct that they don't want to raise such questions. They might be branded as Islamophobic or intolerant or something."

"Well," I add, "I just hope that Muslims who go to Australia want to accept Australian values and become good Australian citizens. And I hope they recognise that our constitution, unlike Islam, separates religion from government."

✱

The average Westerner's understanding of Islam is very limited. People don't realise that it's not just a religion. It's a whole system of living, and it demands that political, legal and civil processes should ultimately be controlled by Islam. In Britain, to the consternation of many, Islamic sharia courts have been allowed to join the arbitration system. Some say, "If it helps solve their property and marriage and family disputes that's fine." Other informed Britons are questioning a parallel legal system, especially when sharia clearly does not give equality, particularly to females. It's like the old Afghan proverb: "Two watermelons can't be held in one hand."

✱

"You know, Janna, after years of living in this part of the world, when hear Islam being promoted as a religion of peace and freedom, I cringe

Back in Australia the Muslim communities take up the right to build mosques and schools, use the media and distribute publications. That's fine. It's the right our society gives to every group, providing they operate within the law. But what about a bit of reciprocation? I wish someone would ask if it's okay in their Islamic countries for people of other minority faiths to do the same."

"Of course it's not, Grant—you know that. It's another example of the one-way street."

"Well, it's time people in the West realised how restrictive Islam can be. They don't know that in most Islamic countries it's extremely difficult, if not impossible, to get permission to build a church or temple."

"But the new Afghan constitution says there is religious freedom, doesn't it?"

"Yes, until you read the fine print. As in many Islamic countries, laws cannot be enacted if they are contrary to Islamic values, and that means sharia. And although Islamic countries have varieties of government, there seems to be an international movement insisting on more and more sharia law."

"So what about Australia as its Muslim population gradually increases?"

"Australians should value what they have, keep their brains in gear and not believe everything without checking it out. They should understand that Islam is more than a religion. They should love and respect Australian Muslims, but they should be very alert in case, over a period of time, what they have is compromised by making gradual exceptions for a particular group in society."

*

I've noticed this is the way it often goes: when someone in the West questions Islam too closely, the common response from certain Islamic leaders is "You are discriminating against Muslims".

Now that's a very interesting response, given that Muslims, according to their own Islamic sharia system, discriminate against half of their own population. As there are about one-and-a-half billion Muslims in the world, that means there are three-quarters of a billion women who are discriminated against. In sharia courts a woman's testimony is worth only half that of a man's. In marriage Muslim men can marry non-Muslim women, but Muslim women cannot marry non-Muslim men. Regarding inheritance, a daughter receives half that of a son. A woman has no custody rights over her children after the age of about seven years. Then there is discrimination against any Muslim who wishes to change his or her spiritual value system.

When these things are raised, some Muslims get very defensive. It's as though they are not able to look into the mirror. Others respond with shock, denial and outrage. Rather than join the discussion, they make further complaints of discrimination, and so the wheel goes round. That's why, in the area of human rights, many thinking people in the West are concerned when Islamic groups demand special consideration and rights in the countries to which they come. Things ought to be discussed in an open way, which is one of our great values: freedom of speech. And this is where things get difficult for non-Muslims, and for countless moderate Muslims and Muslim women's groups who want to explore how Islam can adapt to the modern world. Because at the heart of things, Islam adamantly says, "Sharia is sharia and it cannot be changed. Discussion closed." Somehow, while guarding its heritage of freedom, the West needs to keep the discussions open—for the sake of the human rights of those both outside and inside Islam.

*

Janna adds another observation. "On TV we are always hearing about the more violent Islamic groups. I wish the moderate Muslims would speak up more."

"Me too. I reckon it's because they just want to get on with life and educate their kids. They are probably afraid to speak up too much. They don't want to be labelled 'un-Islamic'. That would mean they could be isolated from the rest of their community, and they may be afraid of possible threats against them. And, of course, the media is less interested in moderate views because they lack sensation and the alarm factor, which always scores attention on TV."

*

There is a real struggle going on between the many groups in Islam. Some are trying hard to adapt their religion to modern circumstances. But it also seems there is a strong international undercurrent for the implementation of sharia law, even in societies where Muslims are not a majority. The moderates have a hard time arguing against that when sharia is grounded on their main holy writings, the Quran and the Hadith.

*

"You know, Grant," Janna says, "if you expressed these views for the benefit of Australians, you would probably be labelled Islamophobic by some Muslims."

"That would just prove my point. It would show that they are not open to freedom of speech, and it would again raise the question: what is it about Islam, or any similar group, that it can't handle open discussion?"

"Well, at least they won't be able to say you don't know anything about Islam in practice. Not when we've lived in Islamic countries for twenty-four years, have Muslim friends and have served so many Muslim people."

"Janna, I'm proud of the freedoms we have back in Australia. Our founding fathers did well not to link religion and government while leaving room for them to interact."

"And I'm glad that if you decide to change your personal belief system in Australia," she says, "you still remain a person, not become a non-person like that taxi driver."

SIXTY-SIX

PUL-E-CHARKHI PRISON

2007

Old Zelgai is the master of the cell. He might be riddled with arthritis and struggle every time he goes to the toilet, but he's in charge. Age must be respected everywhere, even in Pul-e-Charkhi prison, and he's well into his eighties. He's also respected because he has upheld his honour. He knows the man who was carrying on with his youngest wife. First he killed her two young children. He was never sure whose they were, but now he is certain. Then he killed her. She was only nineteen years old. Every day he takes an oath that if he ever gets out he will kill his young brother because he is the father. Yes, Old Zelgai is respected, and you'd better get on with him because, if you don't, he has a way of turning everyone in the cell against you.

*

There are sixty bodies crammed into the first cell. Except for a putrid carpet, an eternally overflowing mess in the stinking toilet and a leaking tap, it's entirely bare. The room is filled with captured Taliban, hardened criminals, murderers and the innocent. Every night, all hold their breath when the names of those to be interviewed are called out.

During the suspicion-filled communist regime, fifty political prisoners were executed or tortured to death in Pul-e-Charkhi every day. Whether it's the communists, the Taliban or the current regime, there are men who love to victimise—men who love to find new ways to inflict pain and extract confessions, genuine or otherwise.

Sleep doesn't come easily. Throughout the night the screams reverberate through the corridors. And then there are the repulsive noises of inmates having sex with boys. How they got there Omar doesn't know, and he doesn't ask.

He scans the cell and tries to convince himself that he doesn't belong with the scum of humanity. As he stares, fifty-nine pairs of hollow, angry eyes return his gaze, and each one takes on the face of Omar Bayer. Their curses are his curses. Their anger, his anger. Their bitterness and desire for revenge are his. Their use of boys is his use of women. The jury of fifty-nine Omar Bayers condemns him.

He averts his gaze and sinks into the ooze of personal despair. If only he had paid attention to the man who opened the gates. Omar's mask has disintegrated and its toxic dye has indelibly stained his face and hands. He wraps the sheepskin coat around himself and sags into the corner of his hell-hole cell.

*

The gates are the same—the same gothic gates he walked through twenty years ago. The thirst is as strong as ever, but he's not trying to push his way in. He feels so dirty. Suddenly they are open, and once again he sees the amazing light. The long-haired man stands before him. The beautiful eyes penetrate his being.

The man extends his arms. "Welcome, Omar Bayer. I have been waiting for you. Come inside."

The businessman doesn't dare look up. "But Sir, I am too dirty."

The man raises his hand over Omar's head. The Turk's body glows like gold, from the inside out. "Now you are clean," the man says. He lifts Omar to his feet and talks with him. "I have work for you."

"Yes, Sir," the Turk replies with deep relief. "I am ready."

"You will leave this prison before the end of next month, before the end of March. Do not fear."

Omar's cell mates are perplexed. They already suspect this English speaking Turk has deserted the true faith. Now he is going crazy. He is on his knees talking to someone who isn't there. The guards must be called. But none of them can move.

"Look, he's coming out of his trance."

"Who were you talking to, Turk?"

"Where did you get the drugs?"

The architect slowly focuses on the faces and beards around him. "I am clean!"

There is laughter. "You are just as filthy as the rest of us, Turk!" But there are some, including Taliban, who realise that Omar is different now. His face tells them. They realise he has had a vision and they want to know about it.

Five times a day the inmates line up in rows and fulfil their duty to pray. The black-turbaned Taliban are in the front row. Omar doesn't join in.

"Why don't you pray with us, Turk?"

"Why should I pray the same repetitious prayers five times a day? That is not talking to God. That is just like reciting the alphabet in the classroom. Is God pleased with that? When I pray, I listen to him talk to me. I don't have to be in the front row to show my reverence and devotion."

"You have been polluted by the decadent West. You are a disgrace to Almighty Allah. We think you are a deserting unbeliever." The inmate spits on the floor. "You must be a Christian!"

Omar does not reply.

"Tell us, Turk. Is Jesus the son of God? Did God come and have sex with a woman?" They laugh. "The Christians have it all wrong. They changed the true gospels of the Holy Prophet Jesus. That's why Allah sent the Holy Prophet Mohammad, peace be upon him, to set everything right again. Now answer us! Is the Holy Prophet Jesus Christ a man or the Son of God?" The questioner sneers as he applies the defining test.

To answer yes would be blasphemy. Allah does not have sons and daughters. He is almighty and omnipotent and high in the heavens. Humans are just specks, and their role is to submit to all the laws of Allah, the laws of sharia. Those Christians have distorted everything. They even say that they belong to God's family; they call him "Father"! It's blasphemy, total blasphemy.

Their eyes drill holes in Omar. The Turk responds quietly, "That is a question you should ask God, my friends."

It is not the answer they expect.

The siren blasts and the guards open the gates to the exercise yard. Omar doesn't move out with the mob. It's too risky. Some come and question him quietly. "What has happened to you, Turk?"

"Once I had everything," the Turk tells them. "Now I have nothing, yet I have everything."

*

Now he has been moved to Old Zelgai's fiefdom. With only five in the cell it's easier to read his paperback books in his own little area.

"You read a lot, Turk. What are those books about?" questions the white-bearded tyrant.

"They are paperbacks. They help to keep me going."

The illiterate old murderer takes the new arrival's word for it. He has bigger problems, personal problems. His bladder is weak and his joints are painful. Every night he faces the ordeal of reaching that filthy toilet. Tonight it will be different.

He rises a little easier. He stands a little steadier. His body is more stable as the painful burden of urine is released. Someone is assisting him. It's the Turk: the fashion-conscious businessman who never dreamed he would willingly half-carry an arthritic multiple murderer to a stinking toilet, not once, but three times a night. Every morning they look at each other and there is thankfulness in the eyes of both.

The key turns, the door swings open and three more inmates are thrust into the cell. Old Zelgai soon establishes his sovereignty. Omar doesn't know it, but one of these new arrivals can read, both in Arabic and in English.

An evening shower of rain drifts over Pul-e-Charkhi. In the stench that has become normality, the sweetness of rain on dry earth is perfume drifting through the elevated windows. Omar reaches high to the bars, pulls himself upward and his lungs drink deeply.

Suddenly there is total darkness. A bag is pulled hard over his head. The attackers bash his forehead against the wall. Omar strains his neck to reduce the impact. He wants to shriek, to vent the pain, but he knows they love to hear the screams. Screams are their intoxicating stimulus their nocturnal sustenance.

He falls to the floor.

"We've found your blasphemous books, you unbelieving *kafir*! They are not ordinary paperbacks, are they? You are reading the *Injil* (the Gospels)."

"But the *Injil* is recommended reading for Muslims," the architect protests from muffled darkness. "The Holy Prophet Mohammad said so."

"That was before the Christians changed it all, *kafir*." They tear his shoes off and beat his feet with rubber hoses. It is intensely painful, and no one can easily see the wounds. Omar won't walk comfortably for a fortnight. A voice growls, "Be sure you don't tell anyone about this, *kafir*, or it will be worse for you. Much worse!"

Omar tries to recognise the voices. Is it the guards who are attacking him, or is it some of the inmates? He will never know. And he won't talk. When an International Red Cross team visits the prison and briefly asks him about his welfare, he says nothing. When a surly member of the Turkish Embassy comes for an even briefer time, he says nothing. His eyesight is out of balance and his head goes into periods of confusion, but he remains silent.

The word is truly out among the inmates. The Turk has deserted the faith. The title *kafir* is on every curled lip. Hatred burns in their eyes.

Gordon and his friends visit when they are permitted. That lifts his spirits, but there are two questions that continually recycle in the weary architect's brain: Will they beat me again? And if they do, will I survive?

The fact that he didn't squeal seems to be respected by the inmates. Some recognise a new spirituality in the Turk. Many of the Taliban are just unemployed teenagers. Some signed up for the money, some at the point of a gun. Omar listens and prays for each one.

Time drags on, and, despite the promise of the long-haired man, seeds of despair begin to germinate.

The new prison director's invitation does not help. Ambitious and experienced, the new incumbent is convinced that there is money in the Turk's foreign connections.

The director's heated office is blissfully warm and Omar removes the sheepskin coat for the first time since he accepted it at Number 17. He is just savouring the aromatic cardamom chai, and enjoying the forgotten sweetness of *goolaab jaaman* (confectionary), when the portly director makes an unnerving announcement.

"Mr Bayer, I hope you are comfortable here in Pul-e-Charkhi because think you will be with us for a long time."

Omar is desperately clinging to the promise "before the end of March", but he's tired and hurting and his grip is weakening.

"You understand that your position is very serious, Mr Bayer. You could be here for at least two years."

It's too much for the architect's battered body and mind. "Two years," he gasps. "But there's not even a charge against me!"

"Mr Bayer, your sub-contractors are very angry and they want you to rot in this place. They have seen to it that no case comes up for at least two years, maybe three." Omar's shoulders sag. "Just remember, Mr Bayer"—and the director gives an affirming little smile—"I am always here to help you, in whatever way I can." They both know what that means.

Omar shuffles back to his cell. *Two or three years! I can't possibly survive this hell-hole for that long. I just want to die and be with the Beautiful Eyes. It's too much!*

*

The chinking of chains signals the warder's approach. A guard calls out the name of Omar Bayer. Old Zelgai knows what the manacles mean. He hugs the Turk. "Please come back and visit me. And, dear friend, I have a gift for you." He bends painfully to the floor and pulls something from beneath his grubby, wafer-thin mattress. "These belong to you." He hands the paperbacks to Omar. "I would not let them take them away" he says.

As the Turk's chains rattle toward the waiting vehicle, fifty-nine inmates line the fence. Some of them are weeping. "Remember us, Turk. You have told us good things. Please come back. *Dua kunehn*—Pray fo us."

The vehicle heads into the city. Omar is sure it will be the Turkish Embassy. Then his heart sinks. This is not the embassy; it's the familia gates of Number 17.

They don't get out of the car. After two hours the fidgety warde speaks up. "No one is coming. They have forgotten you. We will retur to Pul-e-Charkhi."

Just as the driver turns the ignition key, a white car pulls into th prison checkpoint. Gordon's young friend leaps out and talks animatedl to the officers. Papers are signed and the manacles are removed. It's March 28 and Omar is free.

"It was totally unexpected," Gordon's friend announces as they drive away. "Your creditors had a sudden change of heart. They finally realised their only chance of getting their money is for you to return to work. Then there was big confusion about the rendezvous, that's why we're so late."

*

Janna and I have just returned from an out-of-country conference. Soon after his release, Omar is standing at our door. He smiles. It's not the suave, self-reliant smile of the old charmer, but a sincere, appreciative grin on a battered, genuine face.

"You are looking at a man who has come back from hell," he says.

SIXTY-SEVEN

THE TREE HUGGER

ADELAIDE, 2008

It's ten months since the returnee from hell stood on our Kabul doorstep. Janna and I are seated amongst slit lamps and eye charts as an Australian eye specialist makes the pronouncement.

"Stargardt's disease has finally caught up with you, Mr Lock. You cannot return to Afghanistan."

He's brusque and could do with a dash of Omar's charm, but he's a top ophthalmologist. Even though I knew the announcement would come one day, I feel like I've been slugged in the belly. Janna squeezes my hand. It's sad news for her as well, but right now she is generously thinking only of me.

"Can't we go back to hand over our responsibilities," I stammer, "to pack up and say farewell to our team?"

He softens a little. "Yes, but it should only be for a couple of weeks. Your central vision could be entirely gone in a month. Or it may be a few years. It's genetic and we just don't know." Then he answers the question I've been asking in hope for the last ten years, since my Stargardt's was first detected.

"Unfortunately, Mr Lock, there is still no known treatment for this form of macular degeneration. But you will retain your peripheral vision. You will not go completely blind."

I stare at the ophthalmologist. It's true; while I can see the office with my peripheral vision, his face is not there, except for his nose. I wonder how I'll manage when I can't read and can't recognise faces at all.

The doctor lifts up the photos of my eye scan, studies them again and then goes into uncharacteristic chat mode. "You've been lucky. Very lucky!"

"Lucky?"

"Most Stargardt's sufferers lose their central vision by the time they are twenty."

I can do the sums, Lord. You've given me forty-five bonus years. The last twenty-four in Afghanistan and Pakistan have been so special, albeit tough and sometimes terrible. Thank you for those years. Help me now to readapt. Help me to manage the anger and frustration that I'm already starting to feel. And thank you for Janna. Help me to be kind to her and to myself.

"And what were you doing in Afghanistan, Mr Lock?"

"Among other things, I was project support director for a huge eye care program."

"That's really ironic."

"Over the last forty years our organisation, NOOR, has trained most of the ophthalmologists and optometrists in Afghanistan. Now they treat a quarter of a million eye sufferers each year."

The specialist is about to ask more questions when he glances at his watch. He rises. "Make an appointment to see me in six months," he says, and is gone.

We walk slowly to the car park. Janna sits immobilised behind the steering wheel while I am lost in my thoughts, inert and grieving. *Well, that's it, I suppose. I did want to be part of the historic handover of a couple of our biggest eye hospitals to the Ministry of Health. And I wanted to support the growth of the vital Primary Mental Health Program at Herat.*

Janna breaks the silence. "What about my widows?" She reaches for her handkerchief. "I couldn't face them; it would break my heart. I've said temporary goodbyes but now they'll have to be permanent. Grant, you'll have to go back and sell most of our gear and pack up the rest. And the team! We're really going to miss the team."

I nod as the faces of over 120 professional volunteers dance across the screen of my memory bank. As a deputy executive director of the organisation, I want to be there for them. Gutsy women. Dedicated men Eye care professionals, physiotherapists, administrators, business trainers, small loan managers, IT specialists, financial managers, member care workers, community developers, micro-hydro engineers, English teachers and more. The faces keep appearing.

Then the Afghan staff zoom onto my mind-screen, scores of them. It's been so rewarding to be their mentor and their student.

*

It's May 2008 and I am back in our rented Kabul house. I sell most of our gear, pack some for shipping and give away the rest. At the office I've sat for long periods with my colleagues and the handovers have been completed.

The *chaokidaar* escorts Malia through the chaos in the yard. She's heard that her much-loved Janna Jaan is not coming back and she is in tears. "Give my best salaams to Janna Jaan. She was the one who gave me hope."

"And how is your family, Malia Jaan?" I respectfully ask.

She raises her hands in despair. "Our relatives came from the village. They were getting letters tossed over the wall at night. The letters said their names were now on the Taliban's list because they kept sending their girls to school. We are now seventeen in two rooms. What will we do when the snow comes? We need plastic to cover the windows. There is no glass in them, and the landlord doesn't care."

I'm glad I have just given her extra Afghanis on top of Janna's parting gift of money for winter firewood.

At last I make contact with Omar. He's been working on Heather's Family Park at Bamian. He insists on taking me to the airport. I couldn't think of a better way to leave. We cruise toward the heavily guarded facility with faithful Daoud at the wheel.

"Now I feel like a bird," chirps Omar, who shares the back seat with me. "When I got out of prison, I hugged the trees, I smelt every flower and I scrubbed myself for days on end to get rid of the stench of Pul-e-Charkhi. We lived like animals, and we smelt like animals. It's a funny thing to say now, but I'm glad I went to prison. I was changed. It's where I learnt to forgive because I was forgiven." He pauses. "But I still can't forgive myself."

We roll in silence past the mosques and damaged buildings. Omar turns to me. "Grant, you will not believe this, but I talk regularly to Serna, my third ex-wife. She wants me to meet her again back in Turkey. She calls me the new Omar because she never heard the old Omar talk like I do now. She even says she might remarry me." He looks pensively at the traffic ahead. "I've wasted so many years."

"And what about your creditors, Omar. Are they still on your trail?"

"I've worked hard and paid them all off. Sister Heather's Family Park is well on the way. You'd be amazed at what I've done up there. I've also won a big contract to design a town over the border in Tajikistan," he says proudly.

The new Omar can't come into the airport terminal. Armed security guards allow only passengers into the building. We hug in the car park.

"Grant, I will most certainly come to see you in Adelaide next year. You and Janna mean so much to me. I will take you to the best hotel and buy you the very best steak." That's a trace of the old charmer showing through, but I know he's genuine.

*

The sixty-seat plane shudders as it climbs eastward toward Pakistan Somewhere down there in the ocean of peaks and valleys are al-Qaeda and the Taliban, enjoying the security of Pakistan's side of the border The Western quick-fix cavalry has charged in with guns blazing, wallets bulging and the flag of Western democracy to plant on Afghanistan's Parliament House. "It's all going to work out fine; we'll be out of here in no time." But the Taliban are patient. Time and the mountains are a potent combination.

There was a period, after the original "defeat" of the Taliban, wher Afghans had hope in their eyes. Roads, bridges, schools, clinics anc police stations could be built with impunity. You could stand in a fiel and discuss alternative crops with the poppy farmers. Now, to do thos things you need a heap of expensive soldiers or security guards to stanc in front of the theodolites, machinery and shovels.

As the Pakistan International Airways plane crosses the Tora Bor Mountains, I can't help but be proud. Our organisation has bee doing the hearts-and-minds work in Afghanistan for forty-three year Through all the regime changes, they have kept on serving the Afgha people. Every eye that regains its vision, every small business loan, ever micro-hydroelectric light bulb in remote villages, every Afghan traine It's only happening one person, one family, at a time, but it's happenin and it has been done on low budgets with every dollar accounted for. It's immensely rewarding to be a small part of all that.

We cross the Pakistan border and I look back at Afghanistan's snow-capped Hindu Kush Mountains for the last time.

It will be so good to have Omar visit us in the New Year.

SIXTY-EIGHT

CAFE OMAR

2009

It is seven months since the Turk took me to the Kabul airport. We haven't found it easy to become Australians again.

"It must be good to be home," they say. We smile graciously. We are not complaining that it's clean, the power is always on and things are organised. And it's good to catch up with people who have faithfully helped us to be volunteers.

Twenty-four years ago we set off from "half way across Australia" and now we have returned, feeling worn and fulfilled, yet incomplete. We live with our feet in Australia and our hearts in Afghanistan, and our minds are somewhere in between.

And while the powers-that-be struggle with the complexities of unlocated al-Qaeda, controversial peace talks with the Taliban, and when and how to pull out of the country, I struggle with my vision problems. Meanwhile, Janna misses the regular pounding on the gate, listening to the stories of her widows and encouraging them with advice on their embroidery, a sympathetic ear and a prayer. Yes, while I launch into my writing with the help of big letter keyboards and specialised computer programs, my wonderful life-companion takes some time to recover from decades of emotion-stretching sacrifice. Apart from the other pressures on us, thirty moves in twenty-five years have really tested my brilliant homemaker. And naturally we miss our friends in Afghanistan.

So we are looking forward to Omar's visit with real expectation. Then Heather's email arrives.

> It was a massive heart attack. Daoud found him on the floor of the shower. They had to break down the bathroom door. The shower was still running. Now Omar's resting in the Turkish graveyard in Kabul. When the arteries of

> his heart were pumping with anger, he said that he would die in Afghanistan and be buried next to his mother. And when his self-centredness finally found real meaning, he said, "This is where I belong, in Afghanistan." Now his prophecy is fulfilled.

We are stunned at the sudden loss of our silver-haired friend. Janna continues to read out Heather's unexpected correspondence.

> Only last week we threw a party for him. It was his seventieth birthday. He enjoyed it immensely. We gathered at the Lebanese restaurant. You remember the place, and how we waited so long for him with the subcontractors hot on his trail? He told me at the party, "Heather Jaan, I remember the night you waited here for me with Janna and Grant. Truly I thought it was all over for me; I could see no escape, no answers. I planned to finish it all, but you kept ringing and waiting and ringing till finally I came. Thank you for persevering with me."
>
> He cut the cake and made a little speech. "I am so happy," he said. "I feel so free. I am delighted to have you as my dear friends, real friends. I only regret that I was so selfish for so long, and I'm sorry that I've hurt so many people. Although I still cannot forgive myself, I have forgiven all those who have hurt me. Even those who took the money and those who beat me in prison. That was the old Omar. Now you see the new Omar."

I'm often asked, "Is there any hope for Afghanistan?" Like Omar on that suicidal night, there doesn't seem to be a way out. There are no answers. But maybe the answer is in Omar himself. He was totally self-centred, corrupt and full of the desire for revenge, yet he changed. And so can Afghanistan. It will take time and much perseverance. But when I look into the faces of the poor, the unemployed men, the uneducated girls and the displaced families, I have to believe it is possible. It may take a lot of waiting and a lot of genuine expressions of concern, but it can happen.

*

There's a Family Park now at the east end of the Bamian Valley. Visitors come and gasp at the architecture and the intricate stonework in the buildings. "This can't be Afghanistan," they say as they enjoy the garden and the fountains.

"This is better than the pizza I ate in Italy," a prince of the Afghan royal family declares, and the widow-cooks in the kitchen beam with pride.

Over the ornately carved door of the tea house is the name "Cafe Omar".

Whether you invest in building structures or building lives, there is always a risk. Will the Taliban return and blow it all up? Even so, it will have been worth it, because the visitors, and the widows in the kitchen, and the villagers trained to serve at tables, and those trained to tend the park's income-generating gardens, all have one thing in common. They have experienced hope.

Lightning Source UK Ltd.
Milton Keynes UK
UKOW031231020712

195348UK00003B/9/P